*Joint ventures between Yugoslav and foreign enterprises*

---

This study consists of two parts. In the first part the Yugoslav socio-economic system is analysed, on the macro - as well as on the enterprise level. Particular attention is given to the actual working of the system in practice, and, as far as the Yugoslav enterprise is concerned, to the differences with Western firms. The second part deals with the legal, contractual and practical aspects of joint ventures between Yugoslav and foreign enterprises. A survey of foreign investors' experiences in Yugoslavia concludes the study, which is the first comprehensive one of its kind in English.

Tilburg Studies on Economics 16

*Edited by the Tilburg Institute of Economics of the Tilburg School of Economics, Social Sciences and Law*



A study on Economics

# Joint ventures between Yugoslav and foreign enterprises

E.A.A.M. Lamers

*Staff member of the European Investment Bank*

Tilburg University Press

*The Netherlands*/1976

Softcover reprint of the hardcover 1st edition 1976



Distributors: Academic Book Services Holland, P.O. Box 66,
Groningen, The Netherlands

ISBN-13: 978-94-011-7764-1 e-ISBN-13: 978-94-011-7762-7

DOI: 10.1007/978-94-011-7762-7

'Oh, it needn't come to that!', Alice hastily said, hoping to keep him from beginning.

'The piece I'm going to repeat', he went on without noticing her remark, 'was written entirely for your amusement.'

(Lewis Carroll, *Through the Looking-Glass*)

# Preface

This study stems from a long association with Yugoslavia: two years at the World Bank and a further two and a half years with the International Investment Corporation for Yugoslavia S.A. in London when I was involved in the financing of joint ventures between Yugoslav and foreign enterprises – part of the subject matter of this study.

I believe that anyone dealing with Yugoslavia has found it difficult to escape the spell of this fascinating country. There is its history, rich in struggles and achievements, its cultural heritage, the beauty of its landscapes and, last but not least, the character and qualities of its people. But while any one of these features (to which others could easily be added) may have its special appeal depending on one's personal inclinations, it is undoubtedly Yugoslavia's socio-economic system that arouses universal interest. For some it represents the only system that eventually can ensure a just society, while for others its theoretical foundations are utopian and its practical implementation an incoherent muddle. The debate in the West about the merits of Yugoslav socialism will continue for a long time, and if at this stage a personal comment is called for then it must be that I have been struck by two things: modesty and courage.

The Yugoslavs are surprisingly modest about the achievements of their system. There is no missionary zeal to export their social philosophy. They will go no further than claim that the self-management system is suited to their own particular circumstances and that other countries will have to find out for themselves whether the system is appropriate – or can be adapted – to their needs. Perhaps even more admirable is their courage. Not just the physical courage which the Yugoslavs so abundantly displayed in fighting the Nazi aggression, but the moral and political courage in going their own way shortly after the war. Here was a small backward Balkan country squeezed between two hostile blocks and under severe pressure from the Soviet Union. Yet its leaders and its people, in spite of the heavy odds against them, did not for one moment hesitate to assert their country's independence and to set up a social and economic system that had never been put to the test before. Moreover, they always had the courage to admit and correct mistakes, and to experiment so as to improve the system. This conscious and continuing effort to develop a better and more just society is to the lasting credit of the Yugoslavs, and an example for other countries.

In writing this study I have been fortunate to benefit from an abundance of good advice. Professor Dr. H. W. J. Bosman provided overall guidance that was firm yet gentle, for which I will remain grateful. My debt to him, moreover, dates back a long time to my days at the Tilburg School of Economics when the interest he showed in my work – and indeed of every student – was a real stimulus.

His colleagues Professors De Jong, Janssen, Van de Klundert, and Tiemstra have been of great help by giving me the benefit of their comments and observations on various chapters of this study. In particular, Professor Tiemstra, who kindly agreed to act as co-promoter, has given considerable support on the study as a whole.

I have also received valuable assistance and encouragement from Professor Dr. Hans-Joachim Heinemann who helped me on Chapters 1 and 3. I owe a special debt to my ex-colleagues at the International Investment Corporation for Yugoslavia S.A. who were always prepared to discuss particular points with me and to review my drafts: Jasa Almuli, Klaus Benz, Dr. Radoje Prica and Charles Schmeder. Of course, the opinions expressed in this study are entirely my own and cannot be attributed either to IICY or to members of its staff.

# Contents


Preface VII

1. Yugoslavia: a labour-managed market economy 1

1.1. Introduction 1
1.2. The evolution of the doctrine 2
1.2.1. The Soviet model: the centrally-planned economy 3
1.2.2. The phase of decentralisation 5
1.2.3. Self-government socialism 13
1.3. Theoretical aspects of the labour-managed market economy 17
1.3.1. Ward 20
1.3.2. Domar 22
1.3.3. Horvat 25
1.3.4. Vanek 26
1.4. Aspects of the 'real system' 32
1.4.1. The real system versus Vanek's model 33
1.4.2. Investment financing and the rôle of the banks 45
1.4.3. Economic policy 53
1.4.4. Regional inequities 56
1.4.5. Post-war economic growth 60
1.4.6. Self-management in practice 62
1.4.7. Development targets 69

2. The Yugoslav enterprise 84

2.1. Introduction 84
2.2. Legal aspects 85
2.3. Self-management 89
2.3.1. The Workers' Council 91
2.3.2. The Management Board 94
2.3.3. The Director 96

2.4. Accounting principles 97
2.4.1. The income statement 99
2.4.2. The balance sheet 101
2.5. Planning 103
2.6. Determination of personal incomes 105
2.7. Financing 107
2.7.1. Need for funds 108
2.7.2. Sources of funds 109

3. PRIVATE FOREIGN INVESTMENT IN A DEVELOPING ECONOMY 117

3.1. Introduction 117
3.2. Private foreign investment in developing countries 118
3.2.1. The case against private foreign investment 120
3.2.1.1. The effect of PFI on the balance of payments of the host country 120
3.2.1.2. High profits 122
3.2.1.3. The effect of PFI on industrialisation strategy 123
3.2.1.4. The effect of PFI on local entrepreneurship and initiative 124
3.2.1.5. Conflicts of interest between host country and foreign investors 125
3.2.2. The advantages of private foreign investment 127
3.2.2.1. The introduction of management skills 128
3.2.2.2. The transfer of technology and know-how 128
3.2.2.3. Training of labour 129
3.2.2.4. Generation of tax revenues and creation of employment 129
3.2.2.5. Productivity spill-overs 130
3.2.2.6. Transfer of capital 131
3.2.3. Incentives for private foreign investment 132
3.3. The international joint venture in developing countries 138
3.3.1. Definition 138
3.3.2. Advantages to a developing country 139
3.3.3. Advantages to the foreign investor 141
3.3.4. Disadvantages to a developing country 142
3.3.5. Disadvantages to the foreign investor 142
3.3.6. Problem areas 142

4. JOINT VENTURES BETWEEN YUGOSLAV AND FOREIGN ENTERPRISES: INSTITUTIONAL ASPECTS 149

4.1. Introduction 149

4.2. Legislation, rules and regulations 153
4.2.1. The first laws–basic issues 153
4.2.2. Subsequent changes 160
4.2.3. The foreign exchange and trade regime 166
4.3. The joint venture contract 171
4.3.1. The general framework of the contract 174
4.3.2. The financial plan 175
4.3.3. Organisational structure 180
4.3.4. Operations 185
4.3.5. Termination 189
4.3.6. Miscellaneous provisions 193

5. JOINT VENTURES BETWEEN YUGOSLAV AND FOREIGN ENTERPRISES: THE EXPERIENCE SO FAR 198

5.1. Introduction 198
5.2. Joint venture agreements registered up to 31–1–1974 198
5.2.1. Registered contracts by year 198
5.2.2. Registered contracts by industrial sector 200
5.2.3. Foreign investment by size of participation 201
5.2.4. Foreign investment by Republic and Autonomous Province 203
5.2.5. Origin of foreign investment 204
5.3. A survey of foreign investors' experience 205
5.3.1. Selected data about a sample of foreign investors 205
5.3.2. Investment decision and selection of the Yugoslav partner 206
5.3.3. Financing 209
5.3.4. Secondment of foreign staff 211
5.3.5. Foreign investors' evaluation of performance 212
5.3.6. Foreign views on Yugoslav legislation and regulations concerning joint ventures 215
5.4. The International Investment Corporation for Yugoslavia S.A. 216
5.4.1. Background 216
5.4.2. Capital structure 217
5.4.3. Operations 218
5.4.4. Prospects 219

6. SUMMARY AND CONCLUSIONS 220

6.1. Introduction 220
6.2. Yugoslavia: a labour-managed market economy 221

6.2.1. History 221
6.2.2. Theory 222
6.2.3. The 'real' system 224
6.3. The Yugoslav enterprise 225
6.3.1. Legal structure 225
6.3.2. Self-management 226
6.3.3. Accounting principles 226
6.3.4. Planning 227
6.3.5. Determination of personal incomes 227
6.3.6. Financing 227
6.4. Private foreign investment in a developing economy 228
6.4.1. The case against private foreign investment 228
6.4.2. Advantages of private foreign investment 229
6.4.3. Incentives for private foreign investment 229
6.4.4. The international joint venture in developing countries 229
6.5. Joint ventures between Yugoslav and foreign enterprises: institutional aspects 230
6.5.1. Legislation 230
6.5.2. The joint venture contract 232
6.6. The experience so far 232
6.7. Concluding observations 234
6.7.1. General evaluation 234
6.7.2. Problems 235
6.7.3. Prospects 238

ANNEX 240

BIBLIOGRAPHY 248

# 1. Yugoslavia: a labour-managed market economy[1]

*'Nothing that has been created must be so sacred for us that it cannot be surpassed and cede its place to what is still more progressive, more free, more human.'*
(1958 Programme of the Yugoslav League of Communists)

## 1.1. INTRODUCTION

It is inevitable that any study dealing with Yugoslavia begins with the statement that the Yugoslav system is unique; no other country has a socio-economic structure that resembles Yugoslavia's. The principle on which this system is based can be summarised in one word: self-management. The simplicity however, begins and ends with the definition. In fact, the Yugoslav system is highly complex, and in constant evolution: a never-ending process of experiments and continuing search for improvements. One might say that this goes for other socio-economic systems as well, but nowhere is the search so deliberate and the willingness to experiment so pronounced as in Yugoslavia. From the moment the Yugoslavs foreswore the Soviet system in the early post-war years, they have never looked backward.

It is, of course, always desirable for the understanding of any given country's social and economic system to have some knowledge of the historical processes which have led to its present-day structure – but in Yugoslavia's case, it is essential. The very uniqueness of the system developed (and is still developing) in leaps and bounds, every change being called for – in an almost Hegelian fashion – by a state of affairs that had for some reason become unsatisfactory. The Yugoslav system, moreover, evolved quite independently from any other existing system, and it is therefore more easily understood if, for a first reconnaissance, a historical perspective is adopted.

This chapter, devoted to the analysis of some aspects of the Yugoslav socio-economic system, will accordingly first trace its evolution since the early post-war years. In the second section an attempt will be made to highlight some theoretical issues of the labour-managed market economy – i.e. the Yugoslav system in its 'pure' form. The chapter will be concluded with an analysis of the 'real' system.

## 1.2. THE EVOLUTION OF THE DOCTRINE

In the relatively short timespan since the Second World War, the Yugoslav socio-economic system has undergone drastic changes. In the words of a Yugoslav author:[2]

- 'State ownership of the means of production has been turned into social ownership;
- income distribution and the share of the workers in the result of their labour have lost the character of state-paid wages and have been transformed into net income containing surplus labour;
- the centralist administrative management of the economy, based on all-embracing and binding state plans, has been replaced by decentralised self-management by working people, and by polycentric planning at various levels ... through consultation and agreement among those concerned.'

From a carbon-copy of the Soviet model the Yugoslav system developed into a unique brand of socialism – not that the Yugoslavs invented an entirely new system. In fact, as will be seen later, they even went to great lengths to prove that the basic principles of their system were laid down in Marx's and Engels' writings. Moreover, there were historical precedents. The cooperatives inspired by Robert Owen (1771–1858), the 'phalanstères' of Charles Fourier (1772–1837) and the 'ateliers sociaux' envisaged by Louis Blanc (1811–1882), all contained important elements of what was to become in Yugoslavia workers' self-management.[3] The Paris Commune of 1871 and the Russian Soviets of 1905 and 1917 were also a source of inspiration for Yugoslav theoreticians.[4]

The transition process was far from smooth and – as stated above – proceeded in leaps and bounds. Several authors have therefore divided the entire period in stages according to their perception of the number and importance of the various leaps. In this study, the categorisation suggested by Horvat[5] and Gorupic[6] will be followed, as they are less concerned with formal changes, such as legislative action, but trace instead the turning points in the broad development of the system.[7] They distinguish three principal stages:

- The centrally planned economy (Horvat) or, as most Yugoslavs still call it, 'the administrative management of the economy' (Gorupic); during this period which ran from the end of the war until approximately early 1952 the Yugoslav economic and social system was modelled strictly on Soviet principles.
- The phase of decentralisation (Horvat), or in Gorupic's terms, 'the

construction of the system of workers' self-management', lasting from 1952 to 1965; essentially this was a period of transition, leading to:
- Self-government socialism (Horvat), or the self-managing socialist society (Gorupic), from 1965 onwards.

Of course, even this division in chronological phases is to some extent arbitrary. The first moves towards decentralisation occurred some time before 1952, and the Economic Reform of 1965 which heralded the beginning of a new stage was in fact a better conceived and implemented version of the reform attempted in 1961. But, however that may be, the system passed through these three major phases, and in order to understand the last and present stage some attention will have to be given to the preceding periods.

1.2.1. *The Soviet model: the centrally-planned economy*

At the outcome of the Second World War Yugoslavia was utterly devastated. About 1.7 million people had been killed – more than a tenth of the population – the transport system was in chaos, almost two-fifths of the manufacturing industry was either completely destroyed or seriously damaged, the financial system was hopelessly disrupted: seven different currencies were in circulation. The loss of national wealth amounted to 17 percent of the total war damage suffered by eighteen countries represented at the Paris Reparations Conference in 1945.[8] It was a situation almost beyond repair, and these odds were faced by a country, backward even before the war, and led by a group of men with little or no experience in government. But whatever they were short of, the Yugoslavs certainly did not lack confidence. Strengthened by the knowledge that they had been the only country that had liberated itself from the fascist invaders, they set about the task of reconstruction without delay. They had an example to go by, however: Soviet Russia. The Yugoslav partisans, who found themselves in charge of the country, were communists. They had a ready made system with which to tackle the problems at hand, and their leaders had seen and studied how the system operated in practice in Russia.

The new regime had set itself two broad tasks: 'to repair war damage as fast as possible and to organise the economy on what were considered to be socialist principles.'[9] The great wave of national enthusiasm generated by the liberation created a momentum of sizeable force and by 1947 pre-war output levels had again been reached.[10] The first step towards the fulfilment of the second major goal was not entirely orthodox: the agrarian reform did not nationalise all farm lands to turn them into state farms. Private farmers were allowed individual holdings of 87 acres. The excess acquired by the state was distributed among poor peasants and farm workers (half of the total), and to cooperative and state farms.[11] It was typically a case of human nature overruling the requirements of ideology. Yugoslavia was an agricultural country[12] and the partisan forces consisted largely of peasants. It would have been surprising indeed if they were to have been deprived of the opportunity to till their own land after having risked their lives in four years of battle against the invading armies.

The agrarian reform was, however, the only instance where Yugoslavia deviated from strict orthodoxy. 'Soviet influence was so complete that the Yugoslavs hastened, well before their comrades elsewhere in Eastern Europe, to nationalise the means of production and to commence with central planning.'[13] This is the more remarkable since Yugoslavia, having no Red troops on its soil, was under no compulsion to follow the Soviet line as was the case in the satellite states. The Yugoslavs, with the absolute faith of newly converted believers, simply 'regarded the Communist Party of the Soviet Union as the sole authority on the interpretation of Marxism.'[14]

The Soviet system was formally established with the adoption of a new Constitution (1946), the 'Basic Law on State Economic Enterprises' (1946), and the 'Law on the State Economic Plan and State Planning Agencies' (1947), the latter introducing the first Five-Year Plan. The Plan was to be the main instrument of the state's economic management. Article 15 of the 1946 Constitution stated: 'In order to protect the essential interests of the people, increase national welfare and make proper use of all economic potentials, the state directs economic life and development through a general economic plan relying on the state and cooperative sector and exercising control over the private sector of the economy.'[15] The Law on planning (1947) was even more explicit, and laid down that 'the long-term and current state plans have the force of law, and are binding on all state agencies and state and cooperative economic enterprises and institutions throughout the entire territory of Yugoslavia.'[16]

At the same time, the (nationalised) enterprises lost all freedom of action. After the introduction of the Basic Law on State Economic Enterprises, every enterprise came under the wings of a government agency which had far-reaching powers. The agency determined the operations and investment plans of the enterprise, fixed prices, controlled relations with 'trade partners', and appropriated the enterprise's surplus funds.[17] As observed by Gorupic, 'enterprises were in fact state agencies. Financial operations of the enterprise were a component part of the state budget. All its profit went into the state budget, and its losses were covered by it.'[18]

There can be no doubt about it: the system, by 1951, was pure Soviet communism. Every single decision was taken at the top, the economy was run by the state.

### 1.2.2. *The phase of decentralisation*

While Yugoslavia was fully engaged in the process of establishing an economic system along the lines of the Soviet model, a remarkable development occurred in the political field. A development that utterly stunned the Yugoslav leadership, and that was described later by Horvat as 'a complete shock': the excommunication of Yugoslavia from the Cominform.[19]

On the whole, relations between the Yugoslav communists and the Russian leadership had been good.[20] There had, of course, been minor tensions during and after the war but these were never taken very seriously by the Yugoslavs who considered them as unimportant differences of opinion between members of one and the same family. What the Yugoslav communists failed to understand at the time, however, was that the Soviet Union was not going to tolerate a socialist state in Eastern Europe over which it had no control. And it was precisely their independence which the Yugoslavs valued most, having fought for it during a vicious war at enormous sacrifice.

After some initial skirmishes, the situation became serious in early 1948 when Stalin accused the Yugoslavs of revisionism and anti-Sovietism. The accusation was really baseless as the Yugoslav communists were doing all in their power to model the economy on the Russian example. Not surprisingly, the Yugoslavs were shocked and their first reaction was 'a somewhat naive but understandable attempt to prove that Stalin and others must have been misinformed, that no-one (in Yugoslavia) questioned orthodoxy in organising a socialist economy, that state ownership and central planning were the keystones of the system.'[21] Of course, the Yugoslav efforts were to no avail and in June 1948, the Yugoslav Communist Party was expelled from the Cominform. Russian loans were cancelled, and trade reduced to a trickle. But still the Yugoslavs adhered to the Soviet economic doctrine and, in fact, speeded up the rate of collectivisation of agriculture. By 1951 – as stated earlier – the economy was a carbon copy of the Soviet system.

The blind faith in all things Russian was, however, irretrievably damaged and the Yugoslavs soon began to question the Soviet interpretation of Marx. During the course of 1950 this developed into an extensive critique of Soviet centralised decision-making and dominance of the state bureaucracy.[22] But Yugoslav thinkers did not limit themselves to criticism of the Soviet Union: they started to re-study the classics – Marx and Engels. The problem, however, was that Marx and Engels 'wrote seldom and very little about socialism.'[23] They had stated that the disappearance of private ownership would entail the elimination of the market and that distribution would be organised, without the intermediary of money, through comprehensive planning.[24] So far it had always been assumed that by comprehensive planning Marx had meant central planning by the state, and state ownership by the elimination of private ownership. But neither Marx nor Engels had ever drawn such conclusions. In fact, they appeared to have said something quite different. Edvard Kardelj, in an important article in the journal *Kommunist* of July 1949, first put forward Marx's notion of the 'withering away of the state'. Referring to Marx's treatise 'The Paris Commune', he maintained that Marx had denounced the state and argued that it would wither away in the classless society which would be based on popular participation and workers' management of the factories. The theme was quickly taken up by other Yugoslav social scientists, and by politicians such as Djilas and Boris Kidric (later to become head of the Federal Planning Commission and President of the Economic Council). It was argued that far from being truly socialist, state ownership was 'state capitalism' under which the workers would still be exploited – not by private owners but by the state bureaucracy.

Having rejected the concept of the state as the decision-making authority in the economic process, the alternative was clear: the economic system should be decentralised (which implied acceptance of the market) and the enterprises should be run by the workers themselves. How this milestone was reached is revealed by Djilas in a fascinating account:

'The idea of self-management was conceived by Kardelj and me with some help from our comrade Kidric. Soon after the outbreak of the quarrel with Stalin, in 1949 ... I began to reread Marx's *Capital*, this time with much greater care, to see if I could find the answer to the riddle of why, to put it in simplistic terms, Stalinism was bad and Yugoslavia was good. I discovered many new ideas and, most interesting of all, ideas about a future society in which the immediate producers, through free associations, would themselves make the decisions regarding production and distribution – would, in fact, run their own lives and their own future ...

One day – it must have been in the spring of 1950 – it occurred to me that we Yugoslav communists were now in a position to start creating Marx's free association of producers. The factories would be left in their hands, with the proviso that they should pay a tax for military and other state needs still remaining essential. With all this, I felt a tinge of reservation: is not this the way for us communists, I asked myself, to shift the responsibility for failures and difficulties in the economy onto the shoulders of the working class, or to compel the working class to take a share of such responsibilities from us? I soon explained my idea to Kardelj and Kidric while we sat in a car parked in front of the villa where I lived. They felt no such reservation, and I was able all too easily to convince them of the indisputable harmony between my ideas and Marx's teaching. Without leaving the car, we thrashed it out for little more than half an hour. Kardelj thought it was a good idea, but one that should not be put into effect for another five or six years[25] and Kidric agreed with him. A couple of days later, however, Kidric telephoned me to say that we were ready to go ahead at once with the first steps... Shortly thereafter began the debates on the issues of principle and on the statutory aspects that went on for some four or five months. Tito, busy with other duties and absent from Belgrade, took no part in this and knew nothing of the proposal soon to introduce a workers' council bill in the parliament until he was informed by Kardelj and me in the government lobby room during a session in the National Assembly. His first reaction was: our workers are not ready for that yet. But Kardelj and I, convinced that this was an important step, pressed him hard, and he began to unbend as he paid more attention to our explanations. The most important part of our case was that this would be the beginning of democracy, something that socialism had not yet achieved; further, it could be plainly seen by the world and the international workers' movement as a radical departure from Stalinism. Tito paced up and down, as though completely wrapped in his own thoughts. Suddenly he stopped and exclaimed: "Factories belonging to the workers–something that has never yet been achieved!" ... A few months later, Tito explained the Workers' Self-management Bill to the National Assembly.'[26]

On June 27, 1950, the 'Basic Law on the Management of State Economic Enterprises and Higher Economic Associations by Work Collectives' was enacted. The law made it mandatory for all enterprises to establish workers' councils elected by the workers of the enterprise.[27] The workers' council chose in turn from its midst a management board which, together with the director, would exercise day-to-day management. The workers' council was empowered by the law to adopt the statutes of the enterprise, to determine general business policy, to approve the annual plan and the year-end accounts, and overrule any decision of the management board.[28] These powers were certainly sweeping, but in practice the system was slow in being implemented. As Gorupic has observed, a dualism was created in the organisation of the enterprise consisting on the one hand of the democratically elected workers' council and the old hierarchical management structure on the other.[29] In fact, the 'one-man management' by the director, supported by the technical and administrative services under his responsibility remained largely intact. Of course, it is not surprising that the radical change of the system envisaged by the law was not immediately turned into a living reality. The workers' councils needed some time to familiarise themselves with the complicated problems of running an enterprise and this was the more difficult since their members lacked the necessary background and knowledge. The director was therefore left with substantial leeway to push his proposals and policies through the workers' council. In addition, initially the state 'continued to play a substantial role in setting the legal and administrative limits within which the workers' councils operated, in levying taxes and in determining wages and prices.'[30] This point, however, was under review. Slowly, the centralised command economy was being dismantled: the former economic ministries were abolished and replaced by 'Higher Economic Associations' in which the enterprises had a voice, prices were liberated to a large extent, and the role of the plan was being reconsidered. On the last day of 1951, a law was passed which tied these various changes together. But once again there was a certain duality: on the one hand, the tendency to grant enterprises increasing independence, on the other the state retained – in spite of the liberalisation measures – a strong influence in the economic affairs of the country.[31]

While detailed central planning was abolished – leaving the enterprises correspondingly more autonomy – the law instituted planning by so-called 'basic proportions'. This meant that the plan could lay down mandatory rules on:[32]

- the minimum level of utilisation of productive capacity;
- large specific projects;
- the average rate of investment;
- the level of wages.

The law introduced the so-called 'Accumulation and Funds System'. The system worked as follows.[33] The total amount of the payroll for the enterprise (wage fund) was established by multiplying the average wage (set by the state) for each category of professional skill with the respective numbers of workers in those categories in the enterprise. The amount the enterprise had to spend on investment (accumulation) was then established by the state as the ratio between the wage fund and 'accumulation'. These rates were set at different levels for the various sectors of the economy. The balance of the enterprise's income remaining after paying out the wage fund and the expenditure on accumulation was at the free disposal of the enterprise. If this balance was paid out to the workers in the form of bonuses, the enterprise had to pay a progressive tax on the total amount of bonus payments. It is obvious that this 'A-F system' rather considerably curtailed the self-management of the enterprise.

It should further be noted that there were only two sources of funds from which the enterprises could finance their investments: internally-generated funds of the enterprise itself and budgetary funds allocated by the state through the General Investment Fund. Since in practice no enterprise was able to finance its investments out of its own resources, this left a powerful tool in the hands of the federal bureaucracy. Initially, these funds were disbursed à fonds perdu, the obligation to repay investment credits was introduced only later. The enterprises were, however, obliged to pay a 'capital rent' (6%) over all funds at their disposal regardless of origin, i.e. including over internally generated funds.

While the Yugoslavs still did not have a very precise idea of the economic system they were striving to introduce[34] – and indeed were, to a large extent, contradictory in their policies – by 1952 it was sufficiently clear on what principles that system would have to be based: workers' management of the enterprises and decentralisation of the economy.

At this point it may be interesting to review the motives which had led the Yugoslavs to reject the Soviet system. Broekmeyer,[35] as indeed most writers on the subject, basically sees two underlying causes: ideological/political and economic. The argument with respect to the first is clear and unobjectionable: the excommunication of Yugoslavia by the Cominform in 1948 invited a rejection of the system of the political adversary. The second cause, however, is open to question. Broekmeyer maintains that the economic difficulties caused by the blockade by Yugoslavia's East-European neighbours, several bad harvests, and increased defence expenditures were too much to handle for the bureaucratic state apparatus and that the enterprises had to be given some freedom to achieve a more rational use of available resources. This is not entirely convincing, what Broekmeyer implicitly is stating is that a centrally planned economy is workable only in a situation without stresses – and that is not proven.

The most common line of argument, however, with respect to the economic motive is that a centralised system is well suited in the initial stages of development but, once certain bottlenecks are broken and the choices open to planners are multiplying, the market system becomes a more attractive method.[36] One might ask, however, whether Yugoslavia had progressed so far and so fast in the few years until 1952 to justify the change of system. As Milenkovitch rightfully points out,[37] all other East-European countries were in a similar stage of the development process and continued to maintain the same high rates of growth without adopting another economic system.

There is, however, another factor which may have helped to set the process of decentralisation in motion: Yugoslavia's historical and economic background. This background is highly diversified, and the country is often characterised as a federation with six constituent republics, five nations, four languages, three religions, two alphabets and one political party. The strong nationalism in the constituent parts of Yugoslavia has its roots in the century-old cultural, religious and political differences. The peasant in Macedonia or Kosovo, with a per capita income of less than $ 200 and a Turkish/Islamic heritage is closer to the peasant of other South-European or Middle Eastern countries than to his countryman in Slovenia or Northern Croatia who, for his part, shares a standard of living and cultural background with his Austrian or Northern Italian neighbours. These differences are so large and are still of such an important influence in present-day Yugoslavia that it may be useful to describe their roots.

The division of the Roman Empire in 395 split the territory of Yugoslavia into two zones. The area comprised by what is now Slovenia and Croatia was oriented towards Western Europe and Roman Catholicism with all its social and cultural implications. The largest part of this region was integrated in the Frankish Empire, except for the coastal area which came under Byzantine rule. For about two hundred years Croatia was an independent kingdom (mid 9th to mid 11th century); for the eight following centuries it was part of Hungary and later of the Austro-Hungarian Empire. The Southern and Eastern regions became part of the Byzantine Empire and adopted later the Orthodox religion. When Byzantium began to weaken around 1200 the first independent states emerged in the territories of Bosnia and Serbia. Their rise, however, was halted by the Turkish penetration in the Balkans. The Ottoman Empire gradually expanded its influence and at the beginning of the 16th century the Yugoslav peoples found themselves again within the frontiers of two great monarchies: Turkey and Austria, with the geographical division being practically the same as a thousand years before. This increased the fundamental differences within the country. Slovenia and Northern Croatia, under Austrian rule, took part in the economic, social and cultural development of Western Europe. The other parts stagnated under Turkish rule.

With the weakening of the Turkish Empire in the eighteenth century, parts of Yugoslavia acquired an increasing degree of independence. The little mountain Kingdom of Montenegro had never been conquered by the Turks, while Serbia became autonomous in 1830 and an independent principality at the time of the Congress of Berlin (1878). The State of Yugoslavia came into being in 1918 as the result of the amalgamation of Serbia and Montenegro with certain provinces from the dismembered Austro-Hungarian and Turkish Empires. The very name of the new state, 'Kingdom of the Serbs, Croats and Slovenes', highlights the divisions that were caused by sharply divergent cultural traditions, religious and historical background. The strong dominance of Serbia in the new state did nothing to alleviate the differences and the inter-war period saw an almost uninterrupted struggle between the forces of centralism (Serbia) and federalism (Croatia). For about ten years, the country experienced parliamentary democracy. In 1929, however, a royal dictatorship was established as the King saw no other way to end the interminable and increasingly vicious quarrels between Serbs and Croats. Initially, the King found wide support for his efforts to install a more efficient public administration, but the old antagonisms soon re-emerged. The King's assassination in 1934 plunged the country again into political chaos, which was to continue until 1939 when finally Serbs and Croats came to an agreement. External events, however, precluded further political stabilisation. In April 1941 the German-Italian forces invaded the country. The events of the Second World War led to the emergence, for the first time, of a truly national Yugoslav feeling. But once the enthusiasm generated by the liberation had worn off, the old suspicions against Belgrade, capital of the Federation but of Serbia as well, again arose. Each of the Republics, determined to preserve its 'national heritage', resented the fact that in the early post-war years all decisions were made in Belgrade over which they had very little control. And while it may be argued that these deep-rooted differences were not the prime cause of the decentralisation process, they contributed most certainly a great deal to the momentum the process achieved.

Returning now to the development of the system in the early fifties, a significant event had taken place in the political sphere with the Sixth Congress of the Yugoslav Communist Party in November 1952. The voices that for the last couple of years had been arguing that self-management was incompatible with state centralism and the political monopoly of the Party had become so strong that a change was inevitable. At the Sixth Congress it was therefore formally decided that the Party would give up its 'ruling, governing and commanding'[38] position and transform itself into 'an association of political activists.'[39] To symbolise the change, the Party adopted a new name: League of Yugoslav Communists. Of course, this formal decision did not by itself change the role of the Party very much in practice initially. But it was important in the sense that it was another deviation in principle from the Soviet system.

Having redefined the role of the Party, the next task at hand was the dismantling of the centralised state apparatus. The decentralisation process took somewhat longer and was carried out in many intermediate steps. It would require far too much space to treat these in detail, and only the most important will be traced here.

The concept of 'state capitalism' was formally abolished in 1953 when the Constitution was amended. It now ruled that: 'Social ownership of the means of production, the self-government of producers in the economy and self-government of working people in the commune, city and district represent the basis of the social and political system of the country' (Article 4). At about the same time, the planning system was liberalised. Now only the 'basic principles of economic development and not myriads of details were considered the proper subject matter for political determination.'[40] The objectives of the Plan[41] were to be achieved indirectly by such instruments as credit policy, price policy and the like. The enterprises were freed from the fixed rates of the A-F System, and instead profit taxing was adopted as an instrument of income distribution between state and enterprise. Moreover, the enterprises now had the right to determine their own production and investment plans and to dispose of residual income (after payment of taxes and operating costs which included a fixed amount per worker for wages) for bonus payments or reinvestment. The diminishing role of the plan implied an increase in the importance of the market, but direct interference of the state continued in the form of price controls (inflation was causing problems) and through the allocation of investment funds, rebates, subsidies, multiple exchange rates, etc. In 1957 the system of five-year plans was resumed, and the new plan was even more flexible than its predecessors. An innovation was the attention given to the standard of living of the population.

By the end of 1960, the Yugoslavs felt confident enough to make another step forward. The five-year plan had been successfully completed, the economy was booming, and it was felt that the self-management system was well established in the enterprises.[42] In 1961, three reforms were carried out. In the first place, to improve the efficiency of the market 'the hitherto virtually closed economy was to be made more susceptible to the influences of the world market.'[43] The dinar was devalued, multiple exchange rates were abolished, and foreign trade was liberalised to a large extent. Secondly, the entire financial system was reorganised. The banks were transformed from mere windows through which government funds were disbursed into independent, profit-making agencies, although this independence was far more formal than real, as will be seen later. Thirdly, supervision of wage levels and wage differentials were abolished and the share of enterprise income that the workers' council could distribute between personal income, investment funds and social consumption expenditures was increased. Progressive taxes on enterprise income were replaced by a flat rate to provide greater incentives to increase efficiency.

Unfortunately, economic performance in 1961 and 1962 was disappointing. The rate of growth of industrial production was halved (7% as against 14% in 1960), prices rose fast, imports soared and exports stagnated. As could be expected, the discussion on whether liberalisation and decentralisation were the 'correct' policy for Yugoslavia flared up again. In fact, while the country had gone ahead with this policy since about 1950, the protagonists of the Soviet-type system – although in a minority – were never completely silenced and this was the chance they had been waiting for. The debate was acrimonious. The decentralisers, of course, argued that the economic problems were not due to liberalisation but, rather, to mismanagement, half-hearted implementation of the reforms and continued interference by the state. Their opponents blamed the 'anarchy of the market' and advocated a return to mandatory planning – if not on the federal level, then at least by the Republics. In the end, the decentralisers carried the day. By 1964 the principles of a new, even more far-reaching, reform were being discussed all over the country, and in July 1965 the Federal Assembly passed a number of laws inaugurating the 1965 Economic Reform.

### 1.2.3. *Self-government socialism*

It was the Economic Reform of 1965 that finally established the 'labour-managed market economy'. The purpose of the Reform was to achieve three objectives:

a. to consolidate the self-management system by giving greater responsibilities to the enterprises for their production and investment decisions. This required an increasing role of the market and a further reduction in the government's power in the allocation of resources;
b. to correct distortions in the pattern of output which had been caused by subsidies, price controls and other selective regulations;
c. to increase efficiency by integrating the Yugoslav economy in the world economy (especially the industrialised West).

To implement the Reform, a number of specific measures were taken: the dinar was devalued again,[44] the average rate of customs duties was halved, many import and export restrictions were removed, tax laws were changed (the profit tax abolished and the 'capital rent' lowered from 6% to 4%), and subsidies in the form of controlled prices were removed. Government control over investment funds was further reduced by the 'Law on Banks and Credit Operations' (March 1965). The law not only freed the banks – de jure – from political and governmental control, but aimed at introducing competition among the banks. The banks were no longer to receive the bulk of their new resources from the state, they had to compete in the market for deposits. Enterprises were now also completely free to choose their own bank, while the banks for their part had to give more attention to security and liquidity as the state would no longer assist them automatically if they got into difficulties. The only federal investment agency retained was the 'Fund for the Financing of Economic Development in Underdeveloped Republics and Regions'.

The self-management system was further strengthened by the 'Basic Enterprises Act' of 1965, which emphasised the independence of the enterprises. The opening paragraph of the Act reads: 'By freely combining their work through association, the working people in the enterprise permanently organise and expand production, trade and other economic activities on the basis of socialised assets and self-management, thereby satisfying their own individual and joint interests and the general interest of society.'[45] It is interesting to note that 'the general interest of society' is mentioned at the end, after the individual and joint interests of the workers in the enterprise: a clear and definite rejection of the Soviet system.

The changes introduced by the Reform, the increased independence of the enterprises and the decentralisation of the allocation of resources, had obviously considerable consequences for the role to be played by the Plan. And although Yugoslavia was now a 'market economy', such role was still of some importance. As Milenkovitch aptly states: 'The Marxist attitude over the years had been planning *versus* market. The Yugoslavs had slowly freed themselves of the dichotomy of this approach and accepted the principle of plan *and* market.'[46] At the beginning of 1966, the Federal Assembly approved a remarkable document,[47] the so-called 'Theses on the Fundamentals of Social Planning', which exhaustively dealt with the issue of plan and market. As the Theses embody the official point of view, it is worthwhile to quote them at length.

'The plan and the market, and the plan and self-management make one whole and condition each other. If the plan is basically adjusted to the real possibilities, needs and interests of the agents of economic and social activities, then it is not at variance with the action of the laws of commodity production, but directs and stimulates their positive social action ... Planning should accelerate and support objective development processes instead of imposing arbitrary directions and elements of development. If they are objectively conditioned, the social development targets laid down by the plan would also be realised through the free action of economic laws, only in this case their realisation would often require disproportionately more time, resources and effort. Those targets which ignore this objective interdependence would be problematic ... Efficient influence can be exerted by the plan only to the extent to which it is possible to perceive the potentialities, interests and actions of the economic process, and to the extent to which the agents of planning are able to adjust the plan to these while respecting the foundations of the social and economic system. If this borderline is overstepped, the plan inevitably turns into an arbitrary scheme, which ignores the economic laws of the proportional division of labour, and into an element of disharmony and imbalance, and thus narrows the scope of self-management by producers in work organisations.'[48]

From an instrument of coercion, as in the Soviet system, the plan had now turned into an instrument of cooperation. Its role was now simply to 'accelerate' the development process by helping to avoid inefficiencies of the market.

Horvat has summarised the debates on the issue of planning over the last decade in three sets of alternatives:[49]

a. Should the plan be a prognosis or an obligation to act?
b. In the case of planning on different levels (i.e. enterprise – Republic – Federation), should the relationship be one of equality or subordination?
c. Should the national plan be derived from local and partial plans or should the latter be derived from fragmentation of a central plan?

While Horvat acknowledges that the alternatives have been debated in these terms, he rejects himself the 'either-or' propositions as intrinsically faulty. With respect to the first issue, he argues that 'a plan that is not binding on anyone for anything would not be a plan but an intellectual exercise.' State agencies, and, to a lesser extent, banks are held to act according to the directives of the plan, but for the 'autonomous economic organisations the plan is only a prognosis'. On the second issue, Horvat takes an equally qualified position: 'equality of rights' is a necessary precondition for self-government, subordination would effectively destroy it. Horvat makes, however, a distinction between political subordination, which is unacceptable, and social subordination. Since the plan is drawn up in a democratic way, after consultation with 'representative bodies' at all levels, it embodies the social interests of the people. It is therefore 'not contradictory ... to give more social weight to the opinions of representative bodies than to individual economic subjects. In a word, insistence on social interests is not incompatible with the inviolability of autonomy.' This statement is ambiguous; what Horvat probably means is that the plan cannot be enforced by legal means, but that the autonomous enterprise (or Republic) has the moral obligation not to counteract the plan. In practice, the Yugoslavs deal with the problem of potential or actual conflicts between social and individual interests very pragmatically. The normal procedure – which will be dealt with more extensively later on in connection with the 1970 Law on Planning – is one of consultation, in which officials of the government, the party, the trade unions, the Chambers of Commerce may be involved according to the circumstances. It is rare for some kind of solution not to be found and an open conflict to occur. This flexibility has little to do with the system as such – it is a typical Yugoslav quality.

With respect to the third issue, Horvat again rejects the 'either-or'. In working out the social plan there must be a constant flow of information upward from below and vice versa, and a joint solution of the problems of real or presumed divergence of interests.

In his article in the *American Economic Review* of June 1971 Horvat has gone even further in stating that 'social planning' is not in contradiction to the autonomy of the enterprises but, rather, enhances it on three grounds:[50]

- 'It reduces uncertainty, which is a basic restriction on decision making.
- It increases the rate of growth thereby increasing available alternatives (for inputs, output, and sales).
- It equalises business conditions thereby lessening the dependence of the producer on external circumstances which he cannot control and which are "economically and socially irrational."'

For Horvat, and for most Yugoslav policy-makers, the old controversy of plan-versus-market is no longer an issue. Decentralisation and self-management are the guiding principles, but those principles will not be upheld à tout prix. In the background, there is always the notion that the whole is more than the sum of the parts, and that somehow a way has to be found to accommodate what is referred to as the 'social interests'. And it is precisely at this point that a theoretical analysis of the Yugoslav system is bound to fail. Conflicts are solved on an ad hoc basis, pragmatically and with a fine sense for the right compromise. A study of Yugoslav practices in this area is subject matter for a behavioural scientist – the economist can only observe and note that the system works.

In July 1970 parliament enacted a new 'Basic Law on Social Planning' that formalised the changes in planning principles and practices that had evolved since the Theses of 1965. The emphasis of the law is unambiguous: 'Proceeding from their immediate and lasting interests, the working people and citizens in organisations of associated labour (i.e. enterprises), in communities of interests, and in socio-political communities forecast, adjust and direct social and economic development through planning based on self-management.'[51] The targets of the plan are to be determined 'through self-management and social consultation'[52] and these legal provisions are effectively put into practice. The drafting of the Federal plan has become a complicated affair involving literally hundreds of organisations, research institutes and socio-political entities. In this process the role of the Federal Planning Bureau has been reduced to a purely technical one, providing economic analyses of the various options that are being debated or considered. The elaboration of the Federal plan now comprises basically three stages:[53] in the first stage the Federal Assembly reviews the analyses and proposals that have been drafted by the institutions (or, as the Yugoslavs say, planning agents) mentioned above, and issues guidelines for the first draft of the comprehensive plan by the Federal Planning Bureau on the basis of these analyses and proposals. In the second stage, the Assembly reviews the draft plan and submits it for 'public discussion'. This discussion is intensive – it resulted in a considerable delay in the original timetable for the 1971–75 Federal plan. The third stage involves the preparation of a final draft by the Federal Planning Bureau, again based on proposals coming from below, and its review and ultimate adoption by the Assembly.

How the doctrine will evolve further is difficult to foresee.[54] What is certain, however, is that self-management will remain the cornerstone of the system, and that all changes and modifications will be aimed at its strengthening.

## 1.3. THEORETICAL ASPECTS OF THE LABOUR-MANAGED MARKET ECONOMY

It is surprising to note that the Yugoslav system, unique as it is, has not attracted more interest from economic theorists. Apart from the Yugoslavs themselves – about whom more below – only a few authors (Ward, Domar, and Vanek) have attempted a theoretical analysis, and only in the case of Vanek can such analysis be called comprehensive.[55]

Studies by Yugoslav authors are not easily accessible to a Western economist. Firstly, there is the language problem – only rarely are important books or articles translated. But even when a translation is available, problems remain. Theoretical analysis of the kind that is carried out in the West is unfamiliar in Yugoslavia. Most Yugoslav authors, when given to theorising about the nature of their system, tend to dwell on questions of an ideological nature and appear to have little interest in the purely economic aspects. The argument is often difficult to follow since the assumptions are rarely made explicit, and the tendency to consider a point proven by quoting an appropriate passus from Marx's writings cannot satisfy the Western reader. Wiles, rather unkindly, speaks of 'the great tension ... between the large, generous and humane imprecisions characteristic of Yugoslav Marxism and the narrow, petty and technical quest for specific truths (in the plural) for which the Western economist is notorious.'[56] Moreover, it would appear that Yugoslav economists until recently were mostly interested in descriptive analysis and economic policy problems.[57] Horvat explained this phenomenon by the fact that post-war

Yugoslavia was short of economists because the first economic faculties were established only after the war. In addition, there was 'hardly any time left for analysis. Economists were busy changing the organisations, institutions and policies, and keeping themselves informed about all these changes.'[58] It is therefore understandable that, so far, no 'generally accepted' theory of the behaviour of the worker-managed firm has emerged in Yugoslavia.[59] One might even go one step further and say that, with the exception of Horvat, no Yugoslav economist has attempted to analyse – in terms of Wiles's 'technical quest for specific economic truths' – the behaviour or maximising principles of the Yugoslav firm under market conditions. Consequently, since there is very little Yugoslav literature on this subject, the survey will necessarily be limited to Horvat.[60]

Before embarking on a survey of the theoretical analyses of Western economists (and Horvat), it is necessary to make a few preliminary remarks. In the first place, the principal reason for the following brief account of some theoretical aspects of the system in its 'pure form' is to lay a basis for a better understanding of the Yugoslav system as it functions in practice. In order to serve this purpose only those theoretical models which are derived from, or have some resemblance to, the 'real' system will be dealt with. Of course, every theoretical model necessarily implies abstraction, but there is a fundamental difference between abstraction by reducing a system to its bare essentials and abstraction by designing a purely hypothetical economic model. The latter can be a highly interesting exercise, but is of little use when it comes to understanding a given economic system. No attention will therefore be paid, for example, to the otherwise important work of Oskar Lange[61] or Horvat's *Toward a theory of the planned economy.*[62]

A second remark concerns the fact that the (Western) analyses of the theoretical aspects of the Yugoslav economic system are almost invariably couched in terms of a comparison between the 'efficiency' of the Yugoslav and capitalist systems. This raises some definitional problems. One cannot escape the impression that most authors regard 'efficiency' as some absolute yardstick against which systems can be measured in absolute terms and, consequently, compared with each other. It would seem, however, that this concept is too narrow. As Tinbergen has pointed out, the efficiency of a system is the degree to which a particular system, as opposed to another, makes it possible to meet 'the aspirations of the people as a whole.'[63] This would imply that an absolute yardstick does not exist. Inasmuch as the aspirations of the people of one country (and cultural background) may differ considerably from those of another, it is entirely possible that a particular economic system is highly efficient for the former and inadequate for the latter. Moreover, the aspirations of a people are never only economic in nature, which will amplify potential divergencies. Furthermore, the aspirations can be, to some extent, a function of the economic system itself. It is therefore difficult to follow Tinbergen further when he speaks of the optimum order, implying there is only one order that can be characterised as optimal.[64] Moreover, this contention seems to contradict his subsequent statements that 'the theoretical method to judge the distance between any given order and the optimal order is to apply welfare economics and to formulate the conditions the optimum has to satisfy and then compare these with the given order.'[65] These conditions or 'preferences' by which an order must be guided find their expression in the so-called social welfare function. '*The variables occurring in such a function are all phenomena which make for the satisfaction of the members of the community.*'[66] Leaving aside the problem of measuring these variables, it is obvious that – as stated earlier – what makes one country (or a particular community within such country for that matter) happy may be rejected by another. One is therefore inclined to agree with Van den Doel who maintains that the optimal order is not only conditioned by objective factors, but also depends on subjective choices which are made when the targets (or, as Tinbergen would say, the aspirations of a people) are formulated. Consequently, it is not correct to speak of one optimum, since every combination of targets requires a different optimal system.[67]

This inevitably leads to the conclusion that a comparison between the economic efficiency of the labour-managed market economy and the capitalist economy (i.e. a rating of the two systems in the sense of one being superior to the other) is not really valid unless they are compared in relation to one single set of targets and, moreover, that these targets are made explicit. Unfortunately, none of the authors whose analyses of the efficiency of the Yugoslav system will be reviewed here has done so. It would seem, however, that all equate maximum efficiency with equalised marginal factor returns. This, of course, is the conventional concept used by Western economists. Although this definition of efficiency is not above criticism, it will – for the sake of convenience – not be further disputed in the remainder of this section in order to facilitate the review of the literature on the theoretical aspects of the labour-managed market economy. But it should be noted, once again, that from the comparison made between the two systems no conclusions can be drawn with respect to the superiority of one system over the other.

A final remark concerns the necessity to limit this survey to manageable proportions. And in spite of the fact that only a few authors have dealt with the Yugoslav system, a separate study would be required if the entire body of existing theoretical analyses were to be dissected. In what follows, therefore, only a summary account is presented of the more important conclusions emerging from the literature.

### 1.3.1. *Ward*

The first to undertake a theoretical analysis of the Yugoslav system was Benjamin Ward in his article 'The firm in Illyria: market syndicalism.'[68] In Ward's model 'the means of production are nationalised and the factories turned over to the workers who are free to set price and output policy in their own material self-interest.'[69] This hypothetical Illyria comes, in fact, fairly close to the Yugoslav situation.

Ward argued that the Illyrian (labour-managed) enterprise would have a maximising principle different from that of the capitalist firm. Whereas the latter, at least in theory, maximises total profits, the labour-managed firm behaves rationally if it aims to maximise income per worker. This principle, established by Ward, has been accepted by all other Western writers. It is, indeed, not illogical to assume that the 'worker-managers, acting in their own material self-interest, are not necessarily interested in maximising profits as their capitalist counterparts, the stockholders or entrepreneurs would be. Each worker is interested in maximising his own income.'[70] Given these two different maximising principles, the labour-managed firm might find it rational to use different input combinations to produce different outputs than an otherwise similar capitalist enterprise would under the same conditions (identical production functions, and identical prices of output and inputs).[71]

In the simplest case (one product, one variable input i.e. labour, perfect competition, short run), Ward found some surprising results:[72] faced with an increase in fixed costs, the Illyrian firm would increase output and employment, but an upward change in the price of the product would lead to reduced output and employment.[73] Ward concluded that the Illyrian firm has a negatively-sloped supply curve which implies a potential danger for the stability of the economy. This behaviour is different from that of the capitalist enterprise which – under similar conditions – would increase output in the case of a rise in product price and leave output unchanged when an increase in fixed costs occurred.

In the second case, Ward examined the effect of using additional inputs. As far as labour use is concerned, the equilibrium condition for the Illyrian firm would be the same as in the first (one-factor) case: employment will be expanded until the value of the marginal product of labour equals the income per worker. The capitalist firm, of course, hires additional labour to the point where marginal revenue equals marginal costs (i.e. wage). Since income per worker (of the Illyrian firm) is higher than the wage per worker (of the capitalist firm) – except when the latter finds itself in a zero profit situation – the Illyrian firm will reach its equilibrium at lower levels of employment and output than the capitalist firm. With regard to non-labour inputs, however, the behaviour of the capitalist and Illyrian firm is identical: both 'will increase their use of the factor as long as it contributes more to revenue than to costs.'[74] Ward found that in the two-factor case a change in fixed costs would again tend to lead to a change in output in the same direction – just as in the first (one-factor) case. He was, however, more reluctant to come to any firm conclusions with respect to the effect of price changes of input and of output. 'Without a good deal more information it is not possible to state the effect on output of a change in price. The possibility of a positively-inclined supply curve emerges clearly, however, and (of) some presumption that the danger of instability, resulting from a negatively-inclined and relatively elastic supply curve, has diminished.'[75]

Ward's treatment of the behaviour of the Illyrian firm in the case of imperfect markets is not very elaborate. He simply repeats that 'factors are used up to the point at which the marginal revenue product equals the (assumed perfectly elastic) supply price in the case of non-labour inputs, and to the point at which marginal revenue product equals the "full" wage for labour inputs.'[76] He finally stresses the special rigidity of the labour market in Illyria. If the system is in general equilibrium and an excess demand for labour develops, marginal firms will be unable to obtain labour at the existing rate but they will also be unable to pay the new rate since the wage rate was already at a maximum (in the equilibrium position). In the case of an excess supply of labour, workers would be willing to accept lower wages, but Ward assumed that these are not legally possible below a certain rate. (This, in fact, was a realistic assumption: in the real Yugoslav system there is a minimum wage rate set by law.) Ward concluded that the resulting rigidity of the wage offer prevents the achievement of a new equilibrium in the short run.

While Ward deserves considerable credit for his pioneering efforts, his analysis – as he himself admitted – was too limited in scope to allow meaningful comparisons. He examined the Illyrian firm really only under conditions of perfect competition, and he assumed that only one commodity is produced. Moreover, Ward's equilibrium is concerned with the short run and essentially static in nature. It would therefore be premature to come to a judgement on the efficiency[77] of the system based on Ward's findings alone.

### 1.3.2. *Domar*

It took eight years before Ward's analysis was taken up again: in 1966 Evsey Domar published his study on 'The Soviet collective farm as a producer co-operative.'[78] Although Domar did not specifically intend to deal with the Yugoslav system – he was, in fact, interested in the behaviour of a Soviet Kolkhose under certain conditions – his agricultural co-operative resembles closely Ward's Illyrian firm, if the assumptions on which Domar's model is built are examined:[79]

1. 'All non-labour inputs are bought and all outputs are sold at given prices.
2. The production function of the co-operative, if possessed by a profit-maximising firm, would lead to a stable equilibrium under perfect competition.
3. The co-op pays a fixed rent per year.
4. Instead of paying wages, the co-op divides all its net income equally among its members in the form of a dividend.
5. The co-op maximises the dividend per unit of labour.
6. The co-op is actually able to employ the optimum number of labour units maximising the dividend rate.'

To allow comparisons, Domar finally assumes a profit-maximising firm ('the capitalist twin') with the same production function and prices as the co-op, and with a wage rate initially equal to the co-op's dividend rate.

Domar's analysis was broader in scope than Ward's. His production function not only included several factors but several products as well, and – in the second part of his paper – he introduced a supply curve for labour which had some drastic results as will be seen later.

Starting with a given labour input Domar stated that the equilibrium position of the co-op is identical with that of the capitalist twin: both maximise total profit and choose the same outputs and non-labour inputs. When labour becomes a variable factor, the capitalist twin hires additional labour until the value of the marginal product of labour equals the wage, and the co-op takes in labour to the point where the value of the marginal product equals the dividend. But since Domar assumed that initially the marginal product of labour was identical for the two firms and the wage paid by the capitalist twin was equal to the dividend paid by the co-op, both will use the same labour input. In this case, 'use of resources will be identical and allocation of resources in both enterprises is efficient.'[80] It should be noted here that Domar did not point out that his assumption of identical wages and dividend rate implies zero profits for the capitalist firm.

Domar, next, analysed the effect of changes in fixed cost (i.e. rent) and in prices. As Ward before him, he concluded that an increase in rent leads to increased use of labour and output in the case of the co-op, whereas it has no effect on the capitalist twin. The effect of a price change on the co-op is 'more complex because both the dividend rate and the marginal product of labour are affected' as well as of the other inputs. Domar agrees with Ward that, if there is only one output and if labour is the only variable input, both employment and output will contract. The situation becomes more complicated in the case of several outputs and inputs. Domar summarised his findings as shown in Table 1.1:[81]

*Table 1.1. A summary of the effects of an increase in price on the magnitude of outputs and inputs*

| *Effect on* | *Usual capitalist reaction* | *Probable co-op reaction* |
|---|---|---|
| *Increase in the price of an output* | | |
| Output (of product which is increased in price) | Positive | Positive, unless the product concerned has a high labour content or is the only output (in those cases negative) |
| Employment | Positive | Negative |
| Other products | Positive, except when other products competitive with the product of which price was increased | Negative if input proportions remain unchanged: otherwise indeterminate |
| Use of input | Positive | Positive if labour and other input are substitutes; indeterminate for partial complementarity; negative for high complementarity |
| *Increase in the price of an input* | | |
| Use of input | Negative | Negative, except when input and labour are used in constant proportions, in that case the effect is zero |
| Employment | Negative if input and labour are complementary; positive if they are substitutes | Positive, except when input and labour are used in constant proportions, in that case the effect is zero |
| Output | Negative | Indeterminate |

As Table 1.1 shows, the behaviour of Domar's co-op still differs from that of the capitalist firm (which supposedly is behaving rationally). Domar therefore observed that 'the model augurs little good for the allocation of resources among co-ops.'[82] Moreover, Domar agrees with Ward that the labour market will be rigid. 'Indeed, if a rich and a poor co-op[83] should each be in its respective equilibrium, no movement of labour from the poor to the rich is possible (except through a merger) because any movement would reduce the dividend rate in both co-ops. Since the dividend rate in equilibrium equals the net value of the marginal product of labour, there is a definite misallocation of labour, and of course of other resources as well, among the co-ops.'[84]

This rather unfavourable view of the co-op, however, was based on a model that Domar himself admitted was unreal: 'It assumes that labour input can be varied with changing prices and rent in order to maximise the dividend rate ..., a highly unlikely situation once the co-op has been organised.'[85] Since the members of the co-op have other opportunities for employment and for leisure, the co-op is faced with a supply schedule of labour which represents the amount of work members would wish to offer for various levels of dividends. The introduction of this new assumption led to drastic differences in the behaviour of the co-op in response to changes in prices and in rent. In fact, Domar showed that the reaction of the co-op now would be similar to that of the capitalist twin: an increase in rent would lead to a reduction of output and an improvement of output prices to a rise in production. But while this represented a more rational behaviour than that of Ward's Illyrian firm, Domar argued that the equilibrium level of employment was still not likely to be optimal: 'In contrast to the "Pure Model" where the inequality of dividend rates among the co-ops indicated misallocation of labour (and other resources) and where the transfer of labour from the poor to the rich units was clearly in the social interest, the present situation (i.e. assuming a supply curve of labour) is ambiguous because the value of the marginal product of labour no longer (except accidentally) equals the dividend rate.'[86]

Domar's final summing up of his findings was qualified. While 'judged by strictly economic criteria, the co-op has not come out well,'[87] Domar was perceptive enough to realise that efficiency is not determined by economic criteria alone: 'it is quite possible that a co-op may be more efficient than a capitalist or a state-owned firm in societies where membership in the co-op, as contrasted with hiring out for a job, has a strong positive effect on workers' incentives.'[88]

### 1.3.3. *Horvat*

The challenge of Ward's and Domar's, on the whole, negative view of the economic efficiency of the Yugoslav system could not be ignored by Yugoslav economists. And, predictably, it was Horvat who rose to answer it. In 1967 he published his article 'A contribution to the formulation of a theory of the Yugoslav enterprise'[89] in which he attempted to demonstrate that the Yugoslav firm did not behave as Ward and Domar had assumed and that their conclusions therefore were invalid. Horvat firstly pointed out – correctly – that the differences in behaviour between the capitalist and labour-managed firm in response to various stimuli diminished with the increasing generality of the model. Whereas these differences were very large in the one-input one-output case (Ward), they tended to become smaller when two variable inputs were introduced and even more so when several outputs were assumed. Domar's introduction of a labour-supply curve further reduced the difference.

At this point it is interesting to take note of Milenkovitch's observation that 'an increased similarity in response ... should not be confused with showing efficiency. A monopolist and a perfect competitor both respond in the same way to changes in parameters... but they are not equally efficient.'[90] But the increasing similarity of behaviour parallel with the increasing generality of the model was not the main argument Horvat made. His principal objection to the Ward-Domar analysis was directed against the assumption that the labour-managed enterprise maximises income per worker. This might very well be true for the hypothetical Illyrian firm, but it was unrealistic as far as the Yugoslav enterprise was concerned. 'Instead of postulating what should be rational, the present author (Horvat) observes the actual practice of Yugoslav enterprises which fix wages in advance for the current year, and at least once a year make corrections (positive or negative) depending on the income earned. If this behavioural rule is used in the analysis the results are again the same as in the traditional theory of the firm.'[91] Horvat argued that usually the Yugoslav firm – or, more accurately, its workers' council – sets a target for 'income per worker' in the following year. This target normally includes a percentage increase over the previous income to take account of changes in the cost of living, increases in personal incomes in other enterprises, etc. This 'aspiration wage' may be later adjusted (by way of a bonus at the end of the year) but in the meantime it is used as an accounting device for cost calculation and resource allocation.[92] If the 'aspiration wage' is applied as an accounting device, and therefore as a cost item, it is then indeed rational for the labour-managed firm to maximise total profits above the specified personal income payments. Ergo: the maximising principles of the Yugoslav and the capitalist firm are identical, and the inefficiency issue is disposed of.

But this still leaves the question of the distribution of the profit in the labour-managed firm between bonus payments and reinvestment. In his 1967 article, Horvat apparently asserted that profits are reinvested in toto and that the Yugoslav firm therefore maximises investment.[93] In a later publication, however, it would seem that he assumed the answer to be still open: 'How the distribution of the residual (i.e. total profits) is determined, is an interesting question for both the theory and the empirical research concerned with the Yugoslav type of labour-managed firm.'[94] In other words, a dynamic theory is still lacking.

### 1.3.4. *Vanek*

Without any doubt, by far the most important contribution to the understanding of the theoretical foundations of the labour-managed market economy has been made by Vanek. In 1970 he published *The general theory of labor-managed market economies.*[95] It was the first attempt 'to construct a comprehensive theory of a new economic system which hitherto had not been studied in a comprehensive manner.'[96] While Vanek built on the foundations laid by Ward and Domar, he carried the analysis much further and the claim made in the title of the book is not immodest: his theory is truly general and comprehensive. Where Ward and Domar were only concerned with a few aspects of microeconomic theory, Vanek develops the equilibrium theory of the firm in the labour-managed system fully, covering not just the short run and perfect competition, but the long run (and the ultra-long run) and market imperfections as well. In addition, he deals with macroeconomic theory, and such issues as economic policy and planning. It is obviously impossible to review here Vanek's theory in detail, and – as in the case of the other authors discussed earlier – only his assumptions and main conclusions will be taken up. It should be noted in this connection that Vanek wrote a companion volume to his *General theory* in which he expands the scope of his earlier work to include the social and political aspects of the labour-managed economic system.[97]

Vanek defines the labour-managed market economy by five basic characteristics and one derived behavioural principle.[98]

- The first characteristic is that of labour management of firms, i.e. each member of the enterprise participates in the management process, either directly – in major matters – or through elected representatives in day-to-day issues.

- Secondly, all members share equitably in the income of the enterprise, income being defined as the value of sales minus all costs including material costs, capital costs, and tax liabilities of any kind.
- Thirdly, the system is characterised by complete decentralisation of decision-making and reliance on the market mechanism.
- The fourth characteristic is that the members of the enterprise collectively enjoy the usufruct of the assets of the enterprise but not full ownership, in the sense that they can neither destroy nor sell them and subsequently distribute the proceeds as income.
- Finally, there is freedom of employment, i.e. everyone is at liberty to choose or change employment, while each enterprise is free to hire or not to hire a new employee.

The behavioural principle of Vanek's labour-managed enterprise is that of maximisation of income per worker, which Vanek states is implied by the first two characteristics.[99]

Vanek begins his analysis by examining the behaviour of the firm under conditions of perfect competition and full employment, assuming free entry and use of the same technology by all firms in each industrial sector. Like Ward and Domar before him, Vanek postulated that the labour-managed firm will try to equalise factor marginal products with factor marginal costs for all production factors. The only difference between the capitalist enterprise and the labour-managed firm is that the marginal labour costs for the former is the wage rate, while for the latter it is the income per worker. These are equal if the capitalist enterprise makes zero profits, and in that case both firms behave exactly alike and are equally efficient. If, however, the capitalist firm is profitable then the wage rate must be lower than the income per worker in the labour-managed enterprise, and consequently the latter will operate at a lower level of output and employment. This much was also found by Ward and Domar, and the latter had concluded that the system implied a misallocation of resources – in particular because there was no reason to assume that income per worker would be identical for all labour-managed enterprises. Vanek, however, was reluctant to come to the same conclusion. If labour-managed enterprises operate at lower levels of output and employment, it rather meant that the 'impetus to grow infinitely, and thus to control a sizeable portion of the market, in the labour-managed firm can be expected to be considerably less than in the case of its capitalist equivalent. On the whole... the capitalist alternative appears as more Darwinian and the labour-managed system – without being inefficient – as more consistent with the principle "live and let live."'[100] To a certain degree, the disagreement between Domar and Vanek on this particular issue would appear to be pointless. According to the neoclassical theory of the firm, under conditions of perfect competition – i.e. with perfect ease of entry and exit and with perfect foresight – the capitalist firm will, in the long run, make zero profits.[101] It is therefore not correct to introduce into the analysis of the behaviour of the firm under perfect competition the possibility of profits by the capitalist enterprise, except when only the short run is considered.

Vanek agreed with Ward and Domar that the labour-managed system would not reach maximum efficiency in the case that technologies of all firms in the same industry are not identical. In those circumstances, 'the equilibrium behaviour (of the individual firm) will not lead to equalisation of marginal value products of labour among firms,'[102] whereas the capitalist system would achieve maximum efficiency under identical conditions.

Turning next to the equilibrium behaviour of the labour-managed firm under imperfect market conditions, Vanek demonstrated that 'the equilibrium size of a labour-managed firm is considerably smaller than that of a capitalist firm' (and that consequently) 'the degree of monopoly power in, and the structure of, a given industry will tend to be far worse in the capitalist alternative.'[103] In the 'real world', Vanek argued, most firms are faced with a production function of increasing returns at first, followed by 'sizeable or virtually limitless zones of constant returns.'[104] Under those conditions the capitalist firm will aim at a continuing growth – even beyond the point of technical efficiency – in its pursuit of maximum profits. In other words, the equilibrium level of the capitalist firm is infinite, while the labour-managed firm's is finite and indeterminate since it can maximise income per worker at any level of operation.[105] The argument here is that, if a labour-managed firm is operating at a level of output and employment which maximises income per worker, it would not gain anything by, for example, doubling output since this would not result in a corresponding increase in income per worker (assuming constant returns, of course). For the capitalist firm, however, doubling of output would mean doubling of profits. Vanek therefore expects that 'with a considerably number of firms in the labour-managed instance... the long-run equilibria will be quite near the maximum efficiency,'[106] while in the capitalist situation there is a tendency towards a decreasing number of ever larger firms resulting in monopoly power.[107] In this connection, Vanek noted that for the labour-managed market economy it was vital that free entry and exit were secured: 'the most efficient and full (Pareto - optimal) adjustment will occur once labour incomes are equalised through entry and exit.'[108]

Vanek's macroeconomic theory of the system yielded some remarkable conclusions. In the first place, he maintained that in the long run the labour-managed market economy 'effectively does guarantee full employment. It does so in the sense that the economy normally will operate at, or very near, full employment, and if, as a result of some drastic disturbance, unemployment were to arise, there are forces inherent in the system that will tend to restore full employment.'[109] In the short run it is conceivable that unemployment may occur, not because of price-wage inflexibility but mostly because of the special nature of the labour market.[110] Secondly, Vanek stated that variations in effective demand lead not so much to adjustments in income and employment but rather to variations in prices. These adjustments, however, would be small and 'as soon as short-run unemployment arises, long-run forces[111] (largely absent in a capitalist economy) will become operative in the labour-managed system, offsetting both the initial short-run impacts on prices and employment.'[112] There may, of course, be variations in prices, but prices can move down as easily as they move up and, since labour income is of a residual nature, it can be expected that the labour-managed economy is less prone to inflationary pressures than the Western market economy. Vanek's final conclusion was that the labour-managed economy is far less likely to undergo cyclical depressions than the capitalist economies.[113, 114]

On the basis of his micro- and macroeconomic theories Vanek felt no hesitation in claiming that the labour-managed market economy was more efficient than the capitalist system. However, its greatest strength lies in what Vanek calls its 'special dimensions' which are absent in other economic systems. 'These are related to, contained in or emergent from the managerial function of labour, that is, of all participants of the enterprise.'[115] The most important of these special dimensions is, according to Vanek, that the labour-managed firm offers 'among all the existing forms of enterprise organisation the optimal arrangement when it comes to the finding of the utility-maximising effort, i.e. the proper quality, duration and intensity of work, by the working collective.'[116] This is caused by the absence of conflicts between management and labour: the working community of an enterprise will act as 'a single-mind behavioural unit.'[117] Each worker has a vital interest in the overall performance of the firm, and this Vanek sees as the best incentive possible. In the capitalist (and Soviet command-) system, on the other hand, a worker will normally furnish the minimum effort consistent with the retention of his job.[118] This, Vanek claims,[119] can lead to enormous differences: supposing that a reasonable range of variation of each of the three aspects of effort (quality, intensity, and duration of work) is between 100 and 200 percent, the aggregate range for effort as a whole may stretch from 100 to 800 (i.e. 2 × 2 × 2 × 100). It would seem, however, that on this point Vanek is carried away a bit too far in his enthusiasm for the labour-managed firm, when he equates higher effort with proportionally higher output. He overlooks the fact that labour is not the only production factor and that there are therefore constraints (e.g. equipment capacity) on the actual results of higher effort.

Other special dimensions are that the labour-managed firm will provide an environment highly conducive to training and education,[120] that it offers the possibility to choose between monetary income and intangible income (e.g. leisure),[121] that it stimulates minor innovative activity[122] and that it opens possibilities for collective consumption by the workers of the enterprise (housing, recreational facilities, etc.).[123]

A final special dimension concerns the distribution of income among the workers. This process is governed by two sets of forces.[124] In the first place, the labour-managed firm is maximising income per worker when it equalises the income of each category of worker – this force is conditioned by the labour market. The second force derives from the democratic decision-making process within the enterprise: each category of labour will get a share 'consistent with the generally accepted notion of justice.'[125] Vanek fails to point out, however, that these forces may work in different directions. Since it would not be illogical to assume that – even in Vanek's theoretical model – the second force is the stronger one, the maximisation of efficiency could be compromised.

There is, of course, one other issue connected with the distribution of net income, and this issue arises even prior to the decision on incomes of individual workers: the division of net income between reinvestment and disbursement in the form of individual incomes. Vanek is not entirely clear on this point. In fact, he argues rather strongly against the practice of self-financing as 'not only inefficient... (but also) literally against the very nature of labour-management,'[126] and his theory is based on the assumption that all funds for investment are externally supplied. His main argument is 'that in the case of a perfectly competitive (capital) market ruled by a single rate of interest there would be no scope for self-financing.'[127] Of course, the members of the enterprise may save individually or collectively but they should then use the vehicle of the capital market, such saving should be considered an entirely separate operation which has nothing to do with the issue of investment.

It would seem that here lies one of the main weaknesses of Vanek's model. In particular, his observation that self-financing is against the nature of labour-management is incomprehensible. Surely, if the members of an enterprise are assumed to be free in the disposal of the net income of the enterprise, they should not be deprived of the choice of reinvesting directly in their own enterprise in which they – literally – have a vital interest. In addition, there is the practical consideration that no financial institution operating in a market economy is willing to supply all of the funds required by an enterprise. The risk would be simply too great, and a certain amount of self-financing is always insisted upon. It would have been very rewarding if Vanek had developed the criteria governing the distribution of total net income between reinvestment and personal incomes, and secondly the choice between external and self-financing of investment. Of course, this would have meant a relaxation of his assumption that all capital is externally supplied and he may not be willing to do so in view of his bias against self-financing.

A second criticism on Vanek's theory concerns the fact that, while free entry is crucial to the efficiency of the system, the difficulty of actually assuring sufficient possibilities for free entry is seriously underestimated. In the capitalist system, entry of new firms is undertaken by entrepreneurs who see opportunities for a profitable operation. It is hard to see how in the labour-managed system such entrepreneurs could emerge as easily as in the capitalist system. Vanek sees four major sources: local and central government authorities, groups of potential workers organised for the purpose of entry, and existing enterprises.[128] With respect to the first two, Vanek – rather contrary to practical experience – fairly lightly endows them with the entrepreneurial vision to identify investment opportunities and, in addition, the ability to nurse a new enterprise through the infancy period. The third source (groups of workers organised for entry) comes close, according to Vanek, to a Western partnership. But, except for cottage industries and the like, the setting up of a new enterprise requires considerable amounts of capital. Since by definition in Vanek's model all capital comes from external sources, a comparison with a Western partnership is largely incorrect. Moreover, is it realistic to assume that in the labour-managed system a group of people possessing professional qualifications and entrepreneurial ability – because that is what matters – would propose to set up an enterprise only to have to share later the management as well as the entire net income with others?

Vanek feels that existing firms are the most important source of entry, principally through capacity expansion: 'an expansion involving a new plant will normally lead to the creation of an autonomous self-management and income-sharing structure for that plant and thus, de facto, to the entry of a new firm.'[129] This would appear to contain an element of wishful thinking. In the first place, a labour-managed firm that engages in an investment project does so in the expectation that this will increase income per worker (Vanek's own behavioural principle). It would be illogical to assume that the workers of the existing firm would be willing to give up this incremental income for the benefit of the workers in the new plant – there would really be no point in going through the trouble. Secondly, even if the new plant would have a certain degree of independence, can it really be expected to compete rigorously with the parent enterprise? After all, the whole purpose of Vanek's insistence on free entry is to increase or maintain competition. There is, of course, a further constraint on the possibilities of free entry, and that is the size of the market. For a considerable number of industries there is a minimum level of output if losses are to be avoided, and the number of enterprises that can operate in a given market is consequently limited.[130] Therefore, even if free entry is guaranteed, it is quite possible that the supply-capacity (of existing enterprises) for a particular product is large enough to satisfy demand and that there is simply no market for additional supplies.

Summarising this short survey of the – mainly Western – literature on the theory of the labour-managed market economy, one notes that the system was rated as less efficient than capitalism by Ward and Domar, while Vanek considers it more efficient. Inasmuch as the analyses of the first two authors were severely restricted in scope, their conclusions appear premature. Vanek's theory is comprehensive, and internally consistent, although susceptible to minor points of criticism in particular where he leaves the realm of pure economics.

A definite judgement may never be reached – so much depends on the assumptions on which the model is based, and it is the set of assumptions which determine the nature of the system.

If a conclusion is to be drawn, it should perhaps be formulated negatively: so far the labour-managed market economy has not conclusively been proven to be theoretically less efficient than capitalism.

### 1.4. ASPECTS OF THE 'REAL SYSTEM'

In the two preceding sections of this chapter an attempt was made to provide some insights into the 'pure' model that underlies Yugoslavia's social and economic system. The emphasis of the first part was, to a large extent, ideological/political, and in the second section the existing body of economic theory with respect to the labour-managed market economy was briefly surveyed, mainly with a view to bringing out the most important conclusions. The obvious sequence is an examination of the Yugoslav system as it functions in practice.

There can, of course, be no pretension that this review will be complete, or even comprehensive in the sense that all aspects of the system will be touched upon. The approach chosen here – selective and therefore necessarily arbitrary – is to focus first on the differences between the model analysed by Vanek and the economic realities of present-day Yugoslavia. In addition, a few issues will be singled out for analysis that were not dealt with by Vanek but that appear to loom rather large in the Yugoslav context. These concern the financing of investments, economic policy, and the regional differences in economic development. As the analysis up to that point is bound to leave an impression of gloom, the picture will be balanced by a review of Yugoslavia's post-war economic performance. The second principal issue to be examined is related to the subject matter of the first section of this chapter: in concreto, the question whether self-management is a living reality in the Yugoslav enterprise – and this again involves a juxtaposition of theory and practice. The chapter will be closed with a discussion of the targets that Yugoslavia has set for itself – insofar as these have been made explicit – in terms of economic development.

### 1.4.1. *The real system versus Vanek's model*

It will be remembered that Vanek defines the labour-managed market economy by five characteristics and one behavioural principle. These will now be examined in turn to see how far they conform to the Yugoslav reality. The first and most important characteristic is that of labour-management of firms, i.e. 'management by representative bodies elected by the entire working population of an enterprise on a one-man-one-vote basis.'[131] Vanek himself feels that this condition is fulfilled in Yugoslavia[132] and he is certainly correct in the sense that the law of the land is very clear on this point: Yugoslavia is firmly committed to the principle of labour-management or, as the more common expression goes, self-management. No human institution is perfect, however, and the Yugoslavs themselves are the first to admit that the implementation of this basic principle often leaves much to be desired in practice. But this point will be dealt with in more detail later on, suffice it for the moment to agree with Vanek that the condition is fulfilled.

The second characteristic – all members share equitably in the income of the enterprise – is not open to any doubts. Without question, this is the case in Yugoslavia. The same can by and large also be said of Vanek's third characteristic. Decision-making is decentralised and the market is the regulatory mechanism. In fact, decentralisation has been pushed so far that the ability of the federal government to conduct an effective economic policy has been impaired, as will be seen later. With respect to the market, it should be noted that Yugoslavia is, of course, not more papist than the Pope. As is the case in any (capitalist) market economy, the government can intervene – albeit with rather limited powers – to correct imperfections or other undesirable tendencies.

Vanek's fourth characteristic is, again, very close to the real situation. As Vanek says 'the members of the enterprise enjoy the usufruct of the assets of the firm'[133] which means that they cannot sell the assets (except, of course, in the case of a normal commercial transaction) and distribute the proceeds as income. In fact, the enterprise is legally obliged to maintain what in the West would be called its net worth. The question who is the owner of the 'means of production' is legally not very simple. As the Yugoslavs define it: ownership – and control – belongs to the Yugoslav people as an entity and not to the state. This may seem a semantic difference, but it certainly is not. The fact that the state is not the owner means that it has no power over the management of the means of production (as is the case of the Soviet command economy) and that this power is exercised by the working collective of the enterprise, which holds the assets in trust for the Yugoslav people.

The fifth and final characteristic, freedom of employment, equally holds true. There is in Yugoslavia no compulsion to work in a particular enterprise, and the enterprise itself is free to employ whom it wants. Of course, as Vanek points out, this right to engage or dismiss workers lies with the working collective.[134]

Vanek made a further assumption, i.e. that all capital is externally supplied and that no self-financing takes place. This assumption was not qualified by Vanek as a defining characteristic, but since it was rather important for his analytical results, it should be tested against the Yugoslav reality. And, obviously, it is not realistic – in fact, self-financing by enterprises is encouraged in Yugoslavia. As stated in the preceding section, it is to be regretted that Vanek did not build into his model the possibility that investments are financed (partly or wholly) by reinvested earnings. But since he felt that it was contrary to 'the very nature of labour management' and inefficient as well, the assumption is, of course, logical and in accordance with his conviction.

Vanek followed Ward and Domar in assuming that the labour-managed enterprise would behave rationally if it tried to maximise income per worker. Theoretically, the assumption makes good sense. But the fact is that the validity of the assumption in the Yugoslav situation is contested by most Yugoslav authors, and not only by Horvat who was quoted earlier on the matter.[135] Kamusic even goes as far as saying that 'Yugoslav enterprises tend also to maximise profit in relation to the unit of invested capital, especially in cases where an enterprise is not willing or capable of increasing wages beyond an appropriate level.'[136] It is doubtful, however, whether this rather extreme view is true. Practical experience of the present author with Yugoslav enterprises suggests that Horvat is right.[137] This view is confirmed by Wachtel who published several studies on the determination of wages in Yugoslavia[138] and who states that 'the worker's wage in Yugoslavia has two components: a fixed wage, the payment that the worker periodically receives as a result of his own labour input; and a variable wage representing that amount which the worker receives at the end of an accounting period as a supplementary wage payment out of the current profits of the enterprise. This variable wage represents a reward borne by the worker-manager.'[139]

But if the Yugoslav enterprise does not maximise income per worker, what then is its maximising principle? Horvat states that its behaviour (as outlined by Wachtel) implies the same maximising principle as applied by the capitalist firm, and that 'if this behavioural rule is used in the analysis, the results are again the same as in the traditional theory of the firm.'[140] The conclusion is doubtful, however. If the Yugoslav enterprise treats the fixed wage as an accounting device (Horvat) and therefore as a cost item, it would then be not implausible to argue that it will try to maximise the variable wage. And that is still quite different from maximising total profits, or profit per unit of invested capital for that matter.

This section, however, is concerned with the 'real system', and it would be pure speculation to theorise at greater length about the actual maximising principle of the Yugoslav enterprise. What is really required is a thorough empirical study of the matter, which so far has not been made. Until the results of such study are available, all arguments can be safely regarded as conjectural.

Having tested the assumptions on which Vanek's model is built against the Yugoslav situation, the next step is to see how far the conclusions of Vanek's analysis conform to Yugoslav realities.[141] Undoubtedly, his most important finding was that 'the labour-managed market economy is not only highly efficient in absolute terms, but also more efficient than other existing systems.'[142] Quite often it is thought that efficiency can be measured in terms of comparative economic performance, i.e. a country's ranking on the world table of annual growth rates of GNP. This may give a rough and ready indication, but it is a short cut that is not entirely satisfactory. Apart from the many theoretical inadequacies of GNP growth rate figures as a measure of economic performance, there is the further objection that the growth rate is not only determined by the way available resources are used (which should be the yardstick of performance) but also by the country's endowment with resources. To put it crudely: the possession of oil or some valuable mineral makes a big difference. All this is not to say that economic growth is not important – and a separate subsection will be devoted to Yugoslavia's growth later on – but it is advisable to use another yardstick when discussing efficiency.[143]

What that yardstick should be is still open to debate, but it would be fair to say that perhaps theoretically the most satisfactory measure is the increase in factor-productivity. Wemelsfelder, in what must rate as one of the best concise yet comprehensive economic analyses of the Yugoslav system,[144] has examined in detail the various studies that have been made about Yugoslavia on this subject. Most of his sources could only formulate a conclusion in a negative form: there is no indication that self-management has a negative influence on factor-productivity. This is borne out in particular in a study by Balassa and Bertrand[145] who calculated the increase in factor productivity over the period 1953–1965 for ten countries in six different ways.[146] In all computations Yugoslavia scored remarkably well as shown in Table 1.2.

*Table 1.2. Highest score with respect to increase in factor productivity (ten countries)*

| *Computation* | *Rating* | | |
|---|---|---|---|
| | *First* | *Second* | *Third* |
| 1 | Romania | YUGOSLAVIA | Spain |
| 2 | Romania | Spain | YUGOSLAVIA |
| 3 | Romania | Spain | YUGOSLAVIA |
| 4 | Romania | Spain | YUGOSLAVIA |
| 5 | Romania | YUGOSLAVIA | Norway |
| 6 | Romania | Norway | Spain |

Source: Wemelsfelder, *op. cit.* (note 144), Table 9.

In five out of six calculations Yugoslavia ranks among the three highest scoring countries, and in the sixth Yugoslavia came fourth. Remarkable, however, is not so much Yugoslavia's position on this quasi-olympic table as Romania's – a country with a centralised system.

It is indeed difficult to draw a conclusion on the basis of this table other than to state that Yugoslavia has been performing comparatively well.

Whether this is attributable to its particular economic system – or even whether its performance might have been better under another system – must remain an open question.

Second in importance must rate Vanek's conclusion that the labour-managed market economy in the long run guarantees full employment, a goal cherished by every government in the world. Unfortunately, Yugoslavia's experience does not confirm Vanek's conclusion. As a matter of fact, unemployment was considerably lower in 1953 – i.e. at the end of the period of the Soviet-type command economy[147] – than at the time of decentralisation as shown in Table 1.3.

*Table 1.3. Yugoslavia – registered unemployed as a percentage of reported employment*

| *Year* | % | *Year* | % |
|---|---|---|---|
| 1953 | 3.0 | 1968 | 8.0 |
| 1963 | 6.4 | 1969 | 8.2 |
| 1964 | 5.6 | 1970 | 7.7 |
| 1965 | 6.1 | 1971 | 6.7 |
| 1966 | 6.7 | 1972 | 7.0 |
| 1967 | 7.0 | | |

Source: For the period 1953–70, *U.N. Statistical Yearbook 1971*, Table 22; for 1971 and 1972, *U.N. Monthly Bulletin of Statistics*, May 1973, Table 8.

These figures, however, present some difficulties of evaluation with respect to the size of the problem. In the first place, unemployment rates are expressed as a percentage of 'reported employment', and not, as usual, in relation to the economically active population.[148] This would mean that the percentage would be lower if the latter concept was followed. On the other hand, employment in private agriculture and small private enterprises is not taken into account, and there is evidence (although not in reliable statistical terms) of considerable underemployment in the sector of private agriculture.[149] Furthermore, the data on unemployment 'cover only those persons who are registered with the labour exchange services ... as looking for jobs.'[150] To complicate matters even more, there is the fact that large numbers of Yugoslavs are working abroad. Current estimates range from 800,000 to one million.[151] This, incidentally, has the effect of rendering the Yugoslav economy extremely vulnerable to a slow-down in Western Europe. The return of the labour force would aggravate the unemployment situation, and, in addition, it would deprive Yugoslavia of its largest source of invisible earnings (more than $ 400 million in 1972) which would result in severe balance of payments problems.

One thing is clear (cf. Table 1.3), however, unemployment under the decentralised system has been considerably higher than under the centralised regime. There are some theoretical arguments – implicitly refuting Vanek's analysis – which explain this phenomenon.[152] Firstly, in the labour-managed enterprise there will be a tendency to limit employment of additional workers if this would result in a decrease of personal incomes. Secondly, even in the long run enterprises will contribute little to employment creation since it is to the advantage of the existing labour force to engage in 'capital-deepening' investments as these will contribute more to increased income per worker than 'capital-widening' investments. Wemelsfelder has tested this hypothesis statistically and found that the period 1953–63 was characterised by 'capital-widening' investment, i.e. the average amount of invested capital per worker changed very little. After 1963 – i.e. during the period of real decentralisation – investments were clearly 'capital-deepening.'[153] It is further often argued that in the labour-managed market economy there will be little incentive to establish new enterprises when funds are advantageously invested by workers in their own firm. In other words, entry of new firms is not easily achieved. Wemelsfelder has investigated this argument as well and concluded that there was no evidence to confirm it. Employment creation by new firms in Yugoslavia was not noticeably less than in Germany and Holland.[154] It should be emphasised, however, that Vanek attached major importance to the mechanism of free entry as an instrument to ensure the efficient functioning of the system. If free entry is to play such a decisive role there should, ideally, be some indication of new firms being established in Yugoslavia – which is not the case. In fact, the total number of industrial enterprises has gone down (cf. Table 1.9).

While the evidence is perhaps not conclusive, it would seem that Vanek's premise of guaranteed full employment in the long run is not confirmed by Yugoslavia's experience.

Among the major concerns of every country in the world, inflation probably ranks as high as unemployment, and Vanek's claim that the labour-managed market economy offers important advantages on this point is therefore of particular interest. But the Yugoslav experience can hardly be said to confirm Vanek's conclusion. Inflation was kept well under control through the fifties and the early sixties. During this period producer prices in manufacturing and mining rose at an average rate of 0.9% per year, and retail prices including services increased annually 3.9% on average.[155] But from the time decentralisation began to have a real impact on the economy, the rise in prices accelerated very fast as shown in Table 1.4.

*Table 1.4. Yugoslavia – price indices (1963 = 100)*

| Year | Wholesale | Retail |
|---|---|---|
| 1964 | 105 | 109 |
| 1965 | 120 | 150 |
| 1966 | 133 | 184 |
| 1967 | 136 | 197 |
| 1968 | 136 | 207 |
| 1969 | 142 | 224 |
| 1970 | 156 | 248 |
| 1971 | 178 | 286 |
| 1972 | 199 | 339 |

Source: 1964, computed from Horvat (*AER*), page 112.
1965–1972, *U.N. Monthly Bulletin of Statistics*, May 1973, Tables 58 and 60.

It is not necessary to search very far for an explanation of these figures. The relative price stability during the early post-war period is simply due to the fact that the economy was largely centralised and prices were determined by the Federal Government. Later price controls were gradually relaxed but inflation could be held under control because of the fact that 'until 1961 personal incomes were quite efficiently controlled by fiscal and non-fiscal means (Trade Unions).'[156] When income controls were abolished, inflationary pressures started to develop and, in spite of the reintroduction of price controls, prices rose fast. The main reason for the inefficiency of the control system was the fact that it applied in principle only to existing products, and by making small changes in the design of the product an enterprise could claim it was a new product and evade price control.[157]

In 1965, in the framework of the Economic Reform, Yugoslavia tried to get rid of the price distortions that had inevitably accumulated earlier due to the various controls, by aligning domestic prices with world market prices. For those products that are not traded internationally, prices 'were fixed at a level which was to ensure the enterprises concerned normal conditions of operations and possibilities for capital development.'[158] The result was a considerable rise in the general price level – in particular for agricultural products, raw materials and services. The new prices, set by the Reform measures, were initially frozen[159] but slowly a process of liberalisation was set in motion and, by 1970, prices of about two-thirds of products and services were determined by the market.[160] But, contrary to what Vanek wrote about the labour-managed market economy, liberalisation – with the occasional rare exception – never resulted in lower prices, mainly because the rate of increase of personal incomes continued to outrun the rise in productivity.

Probably one of the main weaknesses of the Yugoslav system lies in the fact that, in theory at least, an incomes policy is impossible. If the workers of an enterprise are free to set their own incomes – within the limits imposed by the trading results of the firm – then any attempt to impose restrictions on these incomes would constitute an infringement of the rights of the workers. But the Yugoslavs are pragmatic enough not to let considerations of ideological purity overrule practical exigencies, and by the end of 1971 limits on the increase of personal incomes were imposed in most Republics. It can, in fact, be maintained that the principle of self-management was upheld inasmuch as these limits were not set by the Federal Government but by the parliaments of the Republics, which are elected by the workers. The fact remains, however, that a national incomes policy is not feasible. Moreover, the increases allowed by the assemblies were rather high (up to 15% for the lowest paid workers) and certainly not sufficient to quell inflationary pressures. The instrument of price control has therefore been retained by the Federal Government which, in accordance with the Social Price Control Act of May 1972, 'will continue to regulate the system of social price controls and to ensure direct social control of prices of products and services of concern to the country as a whole.'[161] In fact, intervention by the government continued throughout and, in February 1973, even another price freeze was imposed as inflation went on at an alarming rate.

But although the Yugoslav labour-managed market economy has not lived up to Vanek's expectations, the Yugoslav experience should be seen in the proper perspective. Inflation is, since the sixties, the scourge of all countries that can be classified as market economies. And a cure is yet to be found. It would therefore be unjustified to conclude – as is sometimes done – that inflation is inevitable in a system such as Yugoslavia's, but it is equally clear that it cannot prevent inflation either.

A further interesting conclusion reached by Vanek is that the two sets of forces[162] which determine income distribution among different job categories 'can be expected to lead to income distribution patterns more equal than would result from market forces only.'[163] In his judgement the social advantages of this more egalitarian income structure far outweigh the ensuing 'slight departures from narrow physical Pareto-optimality for the industry and the whole economy.'[164] Wemelsfelder has compared income levels for various job/professional categories in Yugoslavia and the Netherlands, and reached the conclusion that the differences were rather small, except in the case of managing directors of enterprises and their deputies.[165]

*Table 1.5. Income distribution levels in Yugoslavia and the Netherlands*

| *Category* | *Yugoslavia 1967* | *Netherlands 1965* | |
|---|---|---|---|
| | *(skilled labour = 100)* | | |
| Unskilled labour (average) | 68 | 86 | |
| Driver | 114 | 89 | |
| Crane-driver | 114 | 89 | unweighed average |
| Machinist | 118 | | |
| Mechanic | 128 | 100 | |
| Electrician | 118 | | |
| Technician | 135 | 151 | |
| Sociologist/psychologist | 147 | 195 | |
| Economist | 161 | 195 | |
| Engineer | 196 | 208 | |
| Managing director and deputy | 245 | 336 | |

Source: Wemelsfelder, *op. cit.*, Table 19.

Tinbergen came to a similar conclusion when he made a comparison on the basis of educational levels as shown in Table 1.6.

*Table 1.6. Earnings of employees with different educational levels (1967)*

| | *Yugoslavia** | *Netherlands*** |
|---|---|---|
| Graduates of higher education | 194 | 200 |
| Secondary education | 94 | 100 |
| Skilled workers | 94 | 75–80 |
| Trained workers | 79 | |
| Unskilled workers | 71 | 65–70 |

* Average wage level = 100.
** Secondary education = 100.

Source: Tinbergen, in Broekmeyer (ed.), *Yugoslav workers' self-management*, page 118.

Prima facie there seems therefore not to be much evidence to confirm or reject Vanek's conclusion. Socialist Yugoslavia is not markedly more egalitarian than capitalist Holland. The only major difference, observed in practice, is that top salaries in Yugoslavia are always fairly near the average in the highest income category, whereas in the Netherlands there are considerable deviations.

In this context it may be interesting to review the question of wage differentials from the sectoral angle. Wachtel[166] and Popov[167] found rather substantial differences, which, as Popov observed, 'are not in line with the principle of income distribution according to work performed.'[168] Moreover, these differences have been remarkably higher in the last years than, for example, in 1960, as shown by Table 1.7.

*Table 1.7. Yugoslavia: intersectoral wage differentials**

| | *1960* | *1963* | *1966* | *1969* | *1970* | *1971* |
|---|---|---|---|---|---|---|
| Manufacturing and mining | 94.4 | 102.0 | 105.2 | 104.0 | 102.5 | 102.5 |
| - Electrical energy | 103.4 | 123.1 | 133.9 | 138.4 | 137.3 | 132.3 |
| - Coal and coke | 104.3 | 109.2 | 103.0 | 101.5 | 102.1 | 109.0 |
| - Oil | 90.9 | 124.1 | 136.5 | 130.9 | 131.9 | 139.4 |
| - Fe-mining & metallurgy | 117.3 | 116.4 | 123.9 | 114.4 | 112.0 | 114.8 |
| - Non-Fe mining and metallurgy | 107.4 | 113.7 | 132.2 | 112.8 | 112.1 | 108.5 |
| - Non-metallic mineral prod. | 106.9 | 97.9 | 100.6 | 98.6 | 97.6 | 99.1 |
| - Metal processing | 97.7 | 109.0 | 104.6 | 105.7 | 102.7 | 101.5 |
| - Shipbuilding | 106.3 | 122.8 | 132.9 | 147.4 | 136.3 | 135.1 |
| - Electrical products | 105.5 | 105.7 | 99.4 | 105.9 | 101.8 | 99.2 |
| - Chemicals & chem. prod. | 107.2 | 112.3 | 119.1 | 114.6 | 108.5 | 105.5 |
| - Building materials | 80.5 | 87.1 | 95.7 | 101.1 | 103.3 | 106.3 |
| - Wood products | 81.1 | 86.3 | 84.6 | 92.4 | 95.8 | 97.5 |
| - Paper & paper products | 116.5 | 118.4 | 106.5 | 109.2 | 110.6 | 106.2 |
| - Textiles | 86.2 | 88.0 | 94.8 | 86.2 | 83.5 | 85.5 |
| - Leather and footwear | 93.2 | 92.0 | 96.7 | 95.4 | 90.7 | 92.7 |
| - Rubber products | 103.3 | 106.8 | 112.9 | 110.7 | 103.2 | 102.3 |
| - Food and beverages | 89.5 | 94.9 | 105.4 | 97.8 | 100.0 | 99.1 |
| - Printing & publishing | 95.1 | 108.3 | 117.5 | 123.0 | 122.7 | 118.2 |
| - Tobacco manufacture | 82.8 | 89.5 | 92.1 | 92.5 | 87.3 | 89.3 |
| Agriculture | n.a. | 81.9 | 92.2 | 88.3 | 87.2 | 90.2 |
| Forestry | n.a. | 83.2 | 92.2 | 92.2 | 104.0 | 106.2 |
| Building and construction | n.a. | 94.5 | 95.9 | 98.2 | 99.7 | 101.2 |
| Transport & communications | n.a. | 103.8 | 106.5 | 107.5 | 108.4 | 108.9 |
| Trade and tourism | n.a. | 99.2 | 104.1 | 106.9 | 107.1 | 105.9 |
| Public utilities & housing | n.a. | 97.8 | 100.5 | 106.8 | 105.8 | 104.2 |
| Ratio of the extremes** | 145.7 | 151.5 | 161.3 | 171.0 | 165.6 | 163.0 |

* Average personal income of all employed in each year = 100.
** Ratio of highest-wage industry to lowest-wage industry.

Source: Popov, *op. cit.* (note 167), Table IV.

Analysing the data presented in this Table, Popov noted that the highest personal incomes occurred in industries that were either capital-intensive or enjoyed a monopolistic position in the market.[169]

Wachtel[170] ran a cross-sectional multiple regression test to determine how far interindustry wage differentials could be explained by a model using two variables, i.e. labour productivity and industrial concentration. He found that this simplified model accounted in 1956 for only 24% of the variance, but thereafter $R^2$ increased rapidly to .81 (1965). When the model was expanded to include two additional variables (respectively, regional concentration and labour quality), the results of the simplified model were not affected. However, the introduction of net profits as a fifth variable, not surprisingly, added significantly to the explanation of the variance. Wachtel therefore concluded that three factors accounted for the increased interindustry wage differentials, of which the average productivity of labour proved to be the most important. Ergo 'to the extent that labour productivity depends upon the capital-labour ratio and the technology in an industry, the increase in interindustry wage differentials could have been caused by the differential allocations to investment among industries.'[171] Examining these allocations, Wachtel found that industries with low average wages tended to have low ratios of reinvested earnings to net income.[172] These differential reinvestment propensities have widened the technological gap between high- and low-wage industries, thereby increasing interindustry labour productivity differentials over time. This increase in interindustry productivity differentials is the principal cause of increasing wage differentials.[173]

It should be noted here that, while interindustry productivity differentials may be considerable in Yugoslavia, Wemelsfelder has found that they are not much larger than, for example, in Germany or the Netherlands.[174] This would imply that allocational efficiency is not much less in Yugoslavia than in Germany and Holland.

Returning to Vanek's analysis, another advantage of the labour-managed market economy lies in the fact that 'the equilibrium size of the labour-managed firm is considerably smaller than that of the capitalist firm' (and that therefore) 'the degree of monopoly power in, and the structure of, a given industry tends to be far worse in the capitalist alternative.'[175] Statistical evidence collected by Wemelsfelder indicates, however, exactly the opposite in Yugoslavia: the average size of the Yugoslav firm is considerably larger than in several West-European countries (see Table 1.8).

*Table 1.8. Size of firms by number of workers (1961/1962)*

| Number of workers per firm | Percentage of total number of workers | | | | | |
|---|---|---|---|---|---|---|
| | *U.K.* | *Germany* | *France* | *Italy* | *Netherlands* | *Yugoslavia* |
| 10–99 | 20.1 | 21.5 | 29.8 | 41.3 | 28.2 | 3 |
| 100–999 | 45.4 | 40.0 | 43.7 | 40.1 | 51.3 | 47 |
| > 1000 | 34.5 | 38.5 | 26.5 | 18.6 | 20.5 | 50 |
| Total | 100.0 | 100.0 | 100.0 | 100.0 | 100.0 | 100 |
| Average number of workers per firm | 141 | 111 | 86 | 50 | 62 | 408 |

Source: Wemelsfelder, *op. cit.*, Table 3.

These findings are confirmed by a more recent study[176] which showed that in 1968 14% of the total number of Yugoslav enterprises[177] employed more than 1000 workers. This compares with 0.7% in the USA, 0.1% in Japan and slightly less than 1% in the Netherlands. These figures gain additional significance if one considers that the size of the market in Yugoslavia is smaller than in the other countries. There is even a tendency towards further concentration of industrial enterprises in Yugoslavia.

*Table 1.9. Yugoslavia: industrial enterprises*

| *Year* | *Number of enterprises* | *Number of workers per enterprise* | *Fixed assets (at constant 1966 prices)* | |
|---|---|---|---|---|
| | | | *Per enterprise (million dinars)* | *Per worker (dinars)* |
| 1958 | 2500 | 371 | 20.3 | 54,608 |
| 1959 | 2557 | 387 | 21.0 | 54,298 |
| 1960 | 2556 | 419 | 22.7 | 54,140 |
| 1961 | 2787 | 408 | 23.1 | 57,159 |
| 1962 | 2684 | 434 | 26.6 | 61,396 |
| 1963 | 2507 | 487 | 31.2 | 64,031 |
| 1964 | 2445 | 539 | 34.5 | 63,976 |
| 1965 | 2466 | 558 | 37.6 | 66,833 |
| 1966 | 2467 | 550 | 40.0 | 72,692 |
| 1967 | 2492 | 542 | 42.3 | 77,970 |
| 1968 | 2508 | 537 | 44.9 | 83,555 |
| 1969 | 2434 | 574 | 50.8 | 88,522 |
| 1970 | 2374 | 612 | 56.1 | 91,642 |

Source: *Statisticki Godisnjak Jugoslavije 1972.*
Number of enterprises and number of workers: Table 109-1; fixed assets computed from Table 106-7.

In particular over the last few years the number of mergers has increased rapidly, and the number of industrial enterprises has dropped from 2,787 in 1961 to 2,374 in 1970, as shown in Table 1.9. Contrary to Vanek's expectations, there is a distinct danger of growing monopolistic inefficiencies if the momentum continues unchecked.

A final point made by Vanek concerns the fact that the labour-managed market economy is less likely to undergo cyclical depressions than the capitalist economies.[178] It is therefore not uninteresting to note that Branko Horvat, a Yugoslav economist, published a sophisticated econometric analysis on the subject 'Business cycles in Yugoslavia.'[179] Horvat found that the Yugoslav economy had gone through five distinct cycles during the period 1949–1967, and he computed the loss in GNP, due to cyclical depressions, at 24.6% of the actually achieved gross social product.

In summary, it can fairly be said that the Yugoslav experience does not confirm Vanek's most important conclusions about the workings of the labour-managed market economy. Of course, this does not invalidate his theory as such; one can only note that the theory is of limited utility when it comes to explaining the Yugoslav system as it functions in practice.

While the confrontation of Vanek's theory and Yugoslav practice has highlighted some important aspects of the system, there are, of course, other issues that need to be dealt with. It would seem that among these three stand out in particular: investment financing, economic policy, and the regional differences in economic development. These will now be examined in turn.

### 1.4.2. *Investment financing and the role of the banks*

The remarkable changes that have occurred since the war with respect to the financing of investments in Yugoslavia cannot be illustrated more vividly than by Table 1.10.

In the early post-war years investment funds were allocated by the plan out of budgetary sources, as could be expected in a Soviet-type command economy.[180] Moreover, the funds were handed out free of charge and without repayment obligation.[181] In 1952, the first change in the system was made: the Federal budget was split into two parts, the first to cover administrative expenses (current expenditures) and the second for capital expenditures. In the latter fund 'the federal government concentrated just about all investment resources.'[182] In fact, 95% of the financing of

*Table 1.10. Yugoslavia: financing of investment in fixed assets by sources (excl. private sector) (percentages)*

| *Year* | *Governmental funds and budgets* | | | | *Non-profit-making inst.* | *Enter-prises* | *Banks* | *Total* |
|---|---|---|---|---|---|---|---|---|
| | *Federal* | *Republic* | *Commune* | *Total* | | | | |
| 1948 | 60 | 27 | 12 | 99 | 0 | 1 | 0 | 100 |
| 1951 | 50 | 41 | 7 | 98 | 0 | 2 | 0 | 100 |
| 1952 | 95 | 2 | 1 | 98 | 0 | 2 | 0 | 100 |
| 1953 | 71 | 11 | 5 | 87 | 0 | 13 | 0 | 100 |
| 1954 | 50 | 12 | 12 | 74 | 0 | 26 | 0 | 100 |
| 1955 | 47 | 9 | 8 | 64 | 8 | 27 | 1 | 100 |
| 1960 | 37 | 7 | 18 | 62 | 6 | 31 | 1 | 100 |
| 1962 | 30 | 9 | 20 | 59 | 8 | 30 | 3 | 100 |
| 1963 | 26 | 9 | 20 | 55 | 8 | 28 | 9 | 100 |
| 1964 | 7 | 8 | 21 | 36 | 6 | 26 | 32 | 100 |
| 1965 | 5 | 4 | 20 | 27 | 8 | 29 | 36 | 100 |
| 1966 | 6 | 3 | 7 | 16 | 6 | 39 | 39 | 100 |
| 1967 | 9 | 2 | 6 | 17 | 5 | 33 | 45 | 100 |
| 1968 | 9 | 3 | 4 | 16 | 6 | 31 | 47 | 100 |
| 1969 | 9 | 3 | 4 | 16 | 6 | 29 | 49 | 100 |
| 1970 | 9 | 3 | 4 | 16 | 6 | 27 | 51 | 100 |
| 1971 | 8 | 3 | 4 | 15 | 7 | 27 | 51 | 100 |
| 1972 | n.a. | n.a. | n.a. | 20 | 7 | 30 | 43 | 100 |

Source: 1948–1960, Horvat (*AER*), Table 10, page 140.
1962–1971, *Statisticki Bilten*, No. 3, 1972, Table 39.
1972, *Mesecni pregled privredne statistike SFR Jugoslavije*, No. 6, 1973, p. 48.

investment in fixed assets was covered by the fund (see Table 1.10). This centralised system did not last long, however, and change followed change in the next several turbulent years. In 1953, 'enterprises established their own investment funds financed out of profits that by the plan were left to them.'[183] At about the same time, 'Social Investment Funds' were created at the federal, republic, district, and commune level,[184] which was one of the first tentative steps towards decentralisation. The following year brought further innovations. In the first place, enterprises now had to pay interest on capital, regardless of the source of finance, i.e. including on their own reinvested earnings. Moreover, external financing was no longer provided in the form of grants but had to be repaid.[185] Secondly, a new way of allocating investment resources was experimented with: the so-called 'loan auctions'. In the description of Neuberger, the procedure was as follows: 'In principle, the applicants would be listed according to the level of the rate of interest they offered and if two offered the same rate, the one who offered the shorter period for repayment of the loan would be given preference. The bank (i.e. the Social Investment Fund concerned) would go down the list until the amount allocated for this auction, or category within the auction, was exhausted, and the rate of interest offered by the first intramarginal applicant would become the one that everyone paid.'[186] This system was, however, quickly abandoned because enterprises showed little restraint in bidding for loans regardless of their needs and possibilities for debt service[187] and the auctions soon 'degenerated into an old-fashioned administrative distribution of investment from government funds.'[188]

In the meantime, the banking system had been in flux as well – although it should be added that until the mid-sixties banks in Yugoslavia were not much more than government agencies, without a significant degree of independence, which served merely as a window through which government funds were disbursed.[189] And while Vucic distinguishes four distinct phases during the period up to 1954,[190] these phases were characterised only by alternate contraction and expansion of the number of banking institutions. By 1954 the pendulum had again reached the point of contraction and Yugoslavia at that time had only one single giant bank: the National Bank which then comprised 550 branch offices and over 16,000 employees.[191]

More significant, however, was the emergence in the early fifties of self-financing by enterprises. As shown in Table 1.10, the share of enterprise funds in total fixed assets formation grew rapidly from 2% in 1952 to 26% in 1954.[192] While this tended to lessen the dependence of enterprises on government funds, the role of the various Social Investment Funds (SIF) in the process of resource allocation remained predominant. Even in 1955 these Funds absorbed still about two-thirds of total investment resources, and this resulted in the establishment of a fair number of 'political' factories: 'The criteria used for investment allocations from SIF had never been very transparent... and had always been greatly influenced by political considerations... All important investment projects were somehow multiplied six times, one for each republic.'[193] This particular problem has continued to haunt Yugoslavia for a long time. In some sectors simply too many products were produced in too small quantities to be economic. Only during the last few years has the process of mergers and associations between enterprises started to make a dent in this situation by effecting some rationalisation of production.[194] This is, of course, a long-term operation. An industrial structure that has evolved over more than a decade leads to vested interests that resist change. Moreover, except in rare cases of really sizeable losses over a long period, factories are not simply closed down in Yugoslavia. The preferred solution is to change the product-mix, either by specialisation or diversification – and that process inevitably takes time.

Returning to the banking system, from 1955 onwards the trend toward decentralisation was there to stay. In 1955, most of the branch offices of the National Bank were transformed into communal banks to administer the SIF of the municipalities. Subsequently, separate federal banks were established to specialise in the financing of foreign trade (Yugoslav Bank for Foreign Trade, or Jugobanka, in 1955), infrastructure and industry (Yugoslav Investment Bank, 1956), and agriculture (Yugoslav Agricultural Bank, 1959). Most of the federal SIF resources were distributed among these banks, although the Federal Government retained a considerable 'General Investment Fund' which was liquidated only as late as 1963. In 1961 Republic's Banks were established which administered the investment resources allocated under each Republic's own development plan. But while this meant that most banks were no longer under the control of the Federal Government, it certainly did not mean that they had become independent. The Republic's and Communal banks obtained most of their resources from governmental authorities (although they could also accept deposits from enterprises and private persons), and they operated strictly on governmental directive. Moreover, they did not compete with each other geographically or, as far as the three Federal banks were concerned, sectorally. For all practical purposes, the banking system in Yugoslavia was up to 1965 predominantly under political control.

The Economic Reform of 1965, which proved to be a turning point in so many respects, brought some important changes in the banking system as well. The 'Law on Banks and Credit Operations' (March 1965) basically aimed at an improvement in the allocation of resources by freeing the banks from political and governmental control and by introducing competition among banks. The latter was promoted by removing all territorial restrictions on bank operations, while the former point was taken care of by new regulations with respect to the legal structure of banks.[195] In the new set-up, banks are established by so-called 'founders', which may be enterprises but also political entities. These founders, or sponsors, must provide the bank with an initial equity-like capital ('Credit Fund'). The law set minimum requirements for the size of the Credit Funds for the various types of banks. The highest organ of the bank is the assembly, in which the founders are represented in proportion to their contribution to the bank's initial Credit Fund and their deposits in the bank.[196] A special voting quota in the assembly is reserved for the workers' council of the bank.[197] The assembly determines the bank's policy and appoints a board of management and a director to carry out the bank's day-to-day business. Initially, most of the Credit Fund was, of course, in the hands of political entities but these 'governmental founders' have been gradually withdrawing their shares and banks increasingly had to rely on enterprises for the expansion of their permanent capital. It should be added that the law fixed the maximum voting power of any one founder at 10% of the total vote,[198] which curtailed control by governmental authorities that they otherwise might have exercised by virtue of their large (initial) share holdings. Since the banks from now on could no longer rely on governmental sources for the bulk of their funds, they had to compete in the market for deposits.

Apart from the National Bank – which now was strictly a Central Bank – all existing banks were transformed into independent business banks, which the law classified in three categories: investment banks (long-term financing), commercial banks (short-term financing), or mixed banks. The Yugoslav Investment Bank, the Agricultural Bank, and the Republic's Banks were transformed into investment banks, Jugobanka became a commercial bank, while the communal banks were transformed either into commercial or mixed banks. In addition, a sizeable number of new commercial banks were established by groups of enterprises.[199] Inevitably the large number of banks (over 200 in 1965)[200] led to a process of mergers and by 1969 the number had decreased to 69 banks. At the end of 1971 the number had further gone down to 55.[201]

Following the reform measures of 1965, the importance of the banks rapidly increased and at the end of the 1960s they financed half of the annual fixed investment (cf. Table 1.10). The banks were also rather successful in mobilising savings from enterprises and households; time deposits rose from 3.5 billion dinars in 1965 to 21.2 billion dinars in 1971.[202] While at first sight this rapid development may seem to give cause for congratulation, the fact is that the Yugoslav banks have come under increasing criticism. A criticism which has led to a rethinking of the role that the banking system would have to play within the framework of the self-management system. What, then, did go wrong?

While most Yugoslav commentators on this issue have different opinions, the basic thrust of all arguments is twofold: firstly, the banks have acquired too rapidly too much power over the enterprises and, moreover, they have used this power injudiciously; secondly, the banks themselves have remained largely under the influence of regional governmental authorities – the formal changes of the 1965 Law notwithstanding. One of the developments of the decentralisation process was that, although the Federal Government relinquished much of its previous powers, the Governments of the Republics strengthened their position considerably both vis-à-vis Belgrade and vis-à-vis the enterprises, banks, and municipalities on their territories. It is probably fair to say that decentralisation of governmental controls effectively stopped at the level of the Republic.

The position of the banks towards the enterprises was, of course, further strengthened by the 'overall scarcity of capital in Yugoslavia, measured against the needs and the opportunities,'[203] a situation which the banks were not slow to exploit. In spite of a formal interest ceiling (abolished only in 1971), effective interest rates could reach 20-30% and even at those rates it was difficult to obtain credits.[204] The banks, moreover, favoured borrowers able to afford comparatively short repayment periods. The situation at the end of the 1960s was summarised by Vucic in the following terms: 'Die Banken haben das Privilegium, denn sie stellen sich als Schiedsrichter über die Wirtschaft und als Quellen bestimmter ökonomischer und politischer Mächte, mit Rücksicht darauf dass alle Vorgänge der Banken durch den Willen politischer Strukturen jenes Gebiets bedingt sind, auf welcher sich die Banken befinden.'[205]

The virtual territorial monopolies of the larger banks led to substantial profits which, except for the dividend paid out to the founders, were reinvested in the bank's Credit Fund. Since the founders had no claim on this Fund beyond their paid-in participations, the reinvested earnings accrued to the bank itself thus increasing its power. Towards the end of the 1960s, this 'anonymous part of the Credit Fund,' as it was called, came under increasing attack. It was felt that the workers, through whose labour this capital had been created, had no control over its use which was a violation of the principle of self-management.

After a debate that lasted close to three years, a new Federal Law on Credit- and Bank Operations was adopted by parliament in December 1971,[206] with the specific purpose of curbing the banks' power over the enterprises. The major changes were the following.[207] First and foremost, the 'anonymous part of the Credit Fund' was abolished. To emphasise the change the Credit Fund was renamed Founders' Fund and the founders of the banks received certificates proportionally to their investment. More important, however, than this change in name was the fact that these certificates were made negotiable. Previously, a founder-enterprise was not entitled to sell its participation in a bank's Credit Fund which meant that it was tied to that bank for all its credit needs since banks quite understandably gave priority to their shareholders in distributing scarce loan funds. At present, if an enterprise feels that its interests are not well-enough served, it has the option to take out its 'shareholding'[208] and it is hoped that this will have the effect of increasing competition among banks. The second change was the introduction of unlimited liability of the founders. While earlier the founders were liable only up to the amount of their participation in the Credit Fund, they now stand, in effect, guarantor with all their assets for the bank's obligations. This 'extension of responsibility for the operations of a bank to include its founders is intended as an incentive to the founders to take more interest in the work of the bank and to show more concern for the efficient operation of the bank.'[209] To use a Western-type analogy: the founders are transformed from shareholders into partners. The law further abolished the difference between investment-, commercial-, and mixed banks. All banks are now called business banks and can engage in both short-term and long-term operations.

The question remains, however, whether the changes introduced by the law will effectively lessen the predominant influence of the banks over the enterprises. There are reasons to believe that they will not. In spite of the high rate of savings,[210] capital will remain a scarce commodity in Yugoslavia for some time to come – as in any, fast-industrialising, developing country – with the virtual disappearance of governmental funds (cf. Table 1.10). The only sources of finance for investment are reinvested earnings and bank credits. Banks will therefore continue to exercise an effective monopoly over external enterprise financing. And although the enterprises have now more power over the bank's operations, because they have a say in the allocation of credits, they are in effect competing with each other for credits from their own bank. They may, of course, switch banks and take their funds with them, but in the new bank they will have to queue up again and find themselves in the same – if not worse, as a newcomer – position as before. It is therefore not unreasonable to assume that the bank's management will remain the decision-making power.

Perhaps the single most important deficiency of the Yugoslav financial system is the lack of a capital market. Contrary to what is sometimes assumed in Western countries, there are no legal barriers in Yugoslavia prohibiting the emergence of such market. Bonds have been issued in the past for various purposes (e.g. the Belgrade-Bar railway project, the ZCZ car manufacturer etc.) and in December 1971 a 'Law on Negotiable Instruments'[211] was promulgated setting out the various types of financial paper that can be issued and the rules governing the issue. There are now three categories of paper:

a. *Bonds*, which can be issued by enterprises, banks, non-profit making (but revenue earning) institutions, and governmental authorities. The issuing entity must have a 'net worth' of at least 20 million dinars, and the total amount of bonds issued cannot exceed its net worth.[212]

Governmental authorities can issue bonds only with the specific approval of their assemblies whereby one of the criteria is whether revenues can cover debt-service. The interest rate can be set as required by market conditions and can even be variable, or linked to profit performance in the case of banks and enterprises. The bonds can be purchased by anybody, i.e. private persons, enterprises, banks, and even foreigners, and can be freely transferred at whatever price buyer and seller may agree on.

b. *Certificates* in joint capital investment. This is a new type of paper, specifically created for joint ventures. It gives the buyer the right to participate in the management and the profits of the venture; the buyer's liability is limited to the amount of his certificates. The certificate must have a minimum lifetime of ten years before redemption may start. Private persons are not allowed to buy certificates which are reserved for enterprises, banks, insurance companies, and governmental authorities. As in the case of bonds, certificates are transferable, but purchases and sales of certificates by foreign persons can only be made in accordance with the legislation on foreign investment.[213]

c. *Treasury notes*, the second new financial instrument, can be issued only by banks (and not by governmental authorities as one might think). The minimum term of the note is one year and the maximum five years. Treasury notes cannot be bought by private persons; they are also negotiable.

As far as the possibility for enterprises to raise funds is concerned, the law did not change very much: bonds could be issued before 1971 as well. The question is, why didn't the enterprises use this avenue more to lessen their dependence on banks? The answer – unsatisfactory, as it raises additional questions – can only be that bonds have never been popular in Yugoslavia. The huge issue for the Belgrade-Bar railway was never fully subscribed in spite of all extra promotional gimmicks (free tickets etc.). People apparently prefer to keep their savings in saving accounts which are considered more liquid and a safer investment. The only bond issues so far that have succeeded were those of industries like ZCZ (passenger cars) or IMT (tractors) which gave the bond-holder priority of delivery, and it can even be argued that these bonds were only advance payments.

It is therefore difficult to see, at present, the raising of funds through bonds as an alternative to bank financing. The development of a real capital market is a long-term prospect only. One way by which the larger, conglomerate, enterprises have sought to lessen their dependence on the banks is by pooling resources in so-called 'internal banks.' Of course, this can only be a partial solution since for most firms there will always remain a need for external financing of investments.

A further and very significant disadvantage of the concentration of financial power in the banks is the lack of capital mobility. Practically all major banks are regionally oriented and rarely venture beyond the borders of their own Republic or Autonomous Province. This phenomenon can be partly explained by historical factors: before 1965 the banks were regional institutions[214] and old habits are not easily discarded. But, in addition, there is the fact that the 'founders' of any bank tend to be enterprises which are located in the same Republic, and it is understandable that these get priority when it comes to allocating scarce resources.

The discussion about the role of the banks in the economy – and all the attendant problems – is continuing in Yugoslavia. At the present time of writing (mid-1973) it is far from clear how the situation will further evolve. One thing is certain, however. Ultimately the Yugoslavs will have to come to grips with the problem of capital mobility – the country simply cannot afford to continue to neglect it.

### 1.4.3. *Economic policy*

As was seen in the first section of this chapter, the dominant theme of the process of decentralisation has been the reduction of the role of the Federal Government and the introduction of the market mechanism as the principal regulatory force in the economy. This relentless drive to decrease the powers of the Federal administration has been so rapid since 1965 in particular, that it has led to a major institutional weakness: Yugoslavia has failed to develop a balanced set of policy tools appropriate to deal with the economic problems of a decentralised system.[215]

Of the main macroeconomic management tools available to a government to pursue internal equilibrium[216] – budgetary and fiscal policy, monetary policy, incomes policy, and price policy – Yugoslavia has almost exclusively relied on monetary policy, and to a limited degree on price policy, to deal with the problems at hand. The result has been that corrective measures were applied too forcefully and thereby continually overshot the mark.[217]

Yugoslav thinking with respect to budgetary policy as a macroeconomic management tool has been succinctly summed up by Horvat: 'A budget is more consistent with a centrally planned economy the more all-embracing it is. Ideally all financial transactions of the economy are to be regulated by the budget. It is the other way round in a self-government economy. Here the budget ought to be restricted to as small a sector of the economy as possible in order not to interfere with the economic activities of work collectives. *Ideally the budget should cover only the actions of various state agencies.*'[218] This statement, while admittedly entirely consistent with the theory of the withering away of the state, is nevertheless somewhat surprising when coming from a socialist source. It would be difficult to find a capitalist government so devoted to Adam Smith's doctrine.

Yugoslav policy, in particular since 1965, has therefore been to foster 'a further decline in the already limited relative importance of federal finances.'[219] Presently, the consolidated budget of all governmental authorities (including social security and all extra-budgetary funds) account for slightly more than 30 percent of the Gross Material Product[220] and, of this, Federal expenditures make up roughly half.

Consistent with the rejection of the Federal budget as a policy instrument is the legal requirement that all budgets must be balanced, at least to the extent that expenditures should not exceed revenues from sources other than borrowing.[221] In addition, there is the fact that a substantial part of governmental revenues are specifically earmarked for certain expenditures, which introduces a further element of inflexibility.

Given the Yugoslav attitude with respect to the role of the budget, it is not surprising that fiscal policy is neglected. Horvat states quite bluntly, 'there is no fiscal policy in Yugoslavia'[222] which he explains by the 'belief in the absence – or with the ignorance of the presence – of business cycles.'[223] Occasionally, the turn-over tax has been used to absorb excessive purchasing power, but most tax changes have either been intended to affect individual prices or to increase or decrease the power of enterprises over the spending of their net income. At no time, however, have these changes been made to affect aggregate demand.[224]

The system of self-management is, of course, not conducive to an active incomes policy at the Federal level. As was seen earlier, the workers of an enterprise are free to dispose of the firm's net income as they see fit and any attempt to limit increases in personal incomes basically violates the principle of self-management. Nevertheless, such limitations have been imposed but not by any Federal authority. The real power rests with the Republics, and even these behave very cautiously preferring voluntary interindustry agreements. These so-called self-managing agreements can be made compulsory by law and this has happened in several Republics.[225] So far, however, these agreements have not resulted in an easing of inflationary pressures.

The two main tools remaining in the hands of the Federal Government consequently are price policy and monetary policy. As far as price policy is concerned, it can of course help to mitigate the effects of inflation to some extent, but unless it is accompanied by a policy to mop up excessive purchasing power it will not suffice to control inflation. Nor is a price policy an adequate tool to stimulate demand in the trough of the business cycle.

Yugoslavia has therefore so far relied on monetary policy as its principal macroeconomic management tool. One gets the impression that this was not so much a question of necessity but rather a deliberate choice for ideological reasons. As put by Aleksandar Bajt, one of Yugoslavia's most prominent economists: 'Wenn der Staat absterben und seine Kompetenz in der Wirtschaft verringert werden soll, warum soll man dann gestatten, dass er auf die Geschehnisse in der Wirtschaft mit seinen Aufgaben, also auf eine sehr direkte Weise einwirken soll? Die Anwendung der Steuerpolitik ist notwendig und mit Rücksicht auf das sozialistische Wesen der Wirtschaft sogar notwendiger als bei den kapitalistischen Wirtschaften. Da kann also nicht viel geändert werden. Ist aber nicht gerade unter unseren Bedingungen die Kredit- und Geldpolitik oder sogar nur die Geldpolitik die, die am meisten dem Charakter der Wirtschaft und der Gesellschaft entspricht? In erster Linie können die Banken, resp. das Banksystem, welche die Träger dieser Politik sind, als Organe der Gesellschaft der unmittelbaren Produzenten aufgefasst werden (dies ist natürlich auch mit dem Staat der Fall, aber die Bank ist doch etwas anderes als der Staat). Was jedoch wichtiger ist: der Einfluss der Kredit- und Geldpolitik auf die wirtschaftliche Tätigkeit ist nur indirekt, es handelt sich mehr um die Induzierung als um die Substituierung der Beschlüsse der Wirtschaft durch staatliche Beschlüsse.'[226] To avoid misunderstanding, it should be added that Bajt's reference to fiscal policy does not contradict what was said above on this subject. By fiscal policy he simply means the raising of revenue to finance expenditures for public consumption, and not that fiscal policy should be used as a tool to influence aggregate demand.

The main instruments[227] of money and credit policy available to the Yugoslav authorities are discount policy and reserve requirements.[228] The traditional third tool, open market policy, is missing since there is no financial market.[229] In addition, 'interest rate policy has little meaning'[230] in view of the overall scarcity of capital.

The almost exclusive reliance on monetary policy has two distinct disadvantages. The first of these derives from the fact that it is precisely the only main tool of macroeconomic management: policy changes have tended to be very frequent,[231] introducing an element of uncertainty in enterprise decision-making, and too forceful. Secondly, as pointed out in the OECD 1970 Economic Survey of Yugoslavia, 'money and credit policy tends to concentrate its impact on investment activity and clearly must play a central role in a developing country.... But investment is precisely the type of activity that needs continuous encouragement if development is to proceed.'[232] Leaving aside the question whether investment activity in Yugoslavia really needs continuous encouragement given the pronounced tendency to embark on overambitious projects, it is a fact that monetary policy has only limited effects on public and private consumption. And this is a major weakness which has severely restricted the possibilities for overall demand management.

There can be little doubt that these, self-imposed, limitations do nothing for the stability of the Yugoslav economy. There is a clear need for a rethinking of the entire field of economic policy, in particular the development of an effective incomes policy will be required to keep inflationary pressures under control.[233] Since it is unlikely that a solution will be sought in the direction of a return of powers to the Federal Government, a mechanism will have to be developed that will make coordination of policy among the Republics more effective.

### 1.4.4. *Regional inequities*

The rich historical and cultural diversity of Yugoslavia is one of the country's greatest tourist attractions, but unfortunately regional differences extend beyond the mere picturesque. No visitor travelling through Yugoslavia from the Western parts to the South East can fail to notice the wide gap that separates Yugoslavia's most developed Republic, Slovenia, from the Province of Kosovo near the Albanian border. These regional differences in the level of economic development are a legacy from the past that the country so far has been unable to shake off. If anything, the gap has widened since the early post-war years as shown in Table 1.11. It is quite evident that since 1947 the three richest areas (Slovenia, Croatia and Vojvodina) have increased their relative advantage, while in particular Kosovo has fallen back considerably.

One might get the impression from these figures that Yugoslavia has neglected the problem, but nothing could be farther from the truth. Since 1945, 'one of the perennial platforms of Yugoslav economic policy'[234] has been the elimination of regional differences in per capita income. But while there was never any doubt about the ultimate aim of that policy, its concrete conception and application has varied a great deal over time. Bogoev essentially distinguishes two periods: before and after the Econ-

*Table 1.11. Yugoslavia: income per capita, as a percentage of the national average*

| | *1947* | *1964* | *1971* |
|---|---|---|---|
| Yugoslavia | 100.0 | 100.0 | 100.0 |
| Slovenia | 162.7 | 195.1 | 185.8 |
| Croatia | 107.9 | 118.9 | 124.7 |
| Serbia* | n.a. | 90.3 | 93.6 |
| of which Serbia proper | 96.8 | 96.4 | 97.9 |
| Vojvodina | 116.9 | 115.0 | 120.8 |
| Kosovo | 50.4 | 37.1 | 33.6 |
| Montenegro | 71.1 | 73.2 | 70.3 |
| Macedonia | 68.6 | 69.4 | 69.6 |
| Bosnia and Hercegovina | 79.8 | 71.1 | 64.2 |

* The Republic of Serbia comprises the territories of Serbia proper and the Autonomous Provinces of Vojvodina in the North and Kosovo in the South.

Source: 1947 and 1964, Milenkovitch, *op. cit.* (note 13), page 181.
1971, computed from Tables 201–1 (Population) and 203–1 (Gross Material Product), *Statisticki Godisnjak Jugoslavije 1972.*

omic Reform of 1965.[235] During the first period, policy changed almost continuously and, as Bogoev put it, 'neither a complete and consistent system nor methods for consistent realisation of that policy were worked out.'[236] To begin with, there was practically uninterrupted political infighting as to what areas should be considered underdeveloped and therefore eligible for Federal assistance. As a result districts were included or excluded inconsistently. This was due to the fact that even in the relatively rich Republics there were pockets of poverty, which could qualify for aid. Not until 1966 was a final agreement reached, when it was decided to limit the definition of underdeveloped area to the Republics of Bosnia and Hercegovina, Macedonia, Montenegro and the Province of Kosovo. Perhaps more importantly, policy wavered with respect to sectoral priorities.[237] At one time it was agriculture, forestry and infrastructure that were the focus of the development effort, at another infrastructure only, and later industrialisation. Finally, the financing of investment took different forms varying from direct budgetary support to special funds.

After 1965, a determined effort was made to formulate a consistent policy. As said above, the regions that qualified as underdeveloped were defined by law. Secondly, 'for the first time..., the achievement of faster development of the less-developed Republics and Province than the average development of the whole Yugoslav economy was explicitly defined as a goal.'[238] It was decided, on the basis of an assessment of the development potential of the underdeveloped areas, that the increase in GMP should be two percentage points above the national average.[239] Thirdly, all development assistance for investment would now be channeled through the 'Fund for Developing Regions', which had been established in 1963. The Fund was to obtain its resources by a levy amounting to 1.85 percent of the 'social product of enterprises in the socialist sector.'[240] For the period 1966–1970 this amounted to 8.2 billion dinars, of which Bosnia-and-Hercegovina was to receive 31 percent, Kosovo 30 percent, Macedonia 26 percent, and Montenegro 13 percent.[241] The levy was increased slightly to 1.94 percent for the period 1971–1975. The Fund is, at present, the only major centrally-administered investment institution, but its powers are very limited. Basically, it is the developing regions themselves that determine for what purposes their share in the Fund's resources is spent. A fourth and final innovation was that federal budgetary support for 'indispensable social services' would now be provided on the basis of firm criteria rather than ad hoc. The Federal budget now meets the difference 'between the funds collected (by the developing region) and the average per capita expenditure in Yugoslavia (for the services in question), or the per capita expenditure of the Republic which is closest to the national average.'[242]

But even this more concerted and consistent attack has failed to achieve the desired results. Table 1.11 showed that the gap has widened rather than narrowed. This, of course, could have been caused by the large initial difference in starting positions, and a higher growth rate per head would eventually catch up with the gap. However, with the exception

*Table 1.12. Yugoslavia: increase in Gross Material Product per capita, 1961–1971 (%)*

| | |
|---|---|
| Yugoslavia | 85.4 |
| Macedonia | 107.4 |
| Vojvodina | 98.0 |
| Slovenia | 93.7 |
| Croatia | 86.6 |
| Kosovo | 85.5 |
| Serbia proper | 85.2 |
| Montenegro | 79.4 |
| Bosnia-and-Hercegovina | 65.7 |

Source: Computed from Tables 203-1 (Gross Material Product at constant prices) and 201-1 (Population), *Statisticki Godisnjak Jugoslavije 1972.*

of Macedonia, per capita increases in Gross Material Product have been lower than, or at most equal to, the national average over the period 1961–1971 (see Table 1.12).

Further evidence of the failure to close the gap in economic development between regions comes from an examination of the figures with respect to investment in fixed assets. On a per capita basis, most developing areas actually spent less on investment than the richer regions despite the inflow of resources from the Fund (see Table 1.13).

*Table 1.13. Yugoslavia: expenditure on investment in fixed assets*

| | *1967* | | | *1971* | | |
|---|---|---|---|---|---|---|
| | *Investment* | | *Population* | *Investment* | | *Population* |
| | *mln. din.* | % | % | *mln. din.* | % | % |
| Yugoslavia | 19,888 | 100.0 | 100.0 | 41,441 | 100.0 | 100.0 |
| Bosnia and Herceg. | 2,213 | 11.1 | 18.1 | 4,898 | 11.8 | 18.3 |
| Croatia | 4,562 | 22.9 | 21.9 | 10,141 | 24.5 | 21.3 |
| Macedonia | 2,050 | 10.3 | 7.8 | 3,110 | 7.5 | 7.9 |
| Montenegro | 536 | 2.7 | 2.5 | 1,617 | 3.9 | 2.6 |
| Slovenia | 2,668 | 13.4 | 8.5 | 6,964 | 16.8 | 8.3 |
| Serbia total | 7,860 | 39.5 | 41.1 | 14,711 | 35.5 | 41.5 |
| Serbia proper | 5,430 | 27.3 | 25.7 | 9,809 | 23.6 | 25.8 |
| Vojvodina | 1,636 | 8.2 | 9.7 | 3,644 | 8.7 | 9.5 |
| Kosovo | 794 | 4.0 | 5.7 | 1,258 | 3.3 | 6.1 |

Note: Percentages figures do not always add up due to rounding.

Source: *Statistical Pocket Book of Yugoslavia 1973,* Federal Institute of Statistics, Belgrade, April 1973, page 52 (investment by regions) and page 22 (population).

Although official Yugoslav policy has been unequivocal in its affirmation of assistance to the less-developed regions, it is not surprising that the failure to make a real dent in the problem is causing growing disenchantment with the concept of aid in the richer Republics who bear the main brunt.[243] In fact, the line of argument voiced against the official policy bears a remarkable resemblance to what became known in Western Europe as 'Cartierism': development funds are wasted because they are never well-spent and the money can better be used at home. But while this debate has occasionally been acrimonious, it is unlikely to lead to a change in policy and it can be expected that the developing regions will continue to receive considerable injections of financial resources.

Nevertheless, the Yugoslav development effort, well-intentioned as it may be, can be said to have one major defect: assistance is seen almost exclusively in terms of transfers of funds.[244] Economic development does not come about simply by pumping in financial resources. The problem is infinitely more complex. It would seem that this is not realised in Yugoslavia, although some lip-service is being paid to the necessity of technical assistance.[245] Much more attention would need to be given to such areas as project identification and implementation, development planning, and financial and managerial techniques. In addition, increased inter-regional cooperation between enterprises would be very useful, but here local antagonism is an important stumbling block.

In the light of past experience and in view of the unlikelihood of a change in emphasis in Yugoslav policy, it must be concluded that the difference in economic development levels between regions will not decrease for some time to come.

### 1.4.5. *Post-war economic growth*

Whatever criticisms one may voice with respect to the principles or practices of the Yugoslav economic system, it is clear that the country's growth record is outstanding. It has been argued that this growth could have been higher if certain inefficiencies and imperfections had been removed, but that applies to any other country including the fastest growing ones.

Yugoslavia's Gross Material Product increased, in constant (1966) prices, from 31.7 billion dinars in 1952 to 134.2 billion dinars in 1971,[246] i.e. more than quadrupled in twenty years which implies a compound annual growth rate of over 7 percent. Compared to other countries, Yugoslavia's performance is among the best in the world. Out of 71 countries for which per capita growth figures (1960–1970) were published by the U.N., Yugoslavia ranked 16th with an average annual rate of 6.1 percent.[247]

This is not the place to examine in detail the factors that have caused Yugoslavia's high economic growth rate, but as a measure of the country's determined development effort the investment ratio is revealing. For the entire period since 1952, the share of Gross Fixed Capital Formation in GMP rarely fell below 25 percent – and then only by a few decimal points – and for most of the time was well above it (see Table 1.14).

*Table 1.14. Yugoslavia: Gross Fixed Capital Formation as a percentage of GMP*

| | | | |
|---|---|---|---|
| 1952 | 26.4 | 1962 | 32.4 |
| 1953 | 26.9 | 1963 | 31.3 |
| 1954 | 28.4 | 1964 | 32.2 |
| 1955 | 24.1 | 1965 | 28.0 |
| 1956 | 25.1 | 1966 | 26.5 |
| 1957 | 24.3 | 1967 | 24.5 |
| 1958 | 27.3 | 1968 | 28.3 |
| 1959 | 26.7 | 1969 | 27.2 |
| 1960 | 30.1 | 1970 | 31.0[248] |
| 1961 | 31.7 | | |

Source: *Statisticki Godisnjak Jugoslavije 1972*, Table 105–3.

Industry, more than any other sector, has been the main engine of Yugoslavia's economic growth. At the end of the war, the country was faced with an industrial apparatus that was either ruined beyond repair or hopelessly obsolescent. Now, the industrial sector accounts for close to 40 percent of a Gross Material Product amounting to 204.5 billion dinars (1971).[249]

Again, the record gets additional perspective when Yugoslavia's indus-

*Table 1.15. Yugoslavia: growth indices of industrial production, 1955-1970 (1955 = 100)*

| *Sector* | *World* | *Centrally-planned economies* | *Market economies* | | |
|---|---|---|---|---|---|
| | | | *De-veloped* | *De-veloping* | *Yugo-slavia* |
| Manufacturing (total) | 256 | 380 | 214 | 269 | 438 |
| – Food, beverage, tobacco | 203 | 265 | 178 | 215 | 373 |
| – Textiles | 186 | 226 | 168 | 192 | 292 |
| – Leather and footwear | 186 | 287 | 151 | 208 | 410 |
| – Wood | 212 | 314 | 170 | 250 | 370 |
| – Paper and printing | 212 | 293 | 204 | 300 | 560 |
| – Chemicals | 373 | 545 | 335 | 316 | 950 |
| – Non-metallic minerals and building materials | 286 | 497 | 194 | 310 | 435 |
| – Metallurgy | 214 | 330 | 175 | 333 | 378 |
| – Metal products | 305 | 573 | 231 | 433 | 555 |
| – Electricity | 340 | 483 | 303 | 460 | 600 |

Source: Nikolic, *op. cit.* (note 250), Table III, page 41.

trial growth is compared to that of other countries. Nikolic has made an interesting computation[250] which shows that Yugoslavia, over the period 1955–1970 has out-performed in practically every industrial subsector the growth achieved by the centrally-planned economies, the developed and developing countries (as groups) as well as the world as a whole (see Table 1.15).

It would seem fair to conclude that, in spite of all the inevitable constraints and the, partly self-imposed, limitations of its economic system, there is ample reason to be optimistic about Yugoslavia's future.

The skill and industriousness of the Yugoslav people, the country's considerably natural resources and its advantageous location – geographically as well as politically between Western and Eastern Europe – should guarantee a sustained impetus for expansion.

### 1.4.6. *Self-management in practice*

A review of the most important aspects of the Yugoslav system as it functions in practice cannot ignore the problems that have arisen with the implementation of the basic principle on which the entire system rests: self-management. Of course, this is an area where the economist has to walk very carefully – it is the hunting ground, rather, of sociologists and political scientists. Obviously, to do justice to this all-important subject a separate study would be required. Nevertheless, precisely because it is so important for the understanding of the Yugoslav system, a few basic observations should be made. These observations will, moreover, be mainly of a practical nature, no analysis of the theoretical merits or demerits of self-management will be attempted: the system as such will be taken for granted.

One of the most refreshing characteristics of Yugoslav Marxism is its open-mindedness, its willingness continuously to scrutinise and criticise existing institutions. This applies in particular to self-management. Not the principle – there are limits to the acceptability of criticism – but its application. The intensity of the discussion is amazing, it is carried out not only in parliament and other political assemblies, but also within the League of Communists, the trade unions, the enterprises themselves, universities, academic journals and newspapers, special seminars and congresses, etc., etc. And whatever different opinions the Yugoslavs may have on the subject – one is tempted to say that there are as many views as there are Yugoslavs – they all agree on one thing: the implementation of the principle of self-management leaves much to be desired. Ample statistical evidence is available to prove the point. Veljko Rus has published a study[251] in which the results of a number of investigations were summarised. The investigations were all concerned with the perception of workers with respect to the influence, exercised on the operations of the enterprise, by various occupational groups within the enterprise. The seven studies[252] analysed by Rus were based on samples of various sizes and composition. The largest included 1,990 workers from 92 enterprises in Slovenia, and the smallest 56 workers attending a course at the Workers' University in Zagreb.[253] The findings were remarkably similar (see Table 1.16).

*Table 1.16. Yugoslavia: perceived relative influence of occupational groups on enterprise operations*

| | *(1 = most influence ... 9 = least)* | | | | | | | |
|---|---|---|---|---|---|---|---|---|
| | *Rus 1964* | *Zupanov 1966* | *Rus 1968* | *Kavcic et alii 1968* | *Kavcic 1968* | *Mozina/ Jerovsek 1969* | *Mozina/ Rus 1969* | *Average* |
| Top management | 1 | 1 | 1 | 1 | 1 | 1 | 1 | 1 |
| Professional staff | 2 | – | 3 | – | – | 2 | 2 | 2.2 |
| Middle manag. | 3.5 | 4 | 2 | 2 | 4 | – | – | 3.1 |
| Managing board | 5 | 3 | 4.5 | 3 | 2 | 3.5 | 3.5 | 3.8 |
| Workers' Council | 6 | 2 | 4.5 | 4 | 2 | 3.5 | 3.5 | 3.8 |
| Supervisors | 3.5 | 5 | 6 | 5 | – | 5 | – | 4.7 |
| Party | – | – | 7 | – | 5 | – | 5 | 6 |
| Skilled workers | 7 | 6 | 8 | 6 | 6 | 6 | 6 | 6.4 |
| Other workers | 7 | 6 | 9 | 6 | 8 | 8 | 7 | 7.3 |

Source: Rus, *op. cit.* (note 251), Table 1, page 149.

There seems to be little doubt, in the workers' mind, that the management of the enterprise is the most powerful group – more powerful, in any case, than the workers' council which is, legally at least, the decision-making body. As formulated by Rus: 'Top management and staff have power without responsibility, and the council has responsibility without power.'[254] Obviously, this situation is considered unsatisfactory by the workers: in all studies it was the workers' council that was rated as the group that *should* be the most influential. Rus, however, observed a very interesting development. Whereas the earlier studies, dating from 1964 and 1966, found that 'workers' desires ... were consistent with the theory (i.e.) the workers' council should have the most influence, workers slightly less influence, and the various levels of management should have the least,'[255] the later studies showed that the aspirations had 'become considerably more modest. Top management, it is now conceded, should have influence almost equal to that of the workers' council; the workers themselves are resigned to having least influence of all.'[256] This, of course, is quite startling, but Rus concludes blandly that 'workers are more realistic today'[257] in the sense that they have adapted their aspirations to the facts of life.[258]

But while the workers themselves may have become less ambitious, the situation is considered unacceptable to the more active proponents of self-management – a sizeable force including the Party, the trade unions, and the universities. The main thrust of the criticism is, of course, focused on the increasing power of the technocrats (management and professional services, cf Table 1.16), and the corresponding loss of influence of the workers. But, in addition, there is general uneasiness about the fact that the percentage of blue-collar workers in the workers' councils has, on average, decreased (cf. Table 1.17) and that, moreover, managerial staff and specialists have come to dominate the workers' councils proceedings.[259] Finally, the concentration of financial power in the hands of the banks is judged to have put a brake on the development of the independence of the enterprises (and their workers).

*Table 1.17. Yugoslavia: composition of labour-force and Workers' Councils, selected years (percentage)*

| | *Labour force* | | *Workers' Councils* | |
|---|---|---|---|---|
| | *1956* | *1967* | *1956* | *1968* |
| Blue-collar workers | 79.2 | 79.6 | 74.6 | 70.5 |
| White-collar workers | 20.8 | 20.4 | 25.4 | 29.5 |
| Of which with higher education | 3.2 | 6.2 | 3.5 | 8.0 |

Source: Gorupic & Paj, *Workers' self-management in Yugoslav undertakings*, Zagreb 1970, as quoted in P. Verburg et alii, *Wie beslist er nu eigenlijk?* Amsterdam University 1971, page 85.

Of course, there has been no shortage of studies, both in Yugoslavia and abroad, trying to explain why things went wrong. Of the many arguments put forward, a few are common to all analyses. In the first place, it is felt that the increasing complexity of running an industrial enterprise – and it should be noted that industrial development in Yugoslavia has been particularly fast – has not been matched by an increased comprehension of the (blue-collar) worker of the problems. Only specialists seem to be able to understand what is involved and express a reasoned opinion in the deliberations of the workers' councils, which had led to a loss of interest by the shop-floor worker. 'The solving of these problems is generally left to the experts and the proposals by representatives of specialised bodies or of the professional advisory board of the director, who are not members of the workers' council, are generally adopted without discussion.'[260] Secondly, the constitutional amendments of 1968 which gave greater liberty to the enterprise to establish its own organisational structure have, paradoxically, led to a loss of influence of the workers' council. Most enterprises took advantage of the new rules to increase the responsibilities of the board (or committee), chosen from among the members of the workers' council, to which a number of powers of the council were delegated. The members of this board usually were specialists or middle-management staff, and included few blue-collar workers. Thirdly, the initial enthusiasm for the self-management system is thought to have waned, once the country became somewhat more prosperous and a 'consumption mentality' emerged.[261] In other words, workers got more interested in acquiring consumption goods, rather than in the building of the Yugoslav brand of socialism.

Vidakovic, one of Yugoslavia's leading thinkers on the self-management system, has a further argument which is interesting because of its paradoxical nature.[262] He maintains that, during the fifties, the foundations of the system could be laid 'relatively peacefully' because the state at that time was powerful enough to protect this 'development in embryonal form'. When the role of the state started to decline – and it will be remembered that this process was set in motion precisely to give more power to the enterprises – it appeared that the self-management system was still too weak to resist the formidable forces of banks, Republics, and other institutions. The withdrawal of the protection by the state created a vacuum which the self-management organs were unable to fill.[263]

Not only in Yugoslavia, however, have the achievements of self-management come under a barrage of criticism.[264] Practically all Western scholars of the system have expressed their disappointment as well. Broekmeyer – one of the best-informed and most astute observers – who in 1968 had written a fairly positive account of the implementation of self-management,[265] had to change his assessment rather drastically and stated in 1972 that 'the Yugoslav system of workers' self-management has been in a crisis over the last few years.'[266] The arguments on which he based his judgement are basically those that were discussed earlier:

increased power of the technocrats, within the enterprise, and of the banks and other institutions, outside the enterprise.

While Broekmeyer and others are still sympathetic to the Yugoslav efforts to solve their problems, the principle of self-management has been attacked as well.[267] In particular, the French sociologist Albert Meister has not spared the Yugoslavs and their system. It is perhaps of interest to dwell at some length on Meister's analysis[268] because it is a rather good example of what one might call 'well-informed misunderstanding'.

Meister's principal thesis is that self-management is a thing of the past – both in the sense that it is no longer a living reality and that it is no longer necessary because it has fulfilled its historical function. This role was threefold. In the first place, 'l'autogestion a été une institution d'encadrement de la classe ouvrière consentante parce qu'intégrée dans le jeu des mécanismes de participation; consentante parce qu' "idéologisée", et cela au profit de la capitalisation de l'économie.'[269] This, according to Meister, was particularly the case before the Reform of 1965. Secondly, 'l'autogestion a constitué un mécanisme de maintien de la paix sociale durant la phase d'industrialisation de base du pays.'[270] Finally, self-management has led to the emergence of a new class of managers and bureaucrats who now manipulate the levers of power.

Meister's thesis, which seems to be gaining acceptance in Western orthodox Marxist circles, is misleading because it fails to make a distinction between motivation, cause and effect. To take his last point first: of course, it is true that a new managerial class has established itself – but it is a non-sequitur to claim that this was caused solely by the institution of self-management. As Meister admits, at the end of his article, 'je constate que toutes les sociétés ont et ont eu toujours des classes dirigeantes, eh bien l'autogestion a permis de créer une classe dirigeante.'[271] It is therefore hard to perceive any specific historical role of self-management in this respect.

The first two points, essentially, can be reduced to one single argument: self-management has helped to achieve economic development because it has kept the workers in line. This, of course, is an almost grotesque assertion. Surely, Yugoslavia has benefited from social peace but that is an effect of the introduction of self-management and not the reason why it was introduced, as should be clear from the first section of this chapter. But even if one accepts, for the sake of argument, that self-management has mainly been an instrument to maintain a peaceful industrial climate, it is difficult to see why Yugoslavia, at this stage of its development, should do without it. In particular, since Meister himself makes much of the economic problems the country is facing.

More important, however, than his theory about self-management's historical role, is Meister's claim that it no longer exists in practice. He is right in pointing out the many inadequacies and distortions. These are well-known and they have been discussed above. But to conclude that the Yugoslavs, for all practical purposes, have abandoned the system is mistaken. On the contrary, an intensive and determined effort is being undertaken to find remedies for the present problems.

Two of Meister's arguments concerning this point deserve particular attention because they are increasingly voiced by others as well. He states that 'l'autogestion ... se trouve en recul devant la progression constante du secteur privé et aussi devant la progression d'autres formes d'entreprises, qui sont à mi-chemin entre l'entreprise privée et l'entreprise autogérée.'[272] As far as the latter are concerned, Meister includes in this category joint ventures with Western enterprises – which will be discussed in Chapters 4 and 5, although it should be noted in this context that their number is still very limited – and enterprises where the 'technocrats' have come to be the dominating decision-making power. As was seen earlier, this is a real problem and the Yugoslavs are certainly well aware of it. However, Meister seems to imply that this take-over is an inevitable development with the increasing complexity of industrial operations. In fact, he challenges the principle of self-management itself: 'il faut constater qu'il y a une *incompatibilité* entre le travail manuel et la fatigue qu'il entraîne et les tâches de gestion. Ces tâches de gestion constituent un métier.'[273] This is, of course, the crux of the argument that can be made against the system. It is a bit difficult to deal with this point, because it is correct in the sense that for the worker on the shop-floor the issues involved are often beyond his powers of understanding. On the other hand, it reveals a very basic misunderstanding with respect to the meaning of the concept of self-management. What Meister understands by 'métier de gestion' is the day-to-day running of an enterprise as well as making all policy decisions. Self-management is something different: it is basically only the determination of the enterprise's overall policy, the choice between the options open to the enterprise in respect of investment, level of personal incomes, product mix, personnel policy, etc. Surely, to make this choice the worker has to understand what the alternatives imply, and here lies the weakness of the system. A weakness, which the Yugoslavs try to cure by better education, special courses, Workers' Universities, etc.

The role of the management team of the Yugoslav enterprise is to *implement* the policy decisions taken by the workers' council, in other words to take care of the day-to-day running of the business. Of course, there is a difference between theory and practice, and – as said before – the management has quite often usurped the powers of the workers' council. But that does not necessarily mean that it will be impossible to achieve a correct implementation of the theory eventually. After all, it would be unrealistic to expect that Yugoslavia would succeed in a relatively short time-span to solve all problems posed by a system that has never been tried before.

As far as the 'progression constante du secteur privé' is concerned, this is a much overrated issue, and one mainly seized upon by orthodox Marxists. The Yugoslavs themselves have no great ideological trouble with a thriving private sector. What they want to achieve with the system of self-management is to solve the problem of alienation, of exploitation of man by his fellow-man. There is very little doubt that the problem of alienation does not arise in a small, family-size, artisanal workshop, restaurant, or farm. As long as an enterprise does not get beyond a certain size – five employees – the Yugoslavs, very sensibly, leave it alone, since in the large majority of cases this type of firm is a family affair where the problem of alienation is not likely to arise. It is impossible to suggest that the growth of private enterprise threatens the system.

Meister's second objection, which deserves special attention, is riding on the favourite hobby-horse of Yugoslavia's Soviet critics: the abandonment of a compulsory central plan. He admits that 'la déplanification est la condition nécessaire à l'autonomie de l'autogestion dans les entreprises,'[274] but, at the same time, states that this also means that the workers have no further say in the overall investment policy of the country. Moreover, 's'il n'y a plus de plan, comment est-ce que l'Etat, gérant de la propriété sociale, guide les comportements des agents économiques?'[275]

The key to Meister's entire thesis lies in those few words 'l'Etat, gérant de la propriété sociale', and it is here that he makes his most serious mistake. The basic difference between the Yugoslav system and the Soviet-type command economy is centered precisely on this issue. The role of the state in Yugoslavia has been deliberately reduced as a matter of principle, and compulsory planning has been abolished.[276]

The dissatisfaction in Yugoslavia with the implementation of the self-management system has not only given rise to criticism but to various proposals for improvement as well. One of these, which has already come into force, has led to divide enterprises into so-called 'basic organisations of associated labour'. By splitting the enterprises into basic work-units it is hoped that the participation and involvement of the workers will be stimulated and managerial power checked. The units were granted sizeable powers and autonomy, they are even free to withdraw entirely from an enterprise and associate themselves with another.[277] In principle, therefore, all decision-making within the enterprises – pooling of funds, co-ordination etc. – derives now from these 'basic' units. Another proposal, which is being debated at the time of writing, is aimed at a change in the composition of parliament. It is intended that most of the legislature will henceforth consist, not of professional politicians, but of workers' representatives, delegated directly to parliament by enterprises and other organisations. In this way, the Yugoslavs hope to give the workers a large say in the running of the country.

There are, of course, countless other ideas, proposals and measures under consideration. It is not relevant to discuss these as long as they have not reached the stage of implementation. The point to be emphasised is, however, that Yugoslavia is determined not only to maintain its system of self-management but to improve it. This process will take time, and may never be completed. As is the case with any human institution, new problems will appear that require corrective action and perfection will remain an ideal to aim for in the knowledge that it will never be reached.

A definite answer to the question whether self-management really works in Yugoslavia is impossible to give. It all depends on how high one sets one's standards. As stated in *The Economist:* 'Probably the main trouble is that too much has been claimed for self-management and too much is expected of it.'[278] Moreover, it is always dangerous to generalise: in some enterprises self-management has been very successfully applied for years, in others it has been a complete failure. And between those two extremes, there is a whole range of intermediate achievements.

To give the last word to a Yugoslav author: 'Evidently, self-government is not a closed and complete system. Many questions are still open, many problems remain unsolved. The Yugoslav social laboratory is bound to be active for some time to come.'[279]

### 1.4.7. *Development targets*

Since the previous pages were exclusively concerned with Yugoslavia's past and present, it would seem appropriate to bring this chapter to a close by devoting some attention to the future. It is not intended to speculate here on the further evolution of the Yugoslav system, but to concentrate on the country's medium-term development targets. These are defined – Meister's observations to the contrary notwithstanding – in the 1971–1975 Plan. Although the Plan is not legally binding for anybody, the fact that it has been discussed extensively at all political and socio-economic levels and redrafted several times, should be a guarantee that it contains agreed-upon targets.

The Plan envisages an annual increase in GMP of 7.5 percent[280] – as against a growth of 6.7 percent per annum during the period 1966–1970 – which would result in a per capita income of $1,000 by 1975 (in constant 1971 prices and based on the exchange rate prevailing at that time).

The sectoral growth targets are, in general, set slightly above those achieved in the previous plan period. The Plan is more ambitious in the case of several industrial subsectors, notably those where domestic production capacity was insufficient to meet local demand, thus necessitating substantial imports (basic metallurgy, certain basic chemicals, and construction materials). It is hoped that the annual increase in imports, which amounted to 20.9% p.a. during the period 1966–1970, can be brought down to a more manageable 10% p.a. Exports are expected to grow by 12% p.a. (against 11.7% p.a. over the last five years), leading to a current deficit at the end of the Plan period of about ½% of GMP.

But perhaps more interesting than these figures is the development strategy that Yugoslavia intends to follow. Just before the first draft of the Plan was to be prepared – early 1970 – the Federal Institute of Planning drew up a document, which was subsequently issued with the approval of the Federal Executive Council, in which this strategy was outlined in detail.[281] Although since that time the draft of the Plan itself has undergone a number of modifications, the basic thinking behind the planning effort has not significantly changed, and the document therefore remains a good guide to Yugoslav development policy. In the following review of the 'Outline', the emphasis will be placed on what would appear to be the two principal policy decisions on which the Plan is built. In addition, a few points will be singled out which are particularly relevant to the contribution that private foreign investment can make to the economic development of Yugoslavia – a matter which will, of course, be more fully discussed in Chapter 4.

Firstly, the paper makes it very clear that Yugoslavia will continue on the road taken with the Economic Reform of 1965: 'The coming five-year period will represent a further stage in the realisation of the basic goals of the Reform.'[282] In concreto, the Plan should lead to:

a. an improvement in the standard of living;
b. a strengthening of the self-management system through 'the continuation of the assertion of the influence of the working people in the economic and political system, on the basis of the further diminuation of the role of the state in social and economic relations,'[283] i.e. the market should play an increasing role as the principal regulatory mechanism;

c. a relatively faster economic growth of the underdeveloped areas;
d. a further integration of Yugoslavia with the world economy.

The second major point emphasised in the Outline is the strong and unambiguous commitment to economic growth. Without it, none of the goals can be achieved, as stated in the following key paragraph: 'A faster growth is of the utmost importance since this involves, in addition to the further assertion of the socio-political and humanistic implications of the system of self-management, also the optimum utilisation of all resources for the permanent improvement of our material and cultural standard. It is also a question of the ability of our economy to establish links with the economies of other countries; such links are possible only provided that our country succeeds in keeping constant pace with the rest of the world... Fast growth is likewise a pre-condition for the effective solution of a series of problems, e.g. greater employment,... better utilisation of capacities and accelerated growth of economically insufficiently developed regions.'[284]

One of the factors that could contribute most to foster economic growth, it is felt, is an improvement of efficiency (apparently defined as the optimal utilisation of installed capacity rather than as the optimal allocation of new resources, although the latter evidently is also considered of high importance): 'low efficiency is still one of the fundamental problems of our economy.'[285] The paper observes that productivity in Yugoslavia does not lag very far behind the advanced countries in the less complex industries, but that the differences are substantial where more sophisticated industrial operations are concerned, or as the Outline puts it, 'in those activities where the organisation factor plays a relatively more important role.'[286] The term organisation factor covers in Yugoslav parlance such things as managerial ability, financial analysis, marketing techniques and the like. Therefore, 'organisation, beginning with the enterprise and up to the level of the total social economy, represents the factor to which exceptional attention should be devoted in the future development.'[287]

Two further points are made in the paper, which are very relevant as far as the contribution of joint ventures to economic growth is concerned. In the first place, it is felt that the fastest developing LDC's in general are those that have been able to 'skip over some technological and other stages, by making use of the tremendous advancement of science and technology in the world and by applying more and more new achievements.'[288] Whether this is a correct assessment is another question; in any case, the Yugoslavs are determined to modernise their industrial apparatus as fast as possible. And, as will be argued in Chapter 3, private foreign investment can be of help in this respect.

Secondly, the paper states that, in view of the aim to integrate Yugoslavia with the world economy, 'it is essential to apply in our entire production orientation and investment policy basically the same criteria of profitability that are practised today in the policies of the more advanced countries.'[289] One should be careful, of course, not to interpret this statement as an adherence to the principles and practices of the capitalist system. What is probably meant is that Yugoslavia should take advantage of, and adopt, the modern business techniques developed in the West – insofar as these are compatible with the Yugoslav system. Rather contemptuously the Outline argues that 'investment projects based on today's or yesterday's level of technology and organisation typical of Central Europe'[290] impede economic progress. Again, joint ventures with Western enterprises could contribute to the creation of a more modern business climate.

Yugoslavia's objectives are clear: a continuing development of its unique social system, and fast economic growth particularly in the less developed regions. To help achieve these goals, the Yugoslavs seek an increasing participation in world trade and co-operation with industrial partners from the developed countries.

NOTES

1. The definition of the Yugoslav system as a labour-managed economy was introduced by Jaroslav Vanek (cf. his *The general theory of labor-managed market economies*, Cornell University Press, Ithaca and London, 1970).
2. Drago Gorupic, 'The development of the self-managing organisation of enterprises in Yugoslavia', *Yugoslav Survey*, Vol. XI, No. 3, August 1970. Gorupic's terminology may not be entirely clear, and his three points can be paraphrased as follows:
   - Ownership of the means of production has been taken away from the state (as a legal entity) and put in the hands of the people as a whole. (This is more than a semantic difference, the further implications of which will be discussed in Chapter 2).
   - Initially, all wages were determined by the state and the state practically appropriated the remainder of the enterprise's value-added. Now the workers no longer receive wages but instead are entitled to dispose of the enterprise's net income (total revenue minus expenditures and depreciation) as they see fit; they can pay it out as personal income or reinvest. In Marxist terms this means that they are no longer deprived of the surplus value that they create.
   - The Soviet-type command economy was replaced by a decentralised system in which the market plays the main role and the plan has become an instrument of coordination instead of coercion.

3. Cf. Branko Horvat, *An essay on Yugoslav society*, International Arts and Sciences Press, White Plains (N.Y.), 1969, pages 27–28.
4. See M.J. Broekmeyer, *De arbeidersraad in Zuidslavië*, Boom, Meppel, 1968, 2nd edition, page 7.
5. Branko Horvat, 'Yugoslav economic policy in the post-war period: problems, ideas, institutional developments', *American Economic Review*, Vol. 61, No. 3, Part 2, Supplement, June 1971.
6. Gorupic, *loc. cit.*
7. Most authors, quite understandably, tend to see the stages of the evolution of the system from the perspective of their particular subject of interest, e.g. Stajner in his article, 'The system of planning' (*Yugoslav Survey*, Vol. XII, No. 1, February 1971), adopts the various plan-periods as frame of reference, whereas Broekmeyer (*op. cit.*) sees the important legislative actions concerning the workers' councils as milestones.
8. Horvat (*Amer. Econ. Review*), *loc. cit.*, page 73.
9. *Ibidem.*
10. *Ibidem.*
11. *Ibidem.*
12. In 1945, the rural population accounted for 74% of the total. Cf. Anton Vratusa, 'Jugoslavia, 1971', *Foreign Affairs*, No. 1, Autumn 1971, page 149.
13. Deborah D. Milenkovitch, *Plan and market in Yugoslav economic thought*, Yale University Press, New Haven and London, 1971, page 55.
14. *Ibidem.*
15. Horvat (*AER*), *loc. cit.*, page 74.
16. Rikard Stajner, 'The system of planning', *loc. cit.*
17. Cf. Milenkovitch, *op. cit.*, page 61; Ljubo Veljkovic, *Economic development in Yugoslavia*, Interpress, Belgrade, 1968, page 4; Stajner, *loc. cit.*; Gorupic, *loc. cit.*
18. Gorupic, *loc. cit.*
19. The account of events leading up to the break is mainly drawn from Horvat (*AER*) and Milenkovitch (*op. cit.*).
20. A significant event from the period before the war should, however, be noted: in 1937 the leader of the (illegal) Yugoslav communist party was summoned to the Soviet Union and, in line with current practice, executed because of divergent views.
21. Horvat, in *AER*, page 74.
22. Milenkovitch, *op. cit.*, page 65.
23. Horvat, in *AER*, page 75.
24. *Ibidem.* A good account of the philosophical debate on these matters is given by Broekmeyer, *op. cit.*, Chapter 1.
25. This assertion by Djilas is, of course, not consistent with the fact that Kardelj had already in June 1949 written his article in which some of the ideas by Djilas had been put forward.
26. Milovan Djilas, *The unperfect society: beyond the new class*, Harcourt, Bracc & World, N.Y., 1969, pages 220–223.
27. Workers' councils had been introduced in December 1949 on an experimental basis in 215 enterprises. These councils were, however, purely consultative bodies and the enterprise's management was free to disregard any recommendations.
28. Broekmeyer, *op. cit.*, page 32.
29. Gorupic, *loc. cit.*, page 5.
30. Roy Moore, *Self-management in Yugoslavia*, Fabian Research Series, No. 281, Fabian Society, London 1970, page 19.

31. Stajner, *loc. cit.*, page 19.
32. *Ibidem.*
33. The following account is based primarily on Veljkovic, *op. cit.*, pages 5–6.
34. Milenkovitch, *op. cit.*, page 90.
35. See M. Broekmeyer, 'De Arbeidersraad in Joegoslavië', in M. Broekmeyer and I. Cornelissen, *Arbeidersraad of ondernemersstaat*, Van Gennep, Amsterdam, 1969, pages 15–21.
36. See, inter alia, Milenkovitch, *op. cit.*, pages 73–77.
37. Milenkovitch, *op. cit.*, page 76.
38. Broekmeyer, *De arbeidersraad in Zuidslavië (op. cit.)*, page 37.
39. Horvat, in *AER*, page 78.
40. Milenkovitch, *op. cit.*, page 102.
41. For the period 1952–56 the system of 5-year plans was dropped, and only annual plans were formulated.
42. Horvat, in *AER*, page 82.
43. *Ibidem.*
44. The new rate was raised from 750 dinars to the dollar to 1200 dinars. This was followed by the creation of a new dinar equivalent to 100 old dinars.
45. Article 1 of the Act, as quoted by Gorupic, *loc. cit.*, page 11.
46. Milenkovitch, *op. cit.*, page 127.
47. The document was really more a declaration of intent than a law, and it is therefore all the more significant that the Assembly formally endorsed it.
48. As quoted by Stajner, *loc. cit.*, page 22.
49. Horvat, *Essay*, pages 111–112.
50. Horvat, in *AER*, page 159.
51. Stajner, *loc. cit.*, page 24.
52. *Ibidem.*
53. Cf. Stajner, *loc. cit.*, page 28.
54. An interesting, albeit somewhat vague, view has been formulated by Singleton. He sees Yugoslavia develop into 'A commonwealth of self-governing units, competing with each other and held together by a common economic interest and a common belief in socialism. The role of the League of Communists is to act as the ideological cement which will bind together the whole structure' (Fred Singleton, 'Three steps to self-management within an economic commonwealth', *The Times*, Special Supplement on Yugoslavia, February 2, 1972).
55. Of course, there have been other studies dealing with the theory of the labour-managed economy. They will, however, not be analysed here because they are largely variations on themes developed by Ward, Domar or Vanek, and the findings and conclusions did not differ greatly from those of the above authors. See, for example: E.G. Furubotn and S.A. Pejovich, 'Property rights and the behavior of the firm in a Socialist state: the example of Yugoslavia', *Zeitschrift für Nationalökonomie*, Band 30, Heft 3–4, 1970; S.C. Maurice and C.E. Ferguson, 'Factor usage by a labour-managed firm in a socialist economy', *Economica*, February 1972.
56. Peter Wiles, 'A descent toward particulars', in M.J. Broekmeyer (ed.), *Yugoslav workers' self-management*, Reidel Publishing Company, Dordrecht, 1970, page 155.
57. In all fairness, it should be noted that Yugoslav Marxists are far from being the worst offenders; at least they try to develop their own system with an open mind and without any claims to possessing the truth. Criticism on the Yugoslav

economic system coming from the Soviet side, however, has often more in common with theological exegesis than with economic analysis. In this connection, it is interesting to quote a Soviet economist, A. Eremin, as a representative example. He postulates that it may be useful to try to increase the efficiency of socialist production, but only in so far as this is done on the basis of 'Marxist-Leninist positions'. Market socialism, though, is a 'definite anti-Marxist concept', because 'the specific importance of the socialist government in the regulation of production is ignored, former mechanisms for the spontaneous regulation of production are romanticised, the role of planning is in fact denigrated.' According to Eremin, this 'is entirely at odds with the scientific understanding of socialism that was theoretically elaborated by the classicists of Marxism-Leninism, implemented in practice in the USSR, and currently being implemented by socialist countries' (A. Eremin, 'On the concept of market socialism', translated from Russian in *Problems of Economics*, No. 4, August 1970, pages 3–20).

58. Branko Horvat, in *AER*, page 72.
59. Milenkovitch, *op. cit.*, page 188.
60. For an exhaustive, and very readable account of the development of post-war Yugoslav economic thought, see Milenkovitch, *op. cit.*
61. Lange, in 1938, published his paper 'On the economic theory of socialism' in which he worked out a model for an economic system which he characterised as Market Socialism. While this system has certain traits in common with the labour-managed market economy, it differs from the latter in several important aspects – notably in the sense that transfer of goods and services takes place at prices fixed by a Central Planning Board.
62. (Yugoslav Institute of Economic Research, Belgrade 1964). In this study, Horvat is not so much concerned with an analysis of the Yugoslav system, as with 'a rethinking of some major economic problems of contemporary society' (Benjamin Ward, 'Marxism-Horvatism: a Yugoslav theory of socialism', *American Economic Review*, No. 3, June 1967).
63. J. Tinbergen, 'Does self-management approach the optimum order?', in M.J. Broekmeyer (ed.), *Yugoslav workers' self-management*, Reidel Publishing Company, Dordrecht, 1970, page 119.
64. In the same paper he says, for example: 'I have defended the thesis that the optimum order is of a mixed character, somewhere between the extreme freedom of the old type ... and extreme regulation.' And: 'It can be convincingly shown that in the optimum order some tasks must be performed in a centralised way' (p. 120).
65. *Ibidem.*
66. Tinbergen, *loc. cit.*, page 121 (emphasis supplied).
67. Cf. his postscript to an article by Linbeck in *Intermediair* of 20 April 1973.
68. Ward in *American Economic Review*, September 1958, pages 566–589. Ward later presented a more elaborate analysis in *The Socialist Economy*, Random House, New York, 1967.
69. Ward, *loc. cit.* (1958), page 566.
70. *Ibidem.*
71. The detailed argumentation leading to Ward's conclusions is omitted here. It would require too much space to do full justice to Ward's work and, for that matter, to that of the other authors to be discussed later. Therefore only the assumptions on which the analysis is based, and the conclusions, are reviewed here.

72. Ward, *loc. cit.* (1958), page 578.
73. *Ibidem.* The last point sounds rather paradoxical and calls for a brief explanation which is best presented graphically:

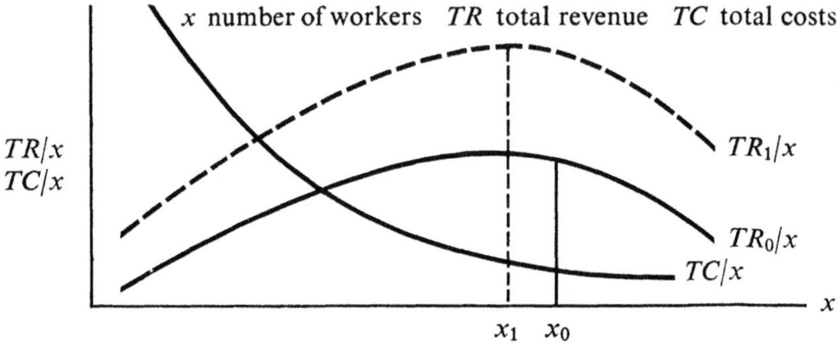


The Illyrian firm maximises revenue per worker, i.e. it will maximise the difference between $TR/x$ and $TC/x$. In the initial equilibrium situation this maximum is reached at $x_0$. An increase in the price of the product means an increase in $TR$ and, as a result, the $TR_0/x$ curve will shift upward to $TR_1/x$, but proportional to the initial values, that is, the curve rises more steeply and declines more rapidly (although the maximum value of $TR_0/x$ and $TR_1/x$ occur at the same value of $x$). Therefore the maximum difference between $TR/x$ and $TC/x$ moves left. This is because the greatest distance between two curves is at the point (on the $x$-axis) where their tangents are parallel. Since the slope of $TR_1/x$ is steeper than of $TR_0/x$, the tangent of $TC/x$ parallel to the tangent of $TR_1/x$ will occur at a lower value of $x$ because the slope of $TC/x$ declines from left to right. Consequently, employment (and output since labour is the only production factor) decreases. (Cf. Milenkovitch, *op. cit.*, page 202.)
74. Ward, *loc. cit.* (1958), page 578.
75. *Idem*, page 579.
76. *Idem*, page 582.
77. Efficiency to be understood here as explained on pages 18/19 above.
78. Evsey Domar in *American Economic Review*, September 1966, pages 734–757.
79. Domar, *loc. cit.*, page 737.
80. Milenkovitch, *op. cit.*, page 204.
81. Domar, *loc. cit.*, page 741. The table reproduced here does not use Domar's symbols as this would require an additional table with the necessary explanations.
82. Domar, *loc. cit.*, page 740.
83. By 'rich' and 'poor' Domar presumably means co-ops with respectively high and low dividend rates.
84. Domar, *loc. cit.*, page 740.
85. *Ibidem.*
86. Domar, *loc. cit.*, page 747. For the full argument, see pages 742–747.
87. *Idem*, page 749.
88. *Ibidem.*
89. Branko Horvat, 'Prilog zasnivanju teorije jugoslavenskog poduzeca', *Ekonomska Analiza*, Nos. 1 and 2, 1967. Unfortunately, a translation of this important article does not appear to be available. The following review of Horvat's study therefore

had to be based on Milenkovitch's rendering of his arguments (Milenkovitch, *op. cit.*, pages 197–211).

90. Milenkovitch, *op. cit.*, page 207.
91. Horvat, in *AER*, page 105.
92. Horvat, 'On the theory of the labour-managed firm', *Florida State University Slavic Papers*, Vol. 4, 1970, pages 7–11.
93. Milenkovitch, *op. cit.*, page 207.
94. Horvat in *Florida State University Slavic Papers*, Vol. 4, page 11.
95. Jaroslav Vanek, *The general theory of labor-managed market economies*, Cornell University Press, Ithaca and London, 1970.
96. Vanek, *General theory* (*op. cit.*), page 1.
97. Jaroslav Vanek, *The participatory economy. An evolutionary hypothesis and a strategy for development*, Cornell University Press, Ithaca and London, 1971.
98. Vanek, *General theory*, pages 1–3.
99. It will be remembered that Ward and Domar made the same assumption. In fact, also Vanek's five basic characteristics were implicitly or explicitly assumed by both Ward and Domar.
100. Vanek, *General theory*, page 34.
101. Cf., *inter alia*, William Fellner, *Modern economic analysis*, McGraw-Hill/Kogakusha, Tokyo, 1960, pages 222–225.
102. Jaroslav Vanek, 'Decentralisation under workers' management: a theoretical appraisal', *American Economic Review*, Vol. LIX, No. 5, December 1969, page 1007.
103. Vanek, *General theory*, page 105.
104. *Idem*, page 120.
105. Vanek, in *AER*, page 1008.
106. Vanek, *General theory*, page 120.
107. Vanek argued also that in a democratic structure, such as the labour-managed enterprise, there would be a strong tendency to subdivisions 'into autonomous decision-making and production units based on location and other functional characteristics' (*AER*, page 1008). This issue will be referred to again, albeit indirectly, when Vanek's position on the question of entry is examined.
108. Vanek, in *AER*, page 1009.
109. Vanek, *Participatory economy*, page 28.
110. Vanek, *General theory*, page 210.
111. The principal corrective force being free entry, and – to a lesser extent – expansion of existing firms.
112. Vanek, *General theory*, page 210.
113. Vanek, *Participatory economy*, page 29.
114. It should be noted here that Vanek's theory is concerned with a closed economy.
115. Vanek, in *AER*, page 1011.
116. *Ibidem*.
117. Vanek, *General theory*, page 244.
118. Vanek, in *AER*, page 1011.
119. Vanek, *General theory*, page 237.
120. *Idem*, page 260.
121. *Idem*, page 258.
122. *Idem*, page 264.
123. *Idem*, page 268.
124. Vanek, in *AER*, page 1011.

125. *Ibidem.*
126. Vanek, *General theory*, page 307.
127. *Idem*, page 303.
128. *Idem*, page 282.
129. *Idem*, page 286.
130. Consistent with Vanek's assumptions of a closed economy, the possibility of foreign trade is not taken into account.
131. Vanek, *Participatory economy*, page 41.
132. *Ibidem.*
133. Vanek, *General theory*, page 2.
134. *Ibidem.*
135. Milenkovitch (*op. cit.*, pages 191–196) discusses the views of several Yugoslav authors on this subject. She experienced, however, some difficulty in interpreting these views and had to conclude that some statements were either unclear or the analysis invalid. In any case, she found only one author (Popovic) who explicitly stated that the rational enterprise would want to maximise income per worker.
136. Kamusic in Broekmeyer (ed.), *Yugoslav workers' self-management*, Reidel Publishing Company, Dordrecht, 1970, page 161.
137. See page 25 above for Horvat's view.
138. Howard M. Wachtel, 'Wages in a labor-managed economy: the Yugoslav case', *The Florida State University Slavic Papers*, Volume 4, 1970; and 'Workers' management and interindustry wage differentials in Yugoslavia', *Journal of Political Economy*, No. 3, May/June 1972. Both studies were based on research done for his Ph.D. dissertation (American University).
139. Wachtel (*Florida State*), page 24.
140. Horvat, in *AER*, page 105.
141. In Chapter 4 of *The participatory economy*, Vanek himself carried out a similar exercise, which was, however, rather limited in scope: he only evaluated Yugoslav performance in terms of economic growth and the investment ratio.
142. Vanek, *General theory*, page 403.
143. Efficiency to be understood in this context as commonly defined in the literature.
144. J. Wemelsfelder et al., 'Arbeiderszelfbestuur in de Joegoslavische industrie; afschrikwekkend of navolgenswaard voorbeeld?', Supplement to *Economisch-Statistische Berichten* of 15 March 1972.
145. D. Balassa and T.J. Bertrand, 'Growth performance of Eastern European economies and comparable Western European countries', *American Economic Review*, May 1970.
146. The following summary of Balassa's and Bertrand's analysis is based on Wemelsfelder. The countries in question were Bulgaria, Czechoslovakia, Hungary, Poland, Romania, Greece, Ireland, Norway, Spain and Yugoslavia.
147. According to Mesa-Lago, 'toward the end of the forties, Yugoslavia claimed that full employment was a national reality and unemployment insurance was suspended' (Carmelo Mesa-Lago, 'Unemployment in a socialist economy: Yugoslavia', *Industrial Relations*, Volume 10, No. 1, February 1971).
148. *Ibidem.*
149. Mesa-Lago quotes a study of the U.S. Labor Department which estimated that in 1965 about one-fourth of the labour engaged in agriculture could be released for other work. In 1967, this was confirmed by a Yugoslav economist who put underemployment in agriculture at over 20% (cf. Mesa-Lago, *loc. cit.*).
150. *Ibidem.*

151. *Arbeiderszelfbestuur in Joegoslavië: Theorie en praktijk*, Stichting Maatschappij en Onderneming, The Hague, 1971, page 20.
152. Wemelsfelder, *loc. cit.*, page 19.
153. *Idem*, page 20. See also Table 1.9.
154. Wemelsfelder, *loc. cit.*, pages 21–22.
155. Horvat, in *AER*, page 112.
156. *Ibidem.*
157. Horvat, in *AER*, page 111.
158. Stevan Govedarica, 'Price system and policy', *Yugoslav Survey*, Vol. XIII, No. 3, August 1972.
159. About 80% of all industrial (factory-gate) prices fell under this measure, as well as almost all wholesale and retail prices of industrial goods, retail prices of the main agricultural and food products, transportation services, rents, and rates of public utilities (cf. Govedarica, *loc. cit.*).
160. *Ibidem.*
161. *Ibidem.*
162. These are resp. market forces and 'the collective expression of the will and distributional attitudes of the working community' (cf. Vanek, *Participatory economy*, page 30).
163. Vanek, *Participatory economy*, page 30.
164. Vanek, *General theory*, page 393.
165. Wemelsfelder, *loc. cit.*, pages 23–24.
166. Howard M. Wachtel, *loc. cit.*
167. Sofija Popov, 'Intersectoral relations of personal incomes', *Yugoslav Survey*, Vol. XIII, No. 2, May 1972.
168. Popov, *loc. cit.*, page 63.
169. *Idem*, pages 76–79.
170. Wachtel, *loc. cit.*, pages 551–558.
171. *Idem*, page 556.
172. *Idem*, Table 2.
173. *Idem*, page 558.
174. Wemelsfelder, *loc. cit.*, page 17.
175. Vanek, *General theory*, page 105.
176. *Arbeiderszelfbestuur in Joegoslavië: theorie en praktijk (op. cit.)*, page 20.
177. Note that the comparison in Table 1.8 was made in terms of the percentage of the total number of workers.
178. Vanek, *Participatory economy*, page 29.
179. B. Horvat, 'Business cycles in Yugoslavia', *Eastern European Economics*, No. 3/4, Spring/Summer 1971.
180. Horvat, in *AER*, page 138.
181. *Ibidem.*
182. *Ibidem.*
183. *Ibidem.*
184. J.J. Hauvonen, 'Postwar developments in money and banking in Yugoslavia', *IMF Staff Papers*, No. 3, November 1970, page 577.
185. Horvat, in *AER*, page 139.
186. E. Neuberger, 'The Yugoslav investment auctions', *Quarterly Journal of Economics*, Vol. 72, No. 1, February 1959, page 93.
187. Hauvonen, *loc. cit.*, page 577.
188. Horvat, in *AER*, page 140.

189. This is demonstrated rather clearly by the figures presented in Table 1.10 (which are directly or indirectly based on official Yugoslav statistics): until 1964 bank financing of fixed asset investment is negligible.
190. Novica Vucic, 'Aenderungen im jugoslawischen Banksystem', *Oesterreichisches Bank-Archiv*, No. 8, August 1972, page 288.
191. *Ibidem.*
192. Unfortunately, the available data do not show separately figures for fixed capital formation by enterprises, but only the total for the whole economy (excl. private sector). One can, of course, safely assume that the percentage of self-financing is higher than the figures shown in the Table.
193. Horvat, in *AER*, page 140.
194. Cf. Table 1.9.
195. Vucic summarised the principles of the Law in two words: 'Deetatisierung' and 'Deterritorialisierung' (Vucic, *loc. cit.*, page 289).
196. Hauvonen, *loc. cit.*, page 581.
197. *Ibidem.*
198. *Ibidem.*
199. Hauvonen, *loc. cit.*, page 580.
200. The National Bank, the three Federal Banks, six Republic investment banks, 206 cooperative banks and the postal savings bank.
201. National Bank of Yugoslavia, *Annual Report, 1971*, page 52.
202. *Statisticki Godisnjak Jugoslavije 1972*, Table 120–5.
203. Hauvonen, *loc. cit.*, page 594.
204. Vucic, *loc. cit.*, page 292. The most common method for banks to circumvent the interest ceiling was to require counter-deposits against credits granted. This practice was continued even after the interest ceiling was abolished.
205. Novica Vucic, 'Finanzierungspolitik der Investitionen in Jugoslawien', *Oesterreichisches Bank-Archiv*, No. 2, February 1971, page 43.
206. 'Law on Banks and on Credit and Banking Operations' (*Official Gazette*, No. 58/71). Early 1972, the overhaul of the banking system was completed by a law dealing with the National Bank. This second law ('Law on the National Bank of Yugoslavia and on the Uniform Monetary Operations of the National Banks of the Republics and the National Banks of the Autonomous Provinces', *Official Gazette*, 23/72) introduced Republic's 'Central Banks' which are endowed with a certain degree of independence thereby strengthening the position of the Republics in the monetary field.
207. The following account is mainly based on Milo Jovanovic, 'Changes in the Yugoslav banking system', National Bank of Yugoslavia, *Quarterly Bulletin*, No. 1, January 1973.
208. The founder can also withdraw his share in the accumulated earnings of the bank, except for that (small) part that has been allocated to the bank's Reserve Fund. The total annual allocation to the Reserve Fund is, at least, 0.5% of the total amount of credits granted by the bank during the year. Only in case of liquidation is this Fund distributed among the founders.
209. Jovanovic, *loc. cit.*, page 44.
210. In 1971, Gross Savings (i.e. including depreciation allowances) amounted to 34% of the Gross Material Product (National Bank of Yugoslavia, *Annual Report 1971*, page 18).
211. *Official Gazette*, No. 58/71.
212. Net worth in the Western sense of the word is not a concept used in Yugoslavia.

However, the Yugoslav 'Business Fund' plus 'Reserve Fund' (the terms used in the Law) comes fairly close to it.

213. This will be further discussed in Chapter 4.
214. Except, of course, for the three specialised Federal banks.
215. See, *inter alia:* OECD, *Economic Survey of Yugoslavia*, November 1970 (page 47) and *Idem*, March 1972 (page 17).
216. While Yugoslavia has experienced severe balance of payments problems in the past, these have not resulted to any significant degree from the specific nature of the Yugoslav system. It is therefore not relevant in this context to discuss the external imbalances.
217. See OECD, *Economic Surveys* 1970 and 1972, *passim*. For a detailed discussion of Yugoslavia's post-war monetary policy, see also Horvat, in *AER*, pages 130–138.
218. Horvat, in *AER*, pages 149–150; emphasis supplied.
219. OECD, *Econ. Surv.* 1972, page 42.
220. The official Yugoslav national accounts are presented in the form of the 'Gross Material Product', which is different from GNP in the Western definition in that it excludes certain services such as public administration and defence, health and welfare, insurance, scientific and cultural activities, and professions. If these were included, GMP would be increased by about 15%.
221. OECD, *Econ. Surv.* 1972.
222. Horvat, in *AER*, page 157.
223. *Ibidem.*
224. *Ibidem.*
225. OECD, *Econ. Surv.* 1972, page 43.
226. Aleksandar Bajt, 'Privredna Kretanja i Ekonomska Politika u 1969 i 1970 Godine', *Ekonomist*, No. 4, 1969, as quoted by N. Vucic, 'Probleme der jugoslawischen Finanzpolitik', *Osteuropa Wirtschaft*, No. 3, September 1972, page 179.
227. See Jovanovic, *loc. cit.*, for a full account of the recent legislation on this subject.
228. OECD, *Econ. Surv.* 1972, page 18.
229. Horvat, in *AER*, page 137.
230. OECD, *Econ. Surv.* 1972.
231. See *Idem*, Annex I-A, for the various policy changes in 1972 alone.
232. OECD, *Econ. Surv.* 1970, page 47.
233. OECD, *Econ. Surv.* 1972, page 44.
234. Milenkovitch, *op. cit.*, page 179.
235. Ksente Bogoev, 'The policy of more rapid development of the undeveloped Republics and Province', *Eastern European Economics*, Vol. X, No. 4, Summer 1972. Bogoev's article is interesting not only because he is one of Yugoslavia's best-known economists, but particularly since he is President of Macedonia, one of the less developed Republics. Yugoslav policy comes in for a fair amount of criticism in this article, which is probably the most cogent exposition of the less developed regions' point of view.
236. Bogoev, *loc. cit.*, page 397.
237. See on this issue, R. Bicanic, *Economic policy in socialist Yugoslavia*, Cambridge University Press, 1973, page 187.
238. Bogoev, *loc. cit.*, page 397.
239. How this percentage was arrived at is not entirely clear.
240. Bicanic, *op. cit.*, page 190.
241. *Ibidem.*
242. Bicanic, *op. cit.*, page 191.

243. Obviously, the less developed regions are not satisfied either. Their argument, not surprisingly, is that there should be more rather than less aid.
244. See, e.g., Bogoev, *loc. cit.*
245. A small amount, 2 percent of its annual lending, is devoted by the Fund for Developing Regions to technical assistance.
246. *Statisticki Godisnjak Jugoslavije 1972*, Tables 105–3 and 203–1.
247. *Yearbook of National Accounts Statistics 1971*, United Nations, New York, 1973, Volume III, International Tables 4A, 4C and 4D. Yugoslavia achieved a similarly high score in the World Bank Atlas (*Finance and Development*, Vol. 10, No. 1, March 1973): 24th out of 127 countries. It would seem, however, that the per capita growth rate – for the same 1960–1970 period – accorded to Yugoslavia by the Bank's economists is too low, i.e. 4.3 percent. According to official Yugoslav data, on which the Bank has to rely as well, GMP almost doubled between 1960 and 1970 (in constant prices). Given a yearly population increase of less than 1 percent, a per capita annual GMP growth rate of about 6 percent is the more probable figure.
248. The figure for 1970 in Table 105–3 of the *Statisticki Godisnjak* is actually 35.0. This would appear too high, and instead the 31.0 listed in Table 2 of the January 1973 *Quarterly Bulletin* of the National Bank of Yugoslavia has been adopted. For other years the figures given by these two sources were virtually identical.
249. *Statistical Pocket Book of Yugoslavia 1973*, page 50.
250. Miodrag Nikolic, 'Changes in the structure of industrial production, 1952–1972', *Yugoslav Survey*, May 1973.
251. Veljko Rus, 'Influence structure in Yugoslav enterprises', *Industrial Relations*, Vol. 9, No. 2, February 1970.
252. See for complete reference to source material, Rus, *loc. cit.*, note 3 on page 149.
253. Rus, *loc. cit.*, page 149.
254. *Idem*, page 151.
255. *Idem*, page 156.
256. *Ibidem.*
257. Rus, *loc. cit.*, page 159.
258. This would seem to be borne out by another study, made in 1969, which reported that about 40% of all respondents thought self-management only marginally useful while another 20% felt it was of no use at all (Dunja Rihtman-Augustin, quoted in *Arbeiderszelfbestuur in Joegoslavië: theorie en praktijk* (*op. cit.*).
259. C.J. Lammers, 'Problemen en prestaties van het Joegoslavische zelfbestuur', *De Groene Amsterdammer*, 24-1-1973.
260. R. Supek, 'Problems and perspectives of workers' self-management', in Broekmeyer (ed.), *Yugoslav workers' self-management* (*op. cit.*), page 231.
261. Lammers, *loc. cit.*
262. Zoran Vidakovic, *Het tweede decennium van arbeiderszelfbestuur* (translated from the Serbo-Croat by M. Broekmeyer), Van Gennep, Amsterdam, 1972.
263. Broekmeyer in his introduction to Vidakovic, *op. cit.*, page 10.
264. Not all of it was particularly well-informed. Ota Sik, the Czech economist behind Dubcek's reform, said in an interview in *Newsweek* when asked whether Yugoslavia was not an example of the economic system he favoured (workers to have a share in profits and decision-making in the enterprise, and long-range planning of national priorities): 'The Yugoslav case is hardly typical. For one thing, their workers have very little industrial experience, and their leadership is new. More important, the Yugoslavs have not matched their self-management

system with political democracy. The country is run by a one-party bureaucracy which constantly interferes with economic forces, weakening the marketing system by subsidies and insists on manipulating the workers' councils in line with the party policies' (*Newsweek*, June 18, 1973).

265. Broekmeyer, *De arbeidersraad in Zuidslavië (op. cit.)*.
266. Broekmeyer in his introduction to Vidakovic, *op. cit.*, page 7.
267. Of course, traditional conservative opinion has condemned self-management as unworkable from the outset.
268. Albert Meister, 'Tendances de l'autogestion yougoslave', *Documentation sur l'Europe Centrale*, Vol. X, No. 3, Louvain, 1972.
269. Meister, *loc. cit.*, page 192.
270. *Idem*, page 193.
271. *Idem*, page 203.
272. *Idem*, page 194.
273. *Idem*, page 195 (emphasis supplied).
274. *Idem*, page 198.
275. *Idem*, page 199.
276. This does not mean, as Meister claims, that there is no planning at all – but this matter has been dealt with earlier in this chapter.
277. The organisational structure of the Yugoslav enterprise will be discussed in Chapter 2.
278. 'Another way: a survey of Yugoslavia', *The Economist*, August 21, 1971, page xxv
279. Horvat, in *AER*, page 161.
280. All figures and data concerning the 1971–1975 Plan are derived from the OECD *Economic Survey of Yugoslavia* (March 1972).
281. Federal Planning Institute, *An outline of the concepts of the social plan of develop ment of Yugoslavia from 1971 to 1975*, Belgrade, 1970.
282. *Outline*, page 7.
283. *Ibidem*.
284. *Outline*, pages 8–9.
285. *Idem*, page 11.
286. *Ibidem*.
287. *Ibidem*.
288. *Outline*, page 13.
289. *Ibidem*.
290. *Ibidem*.

# 2. The Yugoslav enterprise

## 2.1. INTRODUCTION

Having examined in the previous chapter some of the more important macroeconomic aspects of the Yugoslav system, it is time to turn now to the Yugoslav enterprise, and this for two principal reasons. In the first place, private foreign investment in Yugoslavia – the subject of the second part of this study – is allowed only within the framework of the Yugoslav enterprise and this framework therefore needs to be investigated. Secondly, the Yugoslav enterprises are what one might call the building blocks out of which the self-management system is being constructed. It is at the level of the enterprise that the Yugoslavs have been at their most innovative in the search for a solution to the problem of alienation.[1]

In many respects the Yugoslav enterprise is, of course, no different from its capitalist counterpart. It buys the same raw materials, uses the same manufacturing processes, sells the same products, and has the same sort of worries: negotiations with suppliers, customers, and banks. It is also organised in departments for manufacturing, maintenance, services, administration, sales, etc.

But there remain some important differences, and the approach followed in this chapter – as was the case of the previous chapter – will again be selective: the main focus will be on those facets of the Yugoslav enterprise that are different from the capitalist firm. Broadly speaking these differences can be grouped into two principal categories: those of an institutional and those of an operational nature. To the first belong such questions as the legal structure of the Yugoslav enterprise, the system of self-management at the enterprise level, and accounting principles. In the second category are included Yugoslav practices with respect to planning, distribution of income and financing.

## 2.2. LEGAL ASPECTS

Before turning to the question of the legal status of the enterprise within the system, it may be useful to come back again for a moment to the problem of the ownership of the means of production which was briefly touched upon in the previous chapter. It will be remembered that one of the basic changes the Yugoslav socio-economic system has undergone since the Second World War consisted in the fact that, as formulated by Gorupic, 'state ownership of the means of production has been turned into social ownership.'[2] In other words, the state has been divested of legal title to the means of production which now belong to the Yugoslav people. As a legal concept this is, to say the least, somewhat vague. Inevitably, Wiles' remark about 'the large, generous and humane imprecisions characteristic of Yugoslav Marxism'[3] comes forcefully to mind, in particular since the Yugoslavs themselves seemed to be baffled by the precise legal implications. Horvat, who made a thorough review of Yugoslav writing on the subject, found that 'the legal experts agree that social ownership implies self-government, that it is a new social category, that, if it is a legal concept, it does not imply an unlimited right over things characteristic of the classical concept of property, and that it includes property elements of both public and private law.'[4] He drily concluded that on 'practically everything else there is disagreement.'[5] Some writers even go as far as saying that 'in our country it is not possible to speak of ownership. It simply does not exist.'[6] Nor is the legislation very clear. Social ownership is not vested in any specific holder, be it the Federation, other political entities, or enterprises for that matter.

The law, however, recognises a 'right to use'[7] and Milenkovitch has made an interesting attempt to explain this 'right to use' in terms of a division of the property rights normally associated with private ownership as understood in the West between the enterprise and 'Society.'[8] (The rights of the latter are exercised by the various political authorities as its mandatary.) The specific property rights incumbent on the enterprise, which together constitute its 'right to use' are, according to Milenkovitch:[9]

- Right to use property for personal[10] production and consumption.
- Right to use property personally for market production and to sell the produce and retain the proceeds.
- Right to rent property to others and to receive income therefrom.
- Right to keep property without using it.
- Right to alter the nature of property.
- Right to sell physical property.

The enterprise, however, does not have the right to deplete or use up the value of property, to go into liquidation, or to sell shares in its earnings. These property rights remain vested in society.

Milenkovitch's definition of the 'right to use', however, may give the (wrong) impression that the various rights listed above are absolute. This is certainly not the case. The rights of the enterprise are subordinate to those of 'Society', in particular because the enterprise holds its assets in trust for the Yugoslav people as a whole.

It would seem that the Yugoslavs themselves are only marginally interested in exact legal definitions of 'social ownership'. This is not to say that they consider the question of ownership unimportant. On the contrary, as Marxists they emphasise that 'ownership relations are the basic determinants of social relations and thus of the socio-economic system.'[11] Ownership, however, is not so much viewed as a matter of legal title but rather as a question of control, as an economic category. What is important to the Yugoslavs is that the worker is the manager of (social) property and can dispose of the profit or surplus value arising from the use of property.[12]

The legal status of Yugoslav enterprises is regulated in the 'Law on the Assets of Economic Organisations'[13] (1971), which replaced the 'Law on Enterprises' dating from 1965. The basic legal characteristics of the Yugoslav enterprises are summarised by Popovic as follows:[14]

1. The enterprise is an independent organisation.
2. The enterprise is a legal entity, it may acquire rights and enter into contractual relationships.
3. The enterprise is managed by the workers; only labour gives the right to manage.
4. The Statutes and General Regulations of an enterprise are adopted by its workers.
5. The workers of the enterprises establish the management organs, determine their terms of reference and time of mandate, and fix the conditions of their election and dissolution.

It is probably fair to conclude that the Yugoslav enterprise does not differ that much from its capitalist counterpart as far as external relations are concerned. There are no statutory limitations on its operations in the market place. The basic institutional differences lie in the sphere of internal organisation and the way it is established.

As was mentioned in the previous chapter, the increasing concern about the implementation of the self-management system in practice has led to a change in the way enterprises are constituted. The 1971 Law now provides for four forms of 'organisations of associated labour'. These are:

- The '*Basic organisation of associated labour*' (Osnova organizacija udruženog rada, OOUR) which is from now on the elementary work-unit into which all enterprises are divided. The OOUR can be defined as 'a group of workers who produce a product or a service which has a recognisable value and is capable of fetching a price on the market.'[15] There are two types of OOUR – one capable of transacting business on the market in its own name, the other only through the enterprise of which it forms a part. Both have, however, a large degree of autonomy and can withdraw from an enterprise to join another.
- The '*Union of basic organisations of associated labour*' (Zajednica osnovih organizacija udruženog rada), which is a combination of OOUR's within the same enterprise.
- The '*Work organisation*' (Radna organizacija), i.e. the enterprise.[16] It consists of an 'association' (as the Yugoslavs call it) of two or more OOUR's.
- The '*United organisation of associated labour*' (Složena organizacija udruženog rada), which is an association between two or more 'work organisations' (or enterprises).

At the time of writing it is too early to say how far this new legislation will affect enterprise operations. There is, of course, a danger that the large degree of autonomy granted to the OOUR will result in instability of the enterprise as a whole. On the other hand, it may be safely predicted that the independence of the OOUR will be exercised first and foremost in such fields as, e.g., the determination of personal incomes, internal price agreements, etc., rather than in break-aways from the parent enterprise.[17] Since the legislation has been adopted, most enterprises have, in fact, been carrying on as before, the only difference being that relations between the various divisions of the enterprise (i.e. OOUR's) are now the subject of formal contractual agreements.[18]

The system of self-management has, inevitably, some consequences for the way new enterprises can be set up – and existing enterprises liquidated, for that matter.[19] In general, new enterprises can be established by practically anybody, be they political entities, other enterprises, or private persons. The latter are, however, precluded from founding enterprises in certain fields such as banking, wholesale trade, telecommunications and railway transport. The procedure, according to which an enterprise has to be founded, consists basically of two stages. During the first stage, the 'founders' of the new enterprise, as they are called, are responsible – and legally liable – for all operations leading to the establishment of the enterprise. Not only do they carry out all the preparatory work (feasibility studies, planning, etc.), they are also obliged to ensure the availability of the necessary funds. These may come from their own resources or in the form of bank credits, the contracts for which have to be signed by the founders. Once these preparations are completed, the second stage commences: the new enterprise is entered in the Register of Economic Organisations as an 'Enterprise-in-formation'. At this point the enterprise acquires legal personality, and all contractual obligations entered into by the founders (e.g. with banks and suppliers) pass to the enterprise. Simultaneously, any assets that private persons (as founders) have granted to the 'Enterprise-in-formation' become social property to be managed by the new enterprise.

While as of the date of its registration the new enterprise has legal personality, it may only conclude contracts and undertake actions that are directly related to the building up of the enterprise (construction, engaging personnel, etc.). At this stage, the enterprise-in-formation has a managing director, appointed by the founders, who takes all decisions without reference to the workers of the enterprise. He is, however, responsible for his actions to the commune (roughly comparable to a municipality) where the enterprise is located.

When construction and start-up operations are completed, the enterprise-in-formation is 'constituted' (to use the Yugoslav expression) as a fully-fledged enterprise. The act of constitution consists in turning over the enterprise to the workers for self-management. These then proceed to elect the workers' council and, after a public competition for the post, the director. The act of constitution is subsequently registered with the local Economic Court. After registration the enterprise is obliged to adopt its Statutes within six months. Should it fail to keep this time limit, the communal assembly dissolves the workers' council and prescribes elections for a new council.

It will be obvious that the going into liquidation of an existing Yugoslav enterprise is a rare occurrence. Apart from mergers with other enterprises, an enterprise is only liquidated if bankruptcy cannot be further avoided. Before it comes to this stage, however, rescue operations are undertaken under the aegis of the commune in which the enterprise is located. The enterprise is obliged to submit a comprehensive plan to redress its situation and, among other things, has to cut back on personal incomes. The banks normally have an important voice in the formulation and execution of the plan. Only if the plan has failed to yield results, the enterprise goes into receivership. But, even then, an effort is made to keep viable units of the enterprise in existence.

Although not immediately related to the subject of the legal status of the Yugoslav enterprise, it may be useful to add a few words at this stage on the question of risk. From the fact that 'ownership' is a rather diffuse concept in Yugoslavia it should not be deduced that nobody incurs risks in the Yugoslav enterprise. On the contrary, the remarkable thing is that whereas in capitalist society the principal risk lies with those who are best able to carry it, in Yugoslavia it is the labourer who is the main risk-bearer. In fact, the Yugoslav worker carries a double risk: not only as far as his employment is concerned (in this respect, of course, he does not differ from his colleague in the West), but also with respect to reinvested earnings, i.e. that part of the enterprise's net income that is not paid out to the workers but ploughed back – this investment risk is borne, in capitalist society, exclusively by the owners. And, as Neuberger and James have pointed out, 'the Yugoslav worker's investment risk is positively correlated with his employment risk: negative returns may result in the loss of his job.'[20]

One of the disadvantages of the self-management system is therefore that the Yugoslav worker is exposed to greater risks than his counterpart in the West, without being better able to absorb a possible 'loss'. In this connection, it should also be noted that when a Yugoslav worker left an enterprise he irrevocably lost his rights to the (future) benefits arising from his share in the net income of the enterprise that is reinvested. This put him at a disadvantage to the capitalist entrepreneur who, of course, retained his right to any future income stream. The obvious consequence of this state of affairs was a bias against self-financing and a tendency to pay out relatively higher personal incomes to the workers. As was seen earlier, this has been one of the major causes of the persistent inflationary pressures in Yugoslavia. At present efforts are being made to rectify this injustice. In fact, the new Constitution contains a provision which entitles a worker to continuing benefits from his past contribution to an enterprise. It is, however, not yet entirely clear how this constitutional principle is going to be applied in practice. In some cases special bonuses are being paid out to retired workers, but this has already come under criticism as being too restrictive.

## 2.3. SELF-MANAGEMENT

Given its crucial importance for the implementation of the system, it is hardly surprising that the structure and operation of self-management at the enterprise level have been the subject of a substantial amount of legislation.

The principles are even laid down in the Constitution (Article 9, Section 1), and they are important enough to quote them at length:[21]

'Self-management in work organisations[22] shall include in particular the right and duty of the working people:

1. to manage their work organisations directly or through bodies of management elected by themselves;
2. to organise production or other activities, to promote the development of their work organisations, and to lay down their work and development plans and programmes;
3. to decide on the exchange of goods and services and on other business relating to the operation of work organisations;
4. to decide on the use and disposition of social resources and to employ them with economic efficiency so as to insure the highest possible returns for the work organisations and the social community;
5. to distribute the income of their work organisations and provide for the development of the material basis of their labour, to allocate income among the working people; to meet the obligations of the work organisations to the community;
6. to decide on the recruitment of working people into work organisations, and their dismissal, and on other labour relations, to fix working hours in work organisations in accordance with the general conditions of work; to regulate other matters of common concern; to ensure internal supervision and the public character of work;
7. to regulate and improve their conditions of work; to organise industrial safety, and work breaks;
8. to decide on the split-up of parts of work organisations and their constitution into separate organisations, and on the amalgamation and association of their work organisations with other work organisations.'

Prior to 1969, i.e. before the introduction of Constitutional Amendment xv, the Constitution and the 'Basic Law on Enterprises' prescribed what 'self-management organs' – i.e. workers' council, management board and director – each enterprise was obliged to have and regulated their competence in extraordinary detail. Over time, however, the proliferation of additional rules and regulations had made the situation so complicated that 'the legal organs were being short-circuited'[23] thereby rendering the formal legislation virtually ineffective. In typical Yugoslav fashion a radical solution was adopted: doing away with the previous detailed prescriptions, the enterprises were now allowed considerable latitude to set up their own self-management structure and policies – although, of course, the fundamental principles (Article 9 of the Constitution) had to be respected. More particularly: no enterprise may go without a workers' council, and all other (self-) management bodies of the enterprises are elected by the workers' council. The new rules took the form of an Amendment to the Constitution[24] which, again, is worth quoting in full:[25]

'Exercising self-management in work organisations as a whole and in organisations of associated labour making part of the former, working people shall determine matters on which they can decide directly, and shall entrust specific functions of management

**to workers' councils, or according to the nature of the activity of the work organisation concerned, to another appropriate organ of management, and shall entrust specific executive functions to bodies and individuals responsible to this organ of management and elected by the workers' council.**

**Working people in work organisations shall determine the organs of management of their work organisations, specify their province of work and tenure, and lay down conditions for and the mode of their election and removal.**

**A special procedure and mode of appointment and removal of individuals entrusted with executive prerogatives in organisations conducting affairs of special social concern may be laid down by statute.'**

Kamusic has aptly summarised the letter and the spirit of the present legislation as follows: 'Self-managed enterprises ... independently plan their production and business policy, independently define their organs of management and their rights, independently decide on the mode of control over the collective and individual bodies of self-management, elect and dismiss the representative organs of management, their business management and other professionals that take part in the management of enterprises, accept new members into the working relations or decide about the disruption of these relations.'[26]

The remarkable thing, however, is that, although the enterprises are now free to do without a management board, most of them have so far stuck to the old organisational structure.[27] Moreover, as was pointed out in the previous chapter, the increased flexibility of the enterprise with respect to the self-management organs has not led to increased power for the workers but, instead, to more power for management. The overwhelming majority of Yugoslav enterprises therefore still knows three major bodies of (self-) management – the workers' council, the management board, and the director – and these will now be examined in somewhat more detail. In order to give some additional perspective to this review, reference will be made to the concrete case of a Yugoslav enterprise. The enterprise in question is 'SAVA', a factory producing tyres and other rubber products, located in Slovenia. SAVA is known to be not only one of the best-run enterprises in Yugoslavia but also one which from the early days onwards has been in the forefront as far as the development of self-management is concerned. Fortunately, the statute[28] of SAVA is one of the few that has been translated into English, which considerably facilitates the discussion.

### 2.3.1. *The Workers' Council*

The basic organ of self-management is the workers' council. It is 'the supreme policy-maker of the Yugoslav enterprise, with competence to handle all policy questions.'[29] The workers' council is elected by the 'work collective'[30] by universal, direct and secret ballot.[31] All workers, with the exception of the director, are eligible for the council. Usually, members serve a two-year term and half of the membership is renewed each year.[32] The council chooses a chairman from among its members.

Enterprises are now in principle free to determine the number of members of the workers' council. But here again the new regulations have made little difference in practice and the minimum is still 15 members and the maximum 120. It should be noted here that an enterprise with a total employment of less than 30 people does not elect a workers' council. In this case the entire labour force constitutes the council. Large enterprises, consisting of several 'basic organisations of associated labour' (OOUR), on the other hand, normally have a workers' council for each OOUR. The rights and obligations that are incumbent on this type of workers' council, may be illustrated by quoting the more important relevant provisions of the SAVA Statute:[33]

'The department (workers') council, and the workers' assembly in a department without a council,[34] are competent:

- to decide on the proposed operative plans and the manufacturing programs of the department, before they are confirmed by the competent managing bodies of the Enterprise;
- to decide on the socio-economic working conditions set by the Enterprise's technical services (rules, standards, prices and the like);
- to decide on proposals concerning changes in the organisational structure of the department, before they have been decided upon by the Enterprise's Workers' Council;
- to decide on distributing its income according to the provisions of the Regulations on Income Distribution;[35]
- to decide on the proposed bases and criteria for distributing the personal income to the department members before these bases and criteria have been confirmed by the Enterprise's Workers' Council;
- to decide on settling material discussions between departments, by common agreement;
- to give its opinions to the Enterprise's managing bodies in connection with the management, changes of the object of business activity, settling the internal relations within the Enterprise, etc.'

In addition, the department's council deals with hiring and firing within the unit, elects its own chairman, rules on workers' complaints and reports once a year to the Enterprise's workers' council on its activities.

The rights and duties of a SAVA department's council are therefore, in the first instance, related to the operation of the department itself, thus anticipating the increased degree of autonomy granted later to the OOUR's by the 1971 Law, which the SAVA Statute precedes by two years.

The workers' council of the enterprise as a whole is, as stated earlier, elected by direct ballot – and not by the members of the departmental workers' councils. In the case of SAVA, which is fairly usual in this respect, the members of each department elect, directly among themselves, the members of the enterprise's workers' council.[36] Departments with less than 100 workers elect one council member, departments of 100 to 200 members two, and departments with more than 200 members elect three council members. Total membership amounts to about 50 persons at present.

The rights and duties of the enterprise's workers' council are laid down, in great detail, in Article 215 of the Statute. The most important provisions are the following:

'The Enterprise's Workers' Council shall decide on the business policy and other matters important to the work and development of the Enterprise, especially:

a. it decides on the basic principles of the business policy and on the programs for the several fields of the Enterprise's activity;
it decides on the development programs, investment studies and annual economic plans as the basic instruments of the Enterprise's business policy;
it decides on the acquisition of patents, licences, and other industrial properties;
in case of need, it determines measures, gives directions and instructions to the Enterprise's executive boards and to the enterprise's individual executive functionary[37] on how to perform the business policy;
it decides on the rational use of the Enterprise's assets;
..........
it decides on investment maintenance and its calculative degree (sic; i.e. a percentage of the value of investment in fixed assets);
it decides on investment loans for fixed and current assets, and on other loans necessary to the Enterprise;
it decides on authorising the Enterprise's executive functionaries to raise loans;
..........
it determines the bases and criteria for distributing the income (i.e. the net income of the enterprise) and the personal incomes;

b. it checks the management of the Enterprise and decides (sic; i.e. approves) the periodic statements of accounts and reports concerning the fulfilment of the economic plans;
..........
it ratifies the final account of the Enterprise and decides on the distribution of income;

c. it confirms and changes the Statute and other general acts of the Enterprise;
it decides on the organisational and self-management structure of the Enterprise and its departments;
it sanctions acts on status matters of the Enterprise, decided upon by the Enterprise's collective by referendum;

it decides on status change of departments in the Enterprise;

..........

d. it decides on disciplinary expulsions of members of the Enterprise's collective;

e. it issues the writs and appoints the commission for the elections to the Enterprise's Workers' Council and the department's councils, and appoints the commission for the voters' registers;

..........

it elects and recalls members of the Enterprise's executive boards;
it elects its chairman and deputy chairman;

..........

it issues the writs for a referendum, appoints the commission for carrying it out, and closes the referendum;

..........

h. it passes resolutions on other matters under the provisions of the law, of this Statute and other general acts of the Enterprise.'

In theory, the workers' council is clearly the ultimate decision-making authority within the Yugoslav enterprise: 'its decisions control enterprise policy.'[38] Of course, in practice, as was seen in the previous chapter, the real power of the workers' council is often severely limited by the overpowering weight of the managerial bureaucracy.

Apart from its decision-making role, Zupanov has highlighted another interesting function of the workers' council.[39] He points out that, while the council in principle is a representative of the entire working collective (to which, incidentally, the executives belong as well), it also is a body for bargaining between different groups of workers represented in the council. As an example he quotes the (hypothetical) case of a workers' council discussing an allocation of funds to the building of houses for those workers who live in town. The ultimate decision may depend on the employees who live in the country and their vote may be influenced by the way the town-dwellers voted on a previous occasion on the issue of buying buses for the commuters. 'Here we can see the specific role of the workers' council: to be a sort of clearing-house for various intergroup and informal deals.'[40]

### 2.3.2. *The Management Board*[41]

Until the adoption of Constitutional Amendment XV (end 1968), the management board was legally-speaking the second most important self-management organ.[42] Its duties, rights and responsibilities were regulated in detail by law:[43] inter alia, it prepared the draft Statute and other general regulations of the enterprise, and the operational and development plans and programmes (for decision by the workers' council), it had to see to the implementation of the decisions by the workers' council and was in general responsible for the proper functioning of the enterprise. The introduction of Amendment XV – the purpose of which was to give greater powers to the workers – paradoxically led to a shift in decision-making authority from the workers' council to the management board: its rights and duties are exclusively determined by the statute of the enterprise. Of course, this practical result of Amendment XV was not intended by the lawmaker and gave rise to serious objections. In the absence of further legislation it was, however, difficult to correct those enterprises that – in the eyes of their critics – had abused their new freedom.

Some enterprises have taken advantage of the increased flexibility permitted by Amendment XV to set up several management boards. This is, notably, the case of SAVA, which has the following 'Executive Boards':
- Program and Development
- Work and Self-management Organisation
- Production Planning and Quality
- Financial and Commercial Matters
- Distribution of Income and Personal Incomes
- Employment and Instruction
- Vocational Schooling
- Information
- Work Safety
- Distribution of Common Expenditure Assets[44]
- Internal Arbitration
- Damage Appraisal and Settlement
- Violations of Duty.

The members of these 'collective executive bodies' (as the Statute also calls them) are elected, and removed, by the workers' council.[45] Their tenure is fixed at one year and no member can be elected more than twice to the same board. The boards comprise at most seven members.[46] Duties and responsibilities of the executive boards are spelled out in the Statute.[47] Obviously, the powers of the former managing board – which was existing in SAVA before the adoption of its new Statute in 1970 – are now dispersed. Of the new executive boards, those in charge of Program and Development, Financial and Commercial Matters, and Distribution of Income and Personal Incomes are the most important.

The main responsibility of the Program and Development Board concerns the evaluation of all investment proposals, development programs, the annual economic plan, and long-term co-operation contracts with other enterprises. In addition, it provides the follow-up on these matters. The Financial and Commercial Board, inter alia, is responsible for the evaluation of borrowing policies, of depreciation policy, and the accounts of the enterprise. The third board, as indicated by its very name, has the important role of working out the criteria for the distribution of net income between reinvested earnings and personal income.

### 2.3.3. *The Director*

The director is the chief executive of the Yugoslav enterprise, he 'conducts the operations of the enterprise; executes the decisions of the workers' council and the managing board, represents the enterprise; and discharges the other powers and duties prescribed by the law, the statute or other general acts of the Enterprise. The director ... is personally answerable to the workers' council, the managing board and the working community.'[48] He is furthermore personally answerable for any illegal act committed by the enterprise. To avoid this liability he can suspend or veto any decision or action which he considers contrary to the law, the statute of the enterprise,[49] or the policy of the commune.

The director is appointed by the workers' council on the basis of a public competition. Normally, a director serves a four-year term and until the adoption of Constitutional Amendment XV officially could be re-elected only once – although in practice this rule was violated openly and often. At present, it is up to the enterprise itself to regulate (in its Statute) this matter. The SAVA Statute, for example, provides that the director is appointed for a five-year term of office and that he can be reappointed (without limiting the number of terms).[50]

The particular duties and responsibilities of SAVA's director are laid down in Article 235 of the Statute, the most important provisions of which are:

'(The director) is independent in his work and personally responsible to the Workers' Council of the Enterprise. In accordance with the legal prescriptions and the provisions of this Statute, he shall particularly:

a. secure the workers of the Enterprise their socio-economic orientation through medium-term and annual plans,[51] establish the conditions and obligations of management, of investments (for expansion), and of the distribution (of) income and personal incomes according to the business success; ....
   evaluate the co-operation of the Enterprise's executive workers in the self-management process, and their avoiding of dissensions and conflicts within the self-managing relations in regard to business matters pertaining to their province;
b. attend the meetings of the Enterprise's Workers' Council;
   ensure and control the execution of the decisions taken by the Workers' Council and the collective executive bodies of the Enterprise; ....
c. take care of the legality of the work in the Enterprise;

**represent the Enterprise and act for it; ....**
**sign financial and material documents on disposing of the Enterprise's assets; ....**

The director, and the professional services that are answerable to him, occupy a strong position in the Yugoslav enterprise – as was made clear in the previous chapter.[52] He (and his staff) is the initiator of the more important policy decisions which the enterprise faces. All this is not to say that a director, in practice, can do as he pleases. He remains dependent on the workers' council for approval of all major decisions. Of course, in many – and perhaps the majority of – Yugoslav enterprises the director dominates the deliberations of the council, but in some the workers' council is renowned for its nasty, and critical, questioning. Moreover, if the council is not satisfied with its director it can fire him and this happens often enough to act as a brake on an unlimited usurpation of powers.

Quite often the self-management organs of the Yugoslav enterprise are compared to the organs of the capitalist firm,[53] whereby the workers' council usually is equated with the shareholders' assembly[54] and the managing board with the board of directors (in the Anglo-Saxon sense). Formally, there is indeed a similarity as far as decision-making authority is concerned. But the comparison is basically not very fruitful, because the interests represented in the organs of the capitalist firm and the Yugoslav enterprise are radically different. Not only is, therefore, the composition of both types of organ different – in the Western firm many members are outsiders – whereas in the Yugoslav enterprise they are all employees – but also the substance and the emphasis of the deliberations differ. In addition, and this in spite of what was said before about the relatively weak position of the workers' council vis-à-vis the management, there can be little doubt that the workers' council wields, in practice, considerably more power as far as important decision-making is considered than the shareholders' assembly in the capitalist firm.

## 2.4. ACCOUNTING PRINCIPLES[55]

The Yugoslav enterprise relies for its accounting and budgetary control systems basically on the same financial statements that are used for this purpose by capitalist firms: the balance sheet and the income statement. To the uninitiated, however, Yugoslav accounts appear very confusing. This should not be really surprising. Prior to World War II, Yugoslavia was an agricultural country and what little industry there was did not have, even for the standards of that time, a very sophisticated accounting system. After the war, there was practically no tradition or staff to fall back on, and – as Leman has observed – 'für die meisten Betriebe war die Betriebsabrechnung ein unbekannter Begriff.'[56] The rapidly growing number of industries, however, needed an accounting system and very quickly at that. The situation was even further complicated by the fact that Yugoslavia after the war had adopted a totally different socio-economic system, which had rendered pre-war accounting procedures useless. Finally, as was seen in the first chapter, this socio-economic system kept evolving and this, inevitably, led to a continuing stream of new rules and procedures according to which the books of the Yugoslav enterprise had to be kept.[57] These rules were, at all times, also extraordinarily detailed: since the Yugoslav enterprise holds the assets it employs in trust for the Yugoslav people, it must account for their use. The resulting complexity has, of course, done very little for clarity. It is, however, possible for a Western analyst to get reasonably good insight in the financial condition of a Yugoslav enterprise by regrouping some of the items making up the accounts into a classification as usually applied in the West.

It would carry the subject too far to discuss this reclassification in detail, but a review of the main principles on which it is based will probably make the procedure clear enough for the more limited purpose of this study. There is, however, a preliminary general observation to be made with respect to the financial statements of the Yugoslav firm, and that concerns 'the lack of any objective evaluation of the performance and financial position of an enterprise by an outside agency, ... Yugoslavia does not have a professional body of accountants or financial analysts, such as the certified public accountants in the United States or the chartered accountants in the United Kingdom.'[58] Auditing, in Yugoslavia, is carried out by the Social Accounting Service (SDK), a government agency, but this audit is not performed to arrive at a judgement about the enterprise's financial position but merely to check whether all receipts and payments are made in accordance with the provisions of the law. In practice, the audit by the SDK often tends to be cursory[59] and it is therefore surprising that, given the potential dangers inherent to this set-up. so few cases of fraud actually occur. The Yugoslavs are, however, becoming aware of the fact that the present auditing procedures are not entirely satisfactory – and a possible impediment to Western firms contemplating a joint venture with a Yugoslav enterprise – and the possibility of establishing independent auditors is being reviewed.

### 2.4.1. *The income statement*

The self-management system is obviously the principal reason why the financial statements of the Yugoslav enterprise are different from those used in the West. It will be remembered that the workers of the enterprise are its 'managers'. In this connection it is perhaps interesting to note that Yugoslav authors, following Horvat's lead, increasingly refer to the entrepreneurial role played by the workers' collective. The reward for entrepreneurship is – as in capitalist society – not a wage but profit. Personal incomes of the workers are therefore not considered a cost item in Yugoslavia, but that part of the enterprise's revenue that remains after all expenditures have been made and all other financial obligations are met.[60] The absence of labour cost from the profit and loss statement is thus the most important difference between the Yugoslav and capitalist enterprise. A second difference derives from the Yugoslav system of taxation. There is no profit tax,[61] the only taxes levied at the enterprise level are taxes on personal income payments. The amount of these payments varies from year to year, and by Republic and/or Commune, but on the average comes to roughly 40% of the net personal income received by the worker. This taxation system has a very important behavioural consequence: there is no incentive – as under the system of most Western countries – for the enterprise to increase its depreciation charges so as to decrease its tax liability. In fact, there is on the contrary a very strong incentive to keep depreciation levels low to permit higher personal incomes. Yugoslav legislation therefore prescribes minimum depreciation rates, principally to protect the erosion of the enterprise's (and society's) assets. It should be added that at this time of writing the possibility of a corporate tax on enterprise income is being considered. If this tax comes into being, there will obviously be a necessity to introduce maximum depreciation rates as well.

Prior to 1970, there used to be another, and rather confusing, difference: revenues and expenditures were charged for on a 'cash' basis rather than on an accrual basis as in the West. Sales revenues are now entered at invoiced values, and cost of sales is determined by valuing the opening inventory at the cost of materials purchased, adding the cost of materials and services purchased, and depreciation, and subtracting the closing inventory valued in the same way. The difference between sales revenue and cost of sales, as defined above, constitutes the enterprise's realised income (Dohodak). Out of its realised income the enterprise next has to meet its so-called Contractual and Legal (or Statutory) Obligations. These concern, first of all, interest payments, in addition to such items as

The income statement of the Yugoslav enterprise can be summarised as follows:[63]

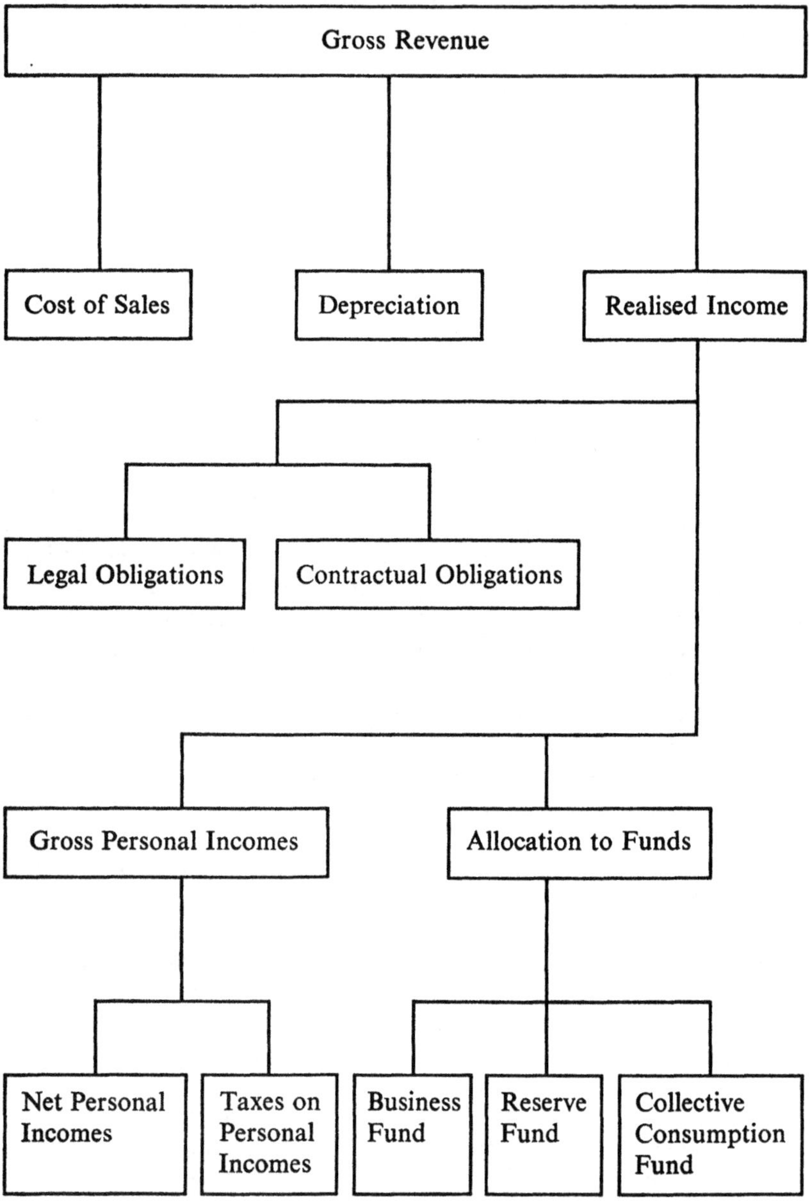

insurance premiums, membership fees for Chambers of Industry etc. Among these obligations there used to figure an item 'Interest on the Business Fund', which constituted a capital tax on the assets used by the enterprise. This capital tax was, of course, highly valued by Western economists as a tool to achieve a rational allocation of capital. Unfortunately, the tax was set too low – 4% – to play this role and moreover, it has been abolished. In its place, the enterprise now is obliged to contribute to the Fund for Developing Regions but this contribution is not à fonds perdu but a loan which ultimately will be repaid.

After contractual and legal obligations have been met, the enterprise is left with its net income (Dobitak). The net income is then divided into gross personal income, i.e. net personal incomes and tax thereon, and the allocation to Funds (see below: balance sheet). There remains one point which sometimes leads to confusion in the mind of the Western analyst: all debt obligations (not only interest payments but also repayment of principal) have a legal claim to funds prior to all distribution to personal incomes. Milenkovitch goes even as far as to conclude that these repayments constitute a 'contractual cost.'[62] This is, of course, not correct and probably due to confusion of a cash-flow and an income statement. A misunderstanding which, incidentally, is easily comprehensible in view of the fact that most Yugoslav enterprises are not familiar with a cash-flow statement. In any case, repayment of credits is a movement of items within the balance sheet and has no place on the income statement.

The income statement of the Yugoslav enterprise can be summarised as shown in the diagram[63] on page 100.

### 2.4.2. *The balance sheet*

The principles underlying the compilation of the balance sheet of the Yugoslav enterprise are rather similar to those employed in the capitalist firm and the regrouping of items presents fewer difficulties than in the case of the income statement. The only major difference with a 'Western' balance sheet is basically that the Yugoslav enterprise is obliged to present three sub-balances: respectively concerning business assets and liabilities, reserve assets and liabilities and Consumption Fund assets and liabilities. The Consumption Fund contains the investments earmarked for the collective use of the workers of the enterprise. It is financed exclusively by the enterprise itself and the funds are invested in such assets as housing, medical and canteen facilities, and in some cases even schools, and holiday resorts. Allocations to the Fund are normally a rather small share of earnings, but may vary considerably between enterprises, or within the same enterprise in different years, depending on the need for such facilities, the needs of the enterprise for business funds, and – obviously – the workers' preference for cash payments.

The Reserve Fund is divided into a compulsory fund and a voluntary fund; allocations to the compulsory fund are related to the level of working capital employed and not to capitalisation or earnings.

For the Western analyst it is only a question to net out the assets and liabilities of these three funds when making calculations for asset turnover or return on fixed assets.

The working capital accounts of the Yugoslav enterprise (current assets and current liabilities) are easy to understand and the usual ratio analyses may be employed. It should be noted, however, that the cash account may somewhat exaggerate the liquidity position of the Yugoslav enterprise because the use of several appropriations out of the earnings made by the enterprise is limited by law to the purpose for which they were allocated. In other words, if a particular bank account is exhausted, say for the variable part of personal incomes, the enterprise may not use another bank account for that purpose.

Two further observations should be made with respect to the balance sheet. In the first place, Yugoslav enterprises from time to time are obliged by law to a revaluation of assets (which, incidentally, has the effect of making year-to-year comparisons difficult). For example, in 1965 at the time of the Economic Reform the dinar was devalued and all enterprises were obliged to revalue inventories and fixed assets financed by foreign exchange debts. On later occasions, a general revaluation of buildings, machinery and equipment had to be made to adjust asset value realistically to price changes. The increase in net worth effected through these changes is then reflected in the Business Fund.

The second observation concerns the Business Fund itself. It is the major fund – the other being the Reserve Fund – representing the accumulated earnings of the enterprise, and it is used in much the same way as that in which retained earnings are employed in the capitalist firm: it supports investments in fixed assets or working capital, and an increase in the Business Fund is reflected in increases in the appropriate asset accounts, or a decrease in long-term debt. One might therefore say that the Business Fund is comparable to the net worth of the capitalist enterprise. In the case of the latter, however, net worth consists not only of the accumulated retained earnings but equity funds as well. Under the system of social ownership equity, of course, does not exist.[64] A newly established enterprise, with no past earnings, must therefore be entirely supported by debt financing.[65] The relation between 'own funds' of an enterprise and long-term debt consequently is partly conditioned by the time the enterprise has been in operation. The usual debt/equity analysis should therefore be applied with some caution.

A final remark should be made with respect to the computation of the profitability of the Yugoslav enterprise. This is somewhat more complicated than in the case of the capitalist firm inasmuch as personal incomes of the workers in Yugoslavia legally are not considered as a cost item but as a reward for entrepreneurship. For practical purposes, however, total personal income distributions may be said to include both a basic payment for services rendered – and it will be remembered that Yugoslav enterprises usually establish at the beginning of the year a basic wage – and a profit-sharing bonus. When considering the profitability of the enterprise this bonus should be considered as a part of the return on capital.

The Yugoslav enterprise does not only differ from the capitalist firm from an institutional point of view – the most important aspects of which were dealt with above – but also in its operational behaviour, albeit to a lesser extent: generally speaking the Yugoslav enterprise operates in much the same way as its capitalist counterpart. The main differences, to which the remainder of this chapter will be devoted, are in the fields of planning, income distribution within the enterprise, and of financing.

## 2.5. PLANNING

Much more than in Western firms, planning at the enterprise level is a firmly established practice in Yugoslavia. There are, it would seem, three principal reasons for this phenomenon. In the first place, immediately after the war the entire Yugoslav economy was organised according to a rigid central plan. Subsequently, as was discussed at length in the previous chapter, a gradual relaxation took place which turned the plan from an instrument of coercion to one of co-operation. But while the plan changed in nature, planning as such was never abandoned. One might say it has become an ingrained habit for all Yugoslav institutions, whether they are political entities or enterprises. Secondly, the Yugoslav attachment to the notion of (voluntary) planning can probably also be explained by the conviction that planning – in the Yugoslav sense – essentially is a process of reaching agreement, of achieving a realistic and valid compromise between various interests (the plan as an instrument of co-operation). Finally, and this argument relates in particular to planning at the enterprise level, the process of drawing up a plan offers an excellent opportunity of participation by the workers in the determination of the enterprise's future operations and policies: it is an exercise of their right to self-management.

Again, the Statute of 'SAVA' provides a good illustration of how the planning process in the Yugoslav enterprise is organised in practice.[66] The Statute emphasises the importance of planning: it is the 'basic instrument' by which departments and 'self-governing bodies' determine business policy (Article 190). SAVA uses the following instruments of planning:

a. the Development Programme for the Enterprise, drawn up for at least a three-year period;
b. the Annual Economic Plan;
c. Operational plans for shorter periods, i.e. months, and in some cases even weeks.

SAVA is in this respect somewhat different from most Yugoslav enterprises as, in addition to the annual and medium-term (3–5 years) plan, an enterprise usually has a long-term (10–15 years) plan as well. In all cases, it is the medium-term plan that is the most important and it constitutes the basis for the succeeding annual plans. SAVA's Development Programme (i.e. the medium-term plan) consists of two parts, in the first a general analysis is given of the past development of the enterprise as well as a comprehensive study of future market conditions, a production programme to meet expected demand and further policy proposals. The second part works these general principles out in more detail, and year by year. In concreto, plans are separately established for production, raw materials and other supplies, investment, staffing, sales and exports, distribution of income, financing, etc. (Article 191).

Responsibility for the preparation of the Development Programme rests with the Planning Department,[67] which distributes the draft to all departments, or basic units, for discussion and comments. After this discussion, which in SAVA's case is limited to 30 days, a final proposal is drawn up and sent to the 'Programme and Development Executive Board' for review and finally to the Workers' Council for formal approval (Article 192).

The annual economic plans are, on the other hand, prepared by the various departments themselves, most of which are large enough to have a special section for this work. The Planning Department, on the basis of these plans, draws up a draft general annual economic plan for the enterprise as a whole which is then sent to all departments for discussion.

Upon completion of the discussion, the draft plan plus all comments and amendments received thereon is submitted to the Executive Board for evaluation, and finally for approval to the Workers' Council not later than the 15th December (Article 195). Basically, the annual economic plan covers the same issues (production, raw materials and supplies, investments for the year in question, sales, staffing, financing requirements, etc.) as the medium-term Development Programme, but – of course – in much greater detail. The same applies also to the monthly or weekly operational plans. In substance these operational plans – and to a considerable extent, the annual economic plan as well – do not differ too much from the type of programming and budgeting that is undertaken in the larger Western enterprises. The basic difference arises, of course, from the fact that in the Yugoslav enterprise the planning procedure involves the workers as the ultimate decision-makers while in the West they are almost totally excluded. For the Yugoslavs, the planning process is therefore not so much a purely technical exercise but rather – as said above – an important feature of the self-management system.

## 2.6. DETERMINATION OF PERSONAL INCOMES

On several occasions the problem of determining the personal incomes of the workers in the Yugoslav enterprise has been touched upon. It may be useful, however, to return to this matter again, and review the principles on which income determination within the enterprise is based in some more detail. Not surprisingly, this question has raised quite a few theoretical and practical problems for the Yugoslavs. On the one hand, they have opted firmly for a market economy and therefore implicitly accepted the principle that the prices of production factors, i.e. including labour, are determined on the market. On the other hand, they are Marxist as well and the basic Yugoslav principle of income distribution is 'Nagradjvanje prema radu' which means 'Reward according to work performed'. In other words, there is a possible conflict between efficiency (market) and equality (Marx). As formulated by Milenkovitch: 'The troublesome question for market socialists, thus, is whether the market mechanism, operating through the use of financial incentives, is compatible with socialist notions about a just distribution of income.'[68]

It would seem that the conflict has been solved in the favour of the market mechanism. As was seen earlier, there is a clear trend of increasing differences in personal income levels between industrial sectors and – for that matter – between regions. No data are available to determine whether the same phenomenon has occurred with respect to the determination of personal incomes within the enterprises. In other words, it is hard to know whether particular skills that are in short supply at a given moment can command higher incomes. Although Milenkovitch maintains that 'the spread in pay for various types of labour grew after the reform, and persons with certain technical skills markedly improved their positions.'[69]

In any case, Yugoslav enterprises enjoy a considerable freedom to decide how much of their net income (Dobitak) is going to be paid out in the form of personal incomes and how much is going to be reinvested. Moreover, they are basically free to determine themselves the range of individual incomes within the enterprise. This principle has even been incorporated in the Constitution in the form of Amendment XXI which was adopted by the Federal Assembly in 1971. The Amendment, however, adds that increases in individual incomes may be restricted by way of 'self-managing agreements', i.e. inter-industry agreements between enterprises.[70] As was mentioned in the previous chapter, these agreements can be made compulsory by law but this happens only at the level of the Republic, and comprehensive national incomes policy has so far been impossible to achieve.

The procedures and policy to be followed by the enterprise in determining the individual incomes of its workers are spelled out in its Statute. In the case of SAVA, it is particularly interesting to note that the chapter on 'Distribution of Personal Incomes' (Articles 70–73) begins with the flat statement that the income of the workers depends, in principle, on achievement: 'the workers' personal income results from their performance, from the success of the department and the Enterprise as a whole.'[71] The income consists of two parts, one determined by 'the bases and standards prescribed by the Statutes and the Regulations on the Distribution of Personal Income,'[72] and the second 'depends on the results of the department's or the total Enterprise's management.'[73] The first part is, to revert to Wachtel's definition,[74] the fixed wage, and the second the variable wage, which represents 'that amount which the worker receives at the end of an accounting period as a supplementary wage payment out of the current profits of the enterprise.'[75]

The fixed wage part is paid out in accordance with a pay scale. Each job within the enterprise is given a certain number of points based on a job evaluation.[76] In addition, the worker himself gets points depending on his individual qualifications, duration of employment, and 'special zeal.'[77] How many points are assigned for each of these factors is determined by the Workers' Council on a proposal either by a special sub-committee of the Council or, as in SAVA's case, by the Executive Board for Distribution of Income and Personal Incomes.[78] The actual wage the worker receives depends then on his accumulated points and the size of the wage fund which is also determined by the Workers' Council.

The variable wage depends, as said above, on the results achieved by the department and the enterprise as a whole. In general, the variable part of the worker's income is computed by increasing the fixed wage by a certain percentage, which can be the same for all workers or differentiated according to some criterion such as, e.g., skill, difficult working conditions, level of responsibility.[79] In some instances (but this is not usual) the distinction between fixed and variable wage gets blurred by the fact that the total income to be received by the worker is computed at monthly intervals and that in this calculation the 'profit' achieved by the enterprise over that period is included.

The personal incomes so determined are 'gross', i.e. the worker does not receive the full amount but only that part that is left after taxes, paid on his behalf by the enterprise. The percentage withheld on account of various taxes and 'obligatory contributions' is the same for all workers in the enterprise.[80] The actual percentage is about 40%, but may differ a little bit depending on the Republic and the Commune in which the enterprise is located.

While, as was mentioned in the previous chapter, the national averages of income levels for various educational or occupational categories do not differ too much between Yugoslavia and the Netherlands,[81] the income structure within the Yugoslav enterprise is on the whole more egalitarian than in its capitalist counterpart. It is highly unusual that the relation between the highest and the lowest net income exceeds a ratio of 5:1. A study group of the Dutch trade union movement, which investigated this issue in Yugoslavia, found in the three enterprises it visited ratios of respectively $4\frac{1}{2}$:1, $4\frac{3}{8}$:1 and 5:1.[82]

The determination of the pay scales is, of course, one of the more hotly debated issues in the workers' councils – and on the shop floor between the workers and their representative(s) in the council. And while the individual worker may, in the end, have little influence on the decision of what his own income will be, the fact that the matter is open for debate can only increase his feeling of participation in the process of self-management.

## 2.7. FINANCING

The last issue which needs to be discussed concerns the financing of the

Yugoslav enterprise, both in terms of the determination of the needs for funds and of the sources available to meet these needs.

### 2.7.1. *Need for funds*

As far as its needs for finance is concerned, the Yugoslav enterprise does not differ too much from its capitalist counterparts: funds are required to finance investment, increases in working capital and the like. One aspect has to be singled out, however, and that concerns the investment decision. All other uses of funds either derive indirectly from the investment decision or are basically of the same character as in the capitalist firm. Theoretically, the investment behaviour of the labour-managed firm is determined by different criteria than in the West and this should be reviewed first. Again in theory, the investment decision of the enterprise in any economic system is governed by the firm's maximising principle. As was seen in the previous chapter, practically every single (Western) author dealing with the labour-managed market economy has assumed that the enterprise operating within such system would try to maximise income per worker. More particularly, this income is to be maximised over time, i.e. the present discounted value of the income generated over a multi-year period; or, as Vanek calls it, 'the net multi-period income per labourer.'[83] Given a minimum desired annual increase in income per worker, all investment yielding a positive net multi-period income should be undertaken. This is, of course, a very neat criterion – but it does present a number of conceptual difficulties which render its practical value doubtful. In the first place, it assumes that all workers of the firm have the same time horizon (i.e. expected length of employment with the firm) and this assumption is too far-fetched to be called realistic. Secondly, it assumes that all workers have identical time preferences which, again, is hardly realistic.

It is therefore not surprising that, in practice, the investment decision of the Yugoslav firm is the result of quite a different process. In an earlier section of this chapter the importance of planning at the enterprise level was emphasised. Based on its views about market development, the availability of raw materials and other inputs, technological developments and the like, the Yugoslav firm establishes its development plan and thereby, implicitly, determines the investments required to implement this plan. Of course, the enterprise aims to achieve a profit, i.e. a positive net income (Dobitak). Any investment which, after a more detailed appraisal than at the time the plan was drafted, will not yield such a profit is abandoned. In practice, there would not seem to exist a specific maximising principle that governs the investment decision of most Yugoslav firms. Neuberger and James are of the opinion that investments are rather made with a view to establishing income and employment.[84] Considering the high rate of unemployment, which appears to be structural in Yugoslavia, this would seem a reasonable argument. It is contradicted, however, by the pronounced tendency of Yugoslav enterprises to launch overambitious investment projects for which in the end no financing is available, a tendency characterised an 'investment megalomania' by President Tito.

Unsatisfactory as it may appear to the economist, the theoretical criteria, developed by Vanek and others,[85] which should govern the investment decision of the labour-managed firm seem to find little application in Yugoslavia. If a conclusion, based on actual behaviour, is to be drawn it can only be that the investment decision of the Yugoslav enterprise is in general determined by the requirements for additional capacity as set out in its development plan. It should further be noted that such concepts as present value and internal rate of return are unknown in Yugoslavia, except perhaps in those few enterprises that have gone through the wringer of a World Bank project appraisal mission.

### 2.7.2. *Sources of funds*

The Yugoslav enterprise finances its assets with own funds and liabilities – just as its capitalist counterpart. There are, however, important differences. In a previous section, dealing with the balance sheet, it was pointed out that the concept of equity or share capital does not exist in Yugoslavia.[86] A new enterprise is therefore necessarily almost completely financed by debt and will build up its own funds (represented on the balance sheet by its Reserve Fund and Business Fund) over time out of retained earnings. The debt/equity ratio of the Yugoslav enterprise is consequently primarily a function of its age.

In the literature considerable attention is given to the question of the retention of earnings in the labour-managed enterprise. Most Western authors have argued that there is a built-in bias against self-financing as the average worker would be inclined to prefer an immediate wage increase over the prospect of higher income in the future resulting from investment. Moreover, on theoretical grounds, several economists have concluded that self-financing is inefficient (Vanek[87] and Wemelsfelder[88]) because it prevents capital from being allocated in the most rational way, i.e. where it yields the highest return. Vanek has even gone as far as suggesting a system whereby self-financing is excluded and all financial resources are pooled: 'In brief and in essence, the method is to require that all users of social productive assets (i.e. of embodied labour) effectively pay an economic price for that use on all assets into a social (i.e. national, republican, or regional) pool of funds. This pool must be used exclusively for investment (simple and enlarged reproduction), never for consumption. To the extent that the real assets being financed are long-run depreciable assets (plant, equipment, buildings, constructions, etc.) the corresponding depreciation allowances (calculated as closely as possible with the life of the asset and the length of the loan) are also to be deposited into the general funding pool, as repayments of the loan.'[89] All savings as well would be transferred to this social fund, which would therefore be the only financial intermediary in a certain area (be it a Republic or the nation as a whole). Vanek's proposal, while theoretically attractive and entirely consistent with his *General theory of labor-managed market economies*, presents two major disadvantages. In the first place, there is the danger that the pooling of financial resources into one single institution will lead to excessive powers which will be difficult to control even in the most democratic of societies. Secondly, and one has to insist on this point, the system proposed by Vanek effectively eliminates the risk that should be borne by the enterprise itself – all risks are transferred to the social fund. One does not have to be a banker to realise that this is not a sound financing practice: 'If proper choices are to be taken in risky situations, there must be not only the prospect of gain but also the possibility of loss.'[90] The Yugoslavs have been well aware of this and from 'the early days of decentralisation, Yugoslav doctrine has required that the enterprise invest some of its own funds in any project.'[91] But while the doctrine may require self-financing, the increasing freedom of the workers to allocate the discretionary income of the enterprise between personal incomes and reinvestment has resulted in a tendency to pay out higher wages. Whereas in 1965, the national average was still 70% to wages and 30% to reinvestment, this had dropped to 80% and 20% in 1970.[92] Within this average, of course, large differences between individual enterprises are hidden as is evident from Table 2.1 which is based on a sample of ten enterprises familiar to the author.

In effect, the range between the highest and lowest rate of reinvestment is almost exactly 100%.

The declining national average reinvestment ratio has led to a curious phenomenon: 'the growth of informal credit extensions outside the banking system.'[93] In other words, in most enterprises there has been a steep increase in accounts payable and, since it is a matter of inter-enterprise

*Table 2.1. Allocation of discretionary income over personal incomes and reinvestment: sample of ten Yugoslav enterprises (1970)*

| *Enterprise* | *Personal incomes* (percentage) | *Reinvestment* (percentage) |
|---|---|---|
| 1 | 69.7 | 30.3 |
| 2 | 78.7 | 21.3 |
| 3 | 77.7 | 22.3 |
| 4 | 67.6 | 32.4 |
| 5 | 82.2 | 17.8 |
| 6 | 69.9 | 30.1 |
| 7 | 75.2 | 24.8 |
| 8 | 66.9 | 33.1 |
| 9 | 69.6 | 30.4 |
| 10 | 83.9 | 16.1 |
| (Weighted average) | (75.0) | (25.0) |

credits, of accounts receivable as well. The Yugoslavs commonly refer to it as the illiquidity problem. Since 'bank credit and other capital market resources were not available in adequate amounts[94] (due in part, perhaps, to the failure of the financial sector to stimulate savings within the growing share of income distributed to the workers) resort was increasingly made to informal credit arrangements.'[95]

The Yugoslav authorities have tried to check this process by requiring that accounts payable are to be met within 45 days and by setting certain standards with respect to the current asset/current liability position of enterprises. These measures are slow to take effect, however, and it may take a few years before the situation has become normal.

Above some of the characteristics of the Yugoslav enterprises have been discussed, in particular those which distinguish it from the capitalist firm. To conclude this chapter one important point should be emphasised again: while different from the Western enterprise, the Yugoslav firm has nothing in common with its state-owned Soviet counterpart. Within the frame-work of the self-management system, the Yugoslav worker-managed enterprise is truly autonomous and independent of the State in its decision-making.

NOTES

1. The Yugoslavs are well aware of the fact that, to be fully effective, self-management should reach beyond workers' participation in the running of enterprises. Man's interests and needs are not only economic in nature. To quote Ratkovic: 'Thus, in our opinion, self-government is not a one-dimensional, but a multi-dimensional phenomenon – economic, social, political, cultural and ideological. .... These various dimensions and spheres of self-government are in mutual dependence upon each other. It is impossible to further develop self-government in the economic field without having developed self-government in politics and in the social consciousness. And vice versa, thence, a developed self-government is only possible in terms of an entire social system. In Yugoslavia we are striving for just exactly that' (Radoslav I. Ratkovic, 'The evolution of the political system and the development of self-government in Yugoslavia', *Florida State University Slavic Papers*, Volume 4, 1970, page 1). A judgement on the question whether or not Yugoslavia is actually making progress towards such multi-dimensional self-government system is beyond the scope of this study.
2. Cf. note 2, Chapter 1.
3. Cf. note 56, Chapter 1.
4. B. Horvat, 'Yugoslav economic policy in the post-war period: problems, ideas, institutional developments', *American Economic Review*, Vol. 61, No. 3, June 1971, page 107.
5. *Ibidem.*
6. Milentije Popovic in *Nasa stvarnost*, Nos. 1–2, Jan.-Feb. 1954, page 18, as quoted on page 96 in D.D. Milenkovitch, *Plan and market in Yugoslav economic thought*, Yale University Press, New Haven and London, 1971.
7. *Ibidem.*
8. Milenkovitch, *op. cit.*, pages 94–99.
9. *Idem*, page 94.
10. The term 'personal' encompasses groups of persons as well, and is used here to mean 'own' production and consumption.
11. Horvat, in *AER*, page 106.
12. Milenkovitch, *op. cit.*, page 92.
13. *Official Gazette*, No. 34, 1971.
14. Slavoljub Popovic, 'The legal status of Yugoslav enterprises', *Florida State University Slavic Papers*, Volume 4, 1970, pages 97–107. Popovic's account, although based on the legislation prior to 1970, remains valid because the innovations introduced by the new Law of 1971 do not affect the legal characteristics described below.
15. David Lascelles, 'Constitutional amendments', *Financial Times*, April 26, 1973.
16. It is, however, not only the enterprise that is constituted in this manner. Institutions, hospitals etc. are set up in the same way.
17. Although the new legislation may achieve its intended purpose, i.e. to make the average worker more involved and therefore more productive, the other side of the coin is that 'the reforms do have the effect of breaking the decision-making process up into thousands of tiny fragments, each of them made up of loquacious Yugoslavs who enjoy a good debate, so it looks as if the country will be spending a lot of time and money for the sake of an ideological principle' (David Lascelles, *loc. cit.*).
18. There was, of course, the problem of how to fit those divisions that serve the enter-

prise as a whole and have no revenues of their own (e.g. personnel, administration, etc.) into the system of OOUR's. It may be interesting to relate how this problem was solved in a concrete case, i.e. the Sisak Ironworks.

'There has also been an innovation at the level of administration, but it does not have its own funds for expansion, since it has no earnings. These are services, and the price of the services is also set by self-managing agreement. The total value of services is divided up among all the organisations of associated labour in proportion to the benefit which they receive from the administration. This is how the administration earns revenue with which it covers expenses and salaries. Of course it is no longer a decision-making executive body, but merely sees to the technical preparation of proposals which the elected organs of self-management submit to the basic organisations of associated labour, the decisions which are made by the assemblies of workers in the basic organisations of associated labour. This right of the workers' assemblies can under no circumstances be transferred to any other person or body' (V. Rokic, 'The Sisak Ironworks: novelties in management', *Yugoslav Life*, Vol. XVIII, No. 4, April 1973).

19. The following account relies heavily on Popovic, *loc. cit.*, pages 99–101.
20. Egon Neuberger and Estelle James, 'The Yugoslav self-managed enterprise: a systemic approach', in Morris Bornstein (ed.), *Plan and Market. Economic Reform in Eastern Europe*, Yale University Press, London and New Haven, 1973, page 262.
21. Text as quoted in Ivan Paj, 'The organisation of self-management in enterprises (managing bodies and their rights)', *Yugoslav Survey*, No. 1, February 1971, pages 31–32.
22. A 'work organisation', in the Yugoslav terminology, includes in addition to enterprises all organisations and institutions in the fields of services, research, health, education, culture, etc. (cf. Paj, *loc. cit.*).
23. Richard B. Glickman and Miodrag Sukijasovic, 'Yugoslav worker-management and its effect on foreign investment', *The Harvard International Law Journal*, Vol. 12, No. 2, Spring 1971, page 266.
24. Constitutional Amendment XV of December 26, 1968 (*Official Gazette*, 55/68).
25. Text as quoted in Paj, *loc. cit.*, page 31.
26. Mitja Kamusic, 'Economic efficiency and workers' self-management', in M.J. Broekmeyer (ed.), *Yugoslav workers' self-management*, Reidel Publishing Company, Dordrecht, 1970, page 80.
27. Cf. *inter alia*, Glickman and Sukijasovic, *loc. cit.*, page 267.
28. 'Statute of the SAVA factory for rubber, leather and chemical products, Kranj', adopted by the Workers' Council at its meeting on 6th January 1970 and published in English on 15th November 1970.
29. Glickman and Sukijasovic, *loc. cit.*, page 267.
30. The 'work collective', in Yugoslav terminology, consists of the entire labour force of the enterprise. There is some difference of opinion as to whether the work collective in itself is also a 'self-management organ'. In fact, some decisions are effectively taken by the work collective either by referenda or at a meeting of all workers of the enterprise (the 'Workers' Assembly'). The decisions referred to the work collective, on the other hand, are few and far between. They only concern mergers with other enterprises, the splitting up of the enterprise into independent parts, and a change in the location of the enterprise. For practical purposes, it is therefore probably correct not to include the work collective in the hierarchy of self-management (cf. Paj, *loc. cit.*, pages 36–37).
31. Paj, *loc. cit.*, page 38.

32. Re-election for two consecutive terms is prohibited by law.
33. SAVA Statute, Article 143.
34. In SAVA's case, a department with less than 25 employees.
35. This provision refers to the decision with respect to the division between reinvested earnings and disbursement to the workers (personal incomes).
36. SAVA Statute, Article 214.
37. The duties and responsibilities of both management organs will be discussed below.
38. Glickman and Sukijasovic, *loc. cit.*, page 270.
39. J. Zupanov, 'Yugoslavia: a socialist alternative', in Ch. de Hoghton (ed.), *The company, law, structure and reform in eleven countries*, Political and Economic Planning, London, 1970, page 331.
40. *Ibidem.*
41. Also known under the names of Executive Committee, Executive Board or Managing Committee.
42. Glickman and Sukijasovic, *loc. cit.*, page 275.
43. Cf. Popovic, *loc. cit.*, page 102, and Paj, *loc. cit.*, page 40.
44. I.e. housing built for the workers of the enterprise, holiday resorts, cafeterias, etc.
45. SAVA Statute, Article 232.
46. *Idem*, Article 218.
47. *Idem*, Articles 219–231.
48. Popovic, *loc. cit.*, page 102.
49. Glickman and Sukijasovic, *loc. cit.* page 277; and Popovic, *loc. cit.*, page 102.
50. SAVA Statute, Article 239.
51. What is probably meant here is that the director has the duty to see to it that the future of the enterprise (and the employment of the workers) is secured by rational planning.
52. A particularly vivid illustration of the pre-eminence of certain directors can be found in a paper presented by Emerik Blum, the nationally known director of the Energoinvest enterprise in Sarajevo. Commenting on the decentralisation versus centralisation issue which had been debated within his enterprise, he said: 'My position in that situation is clear: I must ensure the modern organisation of the enterprise (and a certain level of performance) which does not permit discussion of details at the level of the enterprise but at the same time assures that certain questions will be solved exclusively from one place, meaning somewhere in my immediate vicinity' (Emerik Blum, 'The director and workers' management', in M.J. Broekmeyer (ed.), *Yugoslav workers' self-management*, *op. cit.*, page 192).
53. See, *inter alia*, George A. Wing, 'Impressions of a worker-managed economy', *Business Horizons*, No. 1, February 1971; and *Arbeiderszelfbestuur in Joegoslavië: theorie en praktijk*, Stichting Maatschappij en Onderneming, The Hague, 1972.
54. With the obvious difference, however, that the shareholders' assembly consists, theoretically at least, of all individual shareholders, whereas the workers' council is a representative body elected by the workers.
55. There seems to be no comprehensive study available on the financial framework – and accounting procedures – of the Yugoslav enterprise, which is accessible to the Western reader. As far as could be ascertained, Yugoslav literature on the subject has not been translated. Apart from his experience 'in the field', the present author therefore had to rely basically on two working papers, prepared for their own internal use by the International Finance Corporation and the International Investment Corporation for Yugoslavia. It should be emphasised that only factual information has been extracted from these documents and that all value judgements

are the sole responsibility of the author.

56. Gudrun Leman, *Stellung und Aufgaben der ökonomischen Einheiten in den jugoslawischen Unternehmungen*, Duncker und Humblot, Berlin, 1967, page 76.
57. For an interesting account of the changes in the way the income statement had to be presented over the years 1945–1969, see Ivan Paj, 'The development of the system of distribution of the social product and net income', *Yugoslav Survey*, Vol. XI, No. 3, August 1970.
58. George A. Wing, *loc. cit.*, page 26.
59. *Ibidem.*
60. As was pointed out earlier, for the purpose of cost accounting Yugoslav enterprises normally consider the fixed part of the wages as a cost item.
61. Except, as will be seen in Chapter 4, on the profit of the foreign partner in a joint venture.
62. Milenkovitch, *op. cit.*, page 19, note 4.
63. Based on: Dusan Cobeljic, 'Le mécanisme de la coordination du plan national et des plans des entreprises en Yougoslavie', *Revue Economique*, May 1970, page 360.
64. The situation is different, however, in the case of a joint venture between a Yugoslav and a Western firm. This will be discussed in Chapter 4.
65. There may, however, be a small initial Business Fund representing the value of e.g. land ceded to the enterprise by the commune, or existing buildings, etc.
66. Another example of the planning procedure in a Yugoslav enterprise, i.e. the copper mines at Bor, can be found in: Th. P. van Hoorn and C. A. Koopman, 'De planning-procedure in een Joegoslavische onderneming met arbeiderszelfbestuur', *Economisch-Statistische Berichten*, No. 2821, October 27, 1971.
67. This is, however, not a universally followed procedure. In many enterprises, the draft medium-term plans are in the first instance drawn up by the various 'basic units' and the responsibility of the Planning Department is basically to aggregate (and integrate) these plans into a single plan for the entire enterprise.
68. Milenkovitch, *op. cit.*, page 252.
69. *Idem*, page 259.
70. K. Meneghello-Dincic, 'L'autogestion yougoslave (1950–1972)', *La documentation française, Notes et études documentaires*, July 23, 1973, page 29.
71. SAVA Statute, Article 70.
72. *Ibidem.*
73. *Ibidem.*
74. Howard M. Wachtel, 'Workers' management and interindustry wage differentials in Yugoslavia', *Journal of Political Economy*, No. 3, May/June 1972.
75. *Ibidem.*
76. *Ibidem.*
77. SAVA Statute, Article 71.
78. *Idem*, Article 223.
79. Wachtel, *loc. cit.*
80. A progressive income tax (such as in the West) is levied only on relatively high incomes.
81. Cf. Tables 1.5 and 1.6.
82. Overlegorgaan Vakcentrales, 'Baas in eigen bedrijf', *Interlinks*, Vol. 2, No. 8, June 1970, pages 42–43.
83. J. Vanek, *The general theory of labor-managed market economies*, Cornell University Press, Ithaca (N.Y.), 1970, page 296.
84. Neuberger and James, *loc. cit.*, page 260.

85. See, *inter alia*, Svetozar Pejovich, 'The banking system and the investment behavior of the Yugoslav firm', in M. Bornstein (ed.), *Plan and market, economic reform in Eastern Europe*, Yale University Press, New Haven and London, 1973.
86. Except, of course, in the case of joint ventures with foreign firms, although it is better to speak of risk-sharing capital. This matter will be discussed in Chapter 4.
87. Vanek, *General theory (op. cit.)*; and Vanek, 'The Yugoslav economy viewed through the theory of labor management', *World Development*, Vol. 1, No. 9, September 1973.
88. J. Wemelsfelder, 'Kapitaalvoorzieningsproblemen in een op arbeiderszelfbestuur gebaseerde industrie. Het voorbeeld van Joegoslavië', *De Economist*, No. 2, 1973.
89. Vanek, in *World Development (loc. cit.)*, page 50.
90. Milenkovitch, *op. cit.*, page 214.
91. *Ibidem.*
92. Pejovich, *loc. cit.*
93. OECD, *Economic Survey of Yugoslavia*, June 1973, page 13.
94. This is not in contradiction with what was said in Chapter I about the increasing role of the banks. Their share in the financing of gross fixed asset formation has risen dramatically (cf. Table 1.10). The demand for funds, however, has outstripped supply (which of course reinforces the position of the banks) and the additional financing has taken the form of increasing inter-enterprise credit.
95. OECD, *op. cit.*, page 15.

# 3. Private foreign investment in a developing economy

## 3.1. INTRODUCTION

The remainder of this study will be devoted to the review of a number of aspects of joint ventures between Yugoslav and foreign enterprises.

Joint ventures are – unless, of course, set up by firms of the same nationality in their own country – a special form of private (direct) foreign investment and the discussion in the next chapters may gain some additional perspective if the subject of private foreign investment is dealt with in general terms. This discussion, moreover, will be placed within the framework of the Third World.[1] One may argue that Yugoslavia's socio-economic system and the level of development it has reached make it a unique case. Still, many of the problems that Yugoslavia is facing would appear to be typical for a developing country and the contribution that private foreign investment can make to solving some of these problems is common to Yugoslavia as well as to other less developed countries.

It would seem that of the many controversial issues which are touched upon by development economics none has been the subject of more arguments, misunderstandings and disagreements than private foreign investment.[2] It has been blamed as one of the principal causes of underdevelopment in many LDC's, or, somewhat more mildly, as 'merely the twentieth-century refinement or economic outcome of the gun-boat diplomacy of the imperialist powers of the last century.'[3] On the other hand, the lack of private foreign investment is reckoned severely to hamper economic growth in the Third World. Both criticisms are correct – to a degree. Much harm has been done by ill-conceived projects, and the imposition of outrageous terms and conditions on countries poor in negotiating skills and unfamiliar with the realities of sophisticated business. Often, Western firms have not been reluctant to exploit rampant corruption of government officials to gain valuable concessions or, to use Hirschman's phrase, to resort to 'sheer exploitation of human and natural resources as well as crude power play.'[4]

It is therefore not surprising that private foreign investment has been equated, in some circles, with economic imperialism. But while such sentiment is understandable, it is also wrong. As always, emotional simplifications prevent insight into the many aspects of any given issue. Of course, private foreign investment can be detrimental or beneficial to the LDC's, depending on the form it takes. Provided it is made under the right conditions, private foreign investment can make a vital contribution to economic growth, albeit that such contribution cannot be the prime mover of development as is sometimes hoped or claimed. It is encouraging to note that UNCTAD of 1964, an assembly not known easily to agree on any subject, took the view that the flow of private capital to the LDC's should be stimulated, both on the donor- and the receiving end. That this recommendation was clad in many – eminently sensible – provisos and conditions does not subtract from the important point that many governments of developing countries officially have gone on record in principle to support private foreign investment.

To avoid any misunderstanding: private investment is, of course, not 'aid' in the sense of a deliberate attempt by a donor to help a less fortunate recipient. Private investment is a commercial operation and cannot be expected to be anything else. But while the main *purpose* of foreign investment is profits – be it in the short or the long run – the *result* can help development. To put it differently: private foreign investment is not a zero-sum game. The fact that this obvious point is misunderstood by many governments of the less developed countries is one of the causes for the confusion on this issue.

## 3.2. PRIVATE FOREIGN INVESTMENT IN DEVELOPING COUNTRIES[5]

Before an attempt is made to analyse the contribution private foreign investment can make to the economic development of the Third World, it should be made clear what is understood here by the process of economic development. There are about as many views on this complex concept as there are writers on the subject and this is not the place to review the literature. Of course, all definitions have at least some merit – and some are very perceptive indeed – but ultimately the choice of a particular definition as the framework for analysis is a question of judgement, and therefore subjective. With this explicit proviso, the following, rather long quotation from Professor Harry G. Johnson's *Economic policies towards less developed countries* is put forward as the most succinct and comprehensive explanation of what the development process is all about:

'... the establishment of a modern economy requires "industrialisation". By this term, however, is meant something different from the establishment of "industry" (the production of manufactured goods) as distinct from and in replacement of "agriculture" (the production of commodities from the soil). Industrialisation properly speaking involves the organisation of production in business enterprises, characterised by specialisation and division of labour both within and among themselves; this specialisation is based on the application of technology and electrical and mechanical power to supplement and replace human effort and motivated by the objectives of minimising costs per unit and maximising returns to the enterprise. Industrialisation in this relevant broad sense requires far more than the investment of capital in the establishment of industrial facilities and in the "infrastructure" ... required to power them and link them to markets. Among its more obvious requirements are the development of a skilled, disciplined and acquisitively motivated labour force and the creation of a professional managerial class able to combine disciplined teamwork with imaginative entrepreneurship ... Among its less obvious requirements are the integration of markets for goods, capital, and labour, necessary both for the creation of a competitive environment and for the efficiency of resource allocation and investment decisions and entailing the creation of appropriate institutions, some of which at least require governmental initiative or support. Least obvious but perhaps most important are the institutional, social and motivational changes which may demand radical changes in the system of land tenure (...), the distribution of income (...), as well as abandonment of the practice of exercising close social control over economic life characteristic of traditional societies. Thus economic development and industrialisation require the transformation of the society and the economy, and the transformation must be largely an internal one. The international economic relations of a country can, however, play a crucial role in the process of transformation. First, (through) exposure to the outside world through international trade and investment, (and, secondly, through) the possible contributions that the developed countries can make to the acceleration of economic growth in the less developed countries.'[6]

Industrialisation, in the sense of Johnson's definition, is therefore not so much a question of increasing the supply of inputs (be they capital resources, skilled labour, or even technological know-how) but rather of increasing the ability to make optimal use of available resources, i.e. the effectiveness of management – on the macro- as well as on the micro-economic level.[7]

When the development process is regarded in these terms, it is clear where the potential contribution of private foreign investment should lie. But while few would quarrel with Johnson's view that international investment *can* play 'a crucial role in the process of transformation', private foreign investment is by no means unconditionally welcome in all LDC's. Several developing countries, in fact, have imposed almost prohibitive conditions – although the same countries have often gone to great lengths in encouraging foreign investment a few years earlier. Other countries have gone through the same process in reverse. This ambivalent attitude in the Third World is partly due to misunderstandings about a foreign investor's motives (about which more later) and partly to the fact that private foreign investment is not always an unmixed blessing: it has certain definite advantages, but also a number of drawbacks, real or imaginary. The latter will be dealt with first.

### 3.2.1. *The case against private foreign investment*

Arguments against private foreign investment (PFI) are multiple and widely varied, but they can be grouped into a few major categories.

In the first place, PFI is said to have a detrimental effect on a developing country's balance of payments since it will lead to a net outflow of foreign exchange.

Secondly, it is argued that PFI is an expensive way of obtaining capital, modern technology, know-how and the like, in as much as foreign investors demand high profits.

Thirdly, PFI is alleged to impose wrong industrial strategies on LDC's by forcing the adoption of capital intensive production processes in the face of abundant, unemployed labour resources.

Fourthly, PFI is said to stifle local entrepreneurship and initiative.

Finally, it is argued that there is a divergency between the interests of the foreign investor, optimising profits on his world-wide operations, and the host country in search of a maximum increase in Gross Domestic Product.

#### 3.2.1.1. *The effect of PFI on the balance of payments of the host country*

The most often voiced argument against private foreign investment claims that PFI leads to a net outflow of foreign exchange, and, since the latter is a scarce resource, the ultimate effect of PFI is detrimental to the interests of the host country. The argument is attractive because of its simplicity. Obviously, any foreign company which invests abroad is doing so only if it can be reasonably sure that its investment will pay off in the form of higher return flow.[8] But to consider the effects on the balance of payments of the host country in these narrow terms only is too simple. A straight comparison of direct inflows and outflows of foreign exchange fails to do justice to the indirect effects of PFI. As pointed out by the Pearson Commission: 'Such a comparison neglects to take into account the reinvestment of profits by foreign investors in the host country and fails to note the impact of foreign investment on export promotion and import saving. ... The key question is the productivity of foreign investments for the host economy as a whole.'[9]

Streeten has argued[10] that there are two flaws in this analysis. In the first place, PFI is different from domestic investment only in the sense that it involves an initial inflow of foreign exchange for the construction of the project and a subsequent (higher) outflow in the form of remitted profits. All indirect effects, Streeten maintains, arise from *any* investment and not specifically from PFI. The second flaw is the implicit assumption that the resources employed in the project were previously unused and unusable, and, moreover, that they represent net additions in that they do not replace resources in other sectors of the economy.

But Streeten's analysis is not flawless either. To begin with his second objection, the capital and know-how brought in by the foreign investor are by definition net additions to available resources in the host country. There can hardly be an argument on this point. Where the foreign investor displaces other resources (e.g. labour, raw materials etc.), he is only able to do so if he uses them more efficiently than another investor. If not, he will have to close his plant. But on the other hand, if he does, output of the local economy is increased by the difference between the yield the foreign investor achieves and the yield that would have been achieved by the domestic investor (or any other foreign investor, for that matter). Furthermore, it is difficult to see why the 'displacement of other resources' has really any bearing on the argument. Surely, if it is applicable to the case of foreign investment, it applies to domestic investment as well.

Streeten's first point, i.e. that all indirect effects arise from any investment and not specifically from PFI, is equally open to question. In a way, he seems to retract from his assertion by agreeing that 'the economics of investment is not the same as the economics of P(rivate) O(verseas) I(nvestment), and to credit all indirect effects to POI is to confuse the two.'[11] But this is precisely the point! Foreign and domestic investment do have, in a developing country, different indirect effects on the economy, and it is by comparing these that the advantages of PFI emerge. To consider an investment project merely as a combination of various production factors such as capital, labour, land, and even technology, is too academic a view. It is the ability to coordinate these factors in the most efficient way which is the real scarce resource. And this is the specific advantage of PFI. Of course, the investment 'might have taken place anyway', even without PFI, but that does not mean it would yield the same return. Moreover, it would mean in most cases that another domestic investment would be foregone as LDC's are short of capital resources and – more importantly – entrepreneurs.

There is, however, a more basic point to be made. Streeten, and all other proponents of the balance of payments argument, seem to take an almost mercantilistic view on the question of foreign exchange:

outflows are bad, inflows are good. The real issue, of course, is whether private foreign investment is advantageous for a developing country or not. If it is, a price will have to be paid. It would hardly be realistic to expect that PFI entails only benefits and no cost. Every developing country is therefore faced with the problem of weighing very carefully all potential benefits that PFI can offer, and under what conditions, and compare those with the ensuing costs. If it finds there is a net benefit, then it should be prepared to pay the costs. And it just so happens that an outflow of foreign exchange is one of the costs of PFI.

One could even argue that the main characteristic of PFI is the *import* of scarce resources: know-how, technology, management skills, capital etc. If this is true, then it would be entirely arbitrary to single out this particular category of 'imports' for discriminatory treatment by requiring it to generate its own counter-inflow of foreign exchange. The requirement that foreign investment should be export-increasing or import-decreasing is based, as aptly stated by Kindleberger, 'on the partial-equilibrium fallacy.'[12] And he goes on, 'partial-equilibrium analysis does not apply in an economy that is responsive to market signals. Capital should be invested in the most profitable line in the economy, and the transfer of dividends should be handled through the economy's macroeconomic apparatus.'[13] Of course, in a developing country consumers and producers may fail to respond to correct signals. 'In that case there may be a second-best argument for requiring each investment to provide for transfer of its own dividend income. *This is a weakness of the economy, not of direct investment.*'[14] But then it is this particular weakness that should be remedied on the macroeconomic level by measures to increase exports or decrease imports (e.g. by devaluing overvalued currencies), rather than by discriminating arbitrarily against PFI.[15] In particular, since, as Streeten himself admits, 'it is quite possible that the worsened balance of payment position (i.e. the net outflow of foreign exchange in the form of remitted profits occurs at a higher level of foreign trade and real income than would have been attainable without the foreign investment.'[16] In a sense, PFI is therefore not different from quite a number of other factors which accelerate economic growth but lead to a deterioration of the current account.

3.2.1.2. *High profits*

It is often said that developing countries would be better off to rely less on direct investment and more on bonds or fixed-interest loans since the rate of return on equity investment is higher than interest charges, i.e. PFI is considered too expensive. Before going into the substance of the argument, a look at a few figures is helpful. Over the past several years interest rates on long-term loans have varied between 7 and 9 percent.[17] During the same period the average yields on equity in manufacturing and other industries ranged generally between 8 and 12 percent for U.S. and U.K. investments in developing countries.[18] The Reddaway Report has even computed that the rate of return on U.K. investments in LDC's is not more than 8.5 percent excluding the oil industry.[19] It is therefore obvious that on average profits on foreign investment are not much higher than interest charges on loans, and that no excessive margin is allowed for the transfer of know-how and modern management techniques. Moreover, the return on equity is, of course, always expressed in terms of balance sheet figures which are notoriously undervalued. If one further considers that some compensation is justified for the risk which is implicit in any equity investment, the accusation of too high profits does not seem to hold ground.

There are, however, two additional observations to be made. Firstly, even if average profits on equity were substantially higher than interest charges on loans, one should take into consideration the fact that interest and amortisation payments are fixed regardless of the cash flow generated by the borrower, while the returns from an equity investment will start to flow only if a profit is actually made. Equity capital has therefore a built-in grace period and flexibility which is entirely absent in the case of loans.[20] The second point is that high profits as such are not objectionable. Unless they are the result of a monopoly caused by restrictions on entry, they reflect superior efficiency. The only reasonable action to be undertaken by a developing country in case it feels that the profits of a specific foreign – or domestic – investor are excessive, is to see to it that any artificial barriers to entry are removed. After that, high profits may continue for a limited time until increased production catches up with demand.[21]

### 3.2.1.3. *The effect of PFI on industrialisation strategy*

The third objection against PFI is, briefly, that foreign investment imposes in general the wrong technologies on developing countries: instead of using production processes with a high labour content, PFI basically relies on capital-intensive techniques. This would have two disadvantages: the import of expensive capital equipment is a strain on scarce foreign exchange and the creation of employment opportunities is minimal.

Again, the argument is plausible, but fails to recognise practical difficulties. Contrary to what is taught in most economic textbooks, substitution of production factors is possible only in a very limited number of cases. In general for most production processes, only one specific combination of production factors is technically feasible, and this in spite of all research over the last years into the possibilities of 'intermediate technology.'[22] But there are other problems as well. Even if it is possible to convert a capital-intensive production process to more labour-intensive techniques, such conversion paradoxically requires a highly skilled labour force to replace machine precision and quality and a sophisticated management to organise and control production.[23] In addition, if a developing country wants to be competitive on the world market so as to be able to increase exports, certain standards of quality will have to be met. And it is technically difficult to achieve such standards by labour-intensive technologies, even in the case of so-called light manufactures.

3.2.1.4. *The effect of PFI on local entrepreneurship and initiative*
While the effect of PFI on the local business climate has been the subject of strong criticism, it is striking that the critics seem to hold diametrically opposite views. On the one hand, PFI is thought to be too interfering in the affairs of the host country, on the other PFI has been criticised for not interfering enough. The latter point of view has been most eloquently voiced by Hirschman in his well-known essay 'How to divest in Latin America and why.'[24] After having argued that the cause of economic development is best served by an outspoken group of new industrialists, he states that 'the trouble with the foreign investor may well be not that he is so meddlesome, but that he is so mousy.'[25]

Both points of view, however, come to the same conclusion: PFI is harmful because of its stultifying effect on local policies and initiative in the long run. But even if this were true – and the case has by no means been proven – it still does not imply that therefore PFI should be totally restricted, as Hirschman and other critics suggest. The proper approach of the host country should rather be to develop policies which stimulate local entrepreneurship, and in addition, institute appropriate controls over foreign investment.[26]

With respect to the latter, it is true that the bargaining position of the host country has been weak in the past, but as Kindleberger has pointed out, 'in the bilateral monopoly, non-zero sum game represented by direct investment in the less developed country, there has been a steady shift in the advantages from the side of the company to that of the country.'[27] All developing countries are now well aware of their power to impose a number of conditions on PFI without running the risk of scaring foreign investors away. Among the various instruments at the disposal of any government are tax policies, foreign exchange rate policies, the requiring of local equity participation, of a rising proportion of domestically produced inputs, of training of local labour and management and the like.[28] By a judicious use of its sovereign powers to impose such conditions and policies the negative effects of PFI resulting from too much interference could be kept to a minimum while retaining the advantages.

3.2.1.5. *Conflicts of interest between host country and foreign investors*
This is undoubtedly the most serious argument that can be made against PFI, although – as will be seen later – in practice such conflicts are less common than is usually assumed. Basically, the argument is that any foreign investor is primarily interested in the overall results from his world-wide operations. His investment and operational policies are determined by whatever objectives he has set with respect to growth, flow of profits, market position, or avoidance of foreign exchange risks, for his entire organisation of business interests. And these objectives, of course, take 'precedence over the narrower interest of the individual subsidiaries and the countries in which they are located.'[29] The foreign investor therefore wants as much freedom as possible to arrange his total pattern of production, sales, financing, remittance of profits etc.

It is clear that serious conflicts could arise here between the interests of the foreign investor and of the host country.

Before examining the nature of the problem further, however, two preliminary observations are in order. In the first place, the fact that a possible divergence of interests exists is in itself no cause for alarm. In a sense, this divergence is no less natural or normal than the multitude of differences of interest which occur in the (world) market economy: between producer and consumer, buyer and seller, or producers competing for the same customers. It is only when such a divergence results in a zero-sum game that real damage is done. Secondly, it should not be forgotten that the problem is not peculiar to PFI in the Third World. The developed countries face exactly the same issues when it comes to foreign investment.

The principal manifestations of the possible conflict are decisions of the foreign investor with respect to levels of output and pricing. As far as the former is concerned the foreign investor may decide to increase or decrease the production of his subsidiary to fit his overall output pattern. In the extreme case, he may even decide to close a specific plant altogether. Obviously, a decision calling for a substantial decrease of output – let alone complete cessation of operations – is not in the interest of the host country. There are, however, mitigating factors which lessen the (real) risk. Except for the so-called multinational corporations, most foreign investors lack sufficient alternative production facilities. When a company has only one or two subsidiaries in other countries, it has little scope for significant changes in output levels. But even the multinationals are normally not inclined to make drastic shifts, precisely because they want in general to avoid difficulties with the government of the host country. Unless forced by exogenous factors, such as clear threats of nationalisation, changes tend to be marginal.

The problem of pricing is basically a question of tax avoidance. A foreign company may overprice (imported) inputs and underprice output in order to decrease its tax liability in the host country, or it may follow the opposite policy to avoid taxes in the home country of the parent company. In both cases there are 'losses' to the host country, but some 'gains' as well. If the foreign investor charges too much for the inputs supplied by his other plants and underprices the local output, the local economy suffers in terms of a higher outflow of foreign exchange for imports and of lower tax revenues. On the other hand, assuming that the foreign investor wants to reduce his tax liability in the host country to a minimum, it is likely that he not only overprices inputs but underprices output as well. In that case, the lower prices of the output are a gain to domestic consumers and a boost to exports. In the reverse situation of underpriced inputs and overpriced outputs, the foreign exchange outflow for imported inputs is lower and tax revenue higher, but local consumers pay a higher price and exports may be more difficult.

One of the most flexible tools in the hands of a foreign investor is the manipulation of transfer prices (i.e. prices in intra-company trade).[30] But one should not exaggerate the possibilities for its use. 'A company which varies its prices frequently and by large amounts is asking for trouble from the revenue and customs authorities in the countries where it operates. The variations must be quite small, say a percentage or two either way, and should be justifiable by reference to some plausible factor affecting the trade concerned.'[31] Moreover – and this applies equally to the issue of changes in output levels – most foreign investors are reluctant to disrupt long-range investment planning and sales strategies for the sake of short-term advantages. In particular, tax avoidance schemes can be easily upset by changes in legislation, which in many LDC's can be sudden and unpredictable.

But although one may be prepared to admit the possibility of potentially damaging conflicts of interest, it is encouraging to note that in the largest of developing countries, India, the problem is not considered a serious one: 'Contrary to theoretical dissertations on the subject, we find from experience that the divergencies from the (foreign) firm's interest and the national interest are not very strong, by and large. A project that pays off to the private investor tends also to pay off to the country.'[32]

In conclusion, the disadvantages discussed above do not appear to add up to a convincing case against private foreign investment. A case which is weakened further when the advantages are taken into account.

### 3.2.2. *The advantages of private foreign investment*

At this point, it may be useful to recall once more what the basic elements are of Johnson's definition of the development process, which – as said earlier – in this study will serve as a framework for the analysis of the positive and negative aspects of private foreign investment. The essence of Johnson's definition is that economic development means 'industrialisation,'[33] a process which involves more than the investment of capital: it requires institutional, social, and motivational changes in the field of management, labour, business climate, investment decision-making, and governmental policies. If private foreign investment, therefore, is to make a positive contribution to economic development, it should be analysed in terms of its potential effects on this process of change.[34]

What then are the specific advantages of PFI, and how much do they contribute to the development process?

Again, as in the case of the drawbacks, the advantages are multiple and need to be grouped into a few major categories:

- introduction of management skills;
- transfer of technology and know-how;
- training of labour;
- generation of additional tax revenue and creation of additional employment;
- 'productivity spill-overs';[35]
- transfer of capital.

However, before discussing these categories separately, an observation should be made which applies to all of them. The question of 'how much' private foreign investment contributes to economic development can, as yet, not be answered quantitatively. So far no conclusive studies have been made of this issue, and until that time the beneficial effects of PFI will have to be assessed in qualitative terms. This is not to say that a given specific investment may not be quantitatively analysed. In fact, this is the only instance where it is possible to assess (quantitative) costs and benefits: case by case. The reason is that each of the advantages listed above has a different effect depending on the specifics of an individual investment.

A study, such as this, of the general role of PFI in the development process, is therefore necessarily limited to qualitative analysis.

### 3.2.2.1. *The introduction of management skills*

It is, of course, a question of judgement which particular characteristic of PFI offers potentially the greatest benefit to a developing country. There seems to be, however, a large degree of agreement – among academic writers as well as practitioners of the art – that the major advantage of private foreign investment consists of the introduction of management skills, in the broad sense of the word. It is this combination of entrepreneurial abilities, attitudes, experiences and knowledge, which is commonly referred to as 'management skills', that is a major force in bringing about the process of change and transformation leading to the 'industrialisation' of a developing economy.[36] It is equally obvious that these skills are generally lacking in LDC's and that they are the most important asset of the sophisticated business enterprises of the developed countries.[37]

But even if the opponents of private foreign investment admit its great advantage in this respect, one should recognise that the actual impact of the introduction of management skills may fall short of its potential, and it is therefore easy to exaggerate the benefits of PFI on this point. This would certainly seem to be an area where more research is needed.

### 3.2.2.2. *The transfer of technology and know-how*

Next to the scarcity of managerial skills, what developing countries generally lack most is access to modern technology and know-how, and without those resources it is extraordinarily difficult to succeed in a process of industrialisation. Again, it is hardly necessary to assert that modern technology and know-how are abundantly available in the developed countries and that therefore a way should be found for their transfer to the LDC's.

One can fairly ask the question whether such transfer has to be effected through the vehicle of private foreign investment. It is sometimes suggested that the basic technology, which the developing countries are most in need of, is available through textbooks and other published materials, through foreign training, through assistance of technological research and information centres. While it is certainly possible to acquire a (limited) amount of technology in this way, the application of such technology in industry is an entirely different matter. To be fully effective the transfer of technology has to be accompanied by 'integrated operative experience'[38] and know-how. Some writers have argued[39] that this could be realised through a combination of licensing and the hiring of foreign experts. This is a possibility, but it is doubtful whether by such arrangements the full benefits of the transfer of technology and know-how will be captured. The sale of a licence is a one-shot operation and in general does not involve participation in subsequent developments of new products. Even the combination of a licence agreement with a group of foreign experts under a management contract (whereby remuneration can be made dependent on profits realised) lacks two very important elements. In the first place, the essential link with the 'full arsenal of technical and administrative resources'[40] of the licensor is missing. 'The immediate availability of vital back-stopping services by head office staffs and laboratories, the access to procurement channels and marketing outlets'[41] are the highly desirable complements of a licence that can only be secured through direct private foreign investment. The second element is even more crucial, and that is the element of risk. Without an equity participation the foreign investor has considerably less incentive to make the investment a success. And in practice it is often this extra effort that makes the difference between good profits and an average operation.

3.2.2.3. *Training of labour*

While the beneficial effects of this advantage of PFI have often been overrated, it is nevertheless true that foreign investors generally devote special efforts to the training of local labour. The availability of cheap labour in the host country is, after all, one of the reasons why foreign enterprises invest in developing countries, but this labour has to be educated in the necessary skills to operate the equipment brought in by the foreign investor. The skills thus acquired can often be used in other industries when a change in employment takes place.

3.2.2.4. *Generation of tax revenues and creation of employment*

Much has been made of these advantages of private foreign investment, but even the staunchest advocate of PFI should be ready to admit that it is not the total tax revenue and employment creation resulting from a foreign investment that should be attributed to PFI.[42] Only in the event that there would have been no other domestic (or foreign) investment would the benefits be wholly to the credit of the foreign investor. The benefit of PFI to the host government is limited to the difference between the tax revenue respectively generated by the foreign investment and by the domestic investment foregone. The same line of reasoning applies to employment creation.

While the additional tax revenues may be very substantial – and therefore a clear benefit to the host country – it is likely that the employment creation effect is less significant. If there is no choice between production processes employment creation is the same whether the investment is undertaken by a foreign or domestic entrepreneur, but if there is a choice, the foreign investor is likely to choose a more capital-intensive technique than the domestic entrepreneur.

3.2.2.5. *Productivity spill-overs*

In addition to the effects of private foreign investment which are of direct benefit to the enterprise or venture in which the investment takes place, there are a number of ways in which PFI could contribute to economic development in a broader context: the productivity spill-overs. One instance overlaps with the factor of labour, and even management, training. Employees who are trained by a foreign investor and later move to domestic firms 'may transplant knowledge that provides a basis for imitative productivity gains there without real resource costs.'[43] A second instance is the incentive of the foreign investor to improve the productivity of both his local suppliers and customers: 'given the complex input-output relations characteristic of modern industry and the dependence of profitable utilisation of the product on the knowledge of the user, the firm may have a substantial incentive to invest in the diffusion of production knowledge in two directions: to the local suppliers of the inputs needed in its production process and for which it demands quality standards superior to the customary standards of those industries and to local customers who may have to be taught the technology of using the firm's products effectively.'[44]

The importance of these spill-over effects of PFI is unfortunately rarely fully appreciated. And yet, it is particularly this aspect that could contribute substantially to the process of 'industrialisation'. Moreover, Hirschman's claims to the contrary notwithstanding, PFI is a stimulus to change through its demonstration effect. The results of modern management technique will not go unnoticed even in the most sedate of societies and stimulate their introduction by domestic enterprises. Starting with the local suppliers and customers of the foreign investor the effects will spread – albeit slowly and imperfectly perhaps – through the economy and thus the process of economic development.

3.2.2.6. *Transfer of capital*

**Perhaps because it is the most tangible and immediately beneficial effect of PFI, the inflow of foreign exchange is often cited as its most important advantage. And, in fact, the amounts involved are considerable. Net direct private foreign investment amounted in 1970 to $3.4 billion which was roughly half of the total net private capital flow.**

*Table 3.1. Net flow of financial resources from DAC countries 1966–70 ($ million)*

| | *1966* | *1967* | *1968* | *1969* | *1970* |
|---|---|---|---|---|---|
| Net direct investment | 2,179 | 2,105 | 3,046 | 2,804 | 3,408 |
| Net portfolio and other long-term lending | 655 | 1,269 | 1,738 | 1,696 | 1,152 |
| Net changes in private export credits outstanding | 1,124 | 1,007 | 1,596 | 1,978 | 2,174 |
| Total net private flow | 3,959 | 4,381 | 6,380 | 6,478 | 6,735 |
| Total net flow | 10,390 | 11,440 | 13,407 | 13,670 | 15,542 |

Source: E.M. Martin, *1971 review: development assistance, efforts and policies of the members of the Development Assistance Committee*, Tables II–1 and VI–1, OECD, Paris, 1971.

The share of net direct private investment in the total net flow of financial resources to LDC's ranged thus between 18 and 22 percent over the period 1966–70.

Granted that the amounts involved in PFI are by no means negligible, the impact of PFI in terms of financial transfers can, as yet, not be called decisive. Gross investment of all LDC's in 1970 was estimated at roughly $82 billion and direct private foreign investment constituted therefore about 4 percent of this amount. Whether this proportion will rise in the future is a matter of pure speculation, although the rising interest of firms in the developed world in investment in LDC's gives hope for the long run.

The overall conclusion emerging from this analysis of the pros and cons of PFI can be no other than that private foreign investment can make a definite contribution to economic development. Whether a particular investment will, in fact, be of benefit to the host country depends obviously on the specific circumstances of the case. However, from the general review undertaken in the preceding pages, it would seem fair to conclude that the potential advantages outweigh the possible drawbacks, although – as said before – no conclusive evidence is as yet available to back up this claim.

One important proviso should be added, however. In their desire to attract private foreign investment, LDC's may lose the potential excess of benefits over costs by granting too generous explicit or hidden subsidies to the foreign investor.[45] Obviously, such subsidies should be given sparingly and only if they are really required. The question of the right incentives to stimulate private foreign investment will be examined in more detail in the next section.

### 3.2.3. *Incentives for private foreign investment*

Once a developing country has taken the decision to admit private foreign investment in principle – and it should be emphasised that this is as much a political decision as an economic one – it then becomes a matter of determining the right incentives to attract PFI and to establish the conditions under which it will be allowed to operate. The latter point is as important as the first since, although the potential benefits of PFI in general may outweigh its costs, it is clear that not all foreign investment will be beneficial per se. The contribution of a particular investment to the host country's economic development very much depends on its specific characteristics and circumstances, and a government can definitely influence these by imposing certain conditions.

In order to determine the right incentives – and impose realistic conditions the government of a developing country should be aware of the factors that play a rôle in the investment decision-making process of foreign firms. Without such elementary understanding it is difficult to formulate the right mix of policies. It is therefore rather unfortunate that so far no comprehensive theory of foreign investment has been advanced and tested:[46] 'only fragments of a complete explanation based on economic theory and more recently on the theory of organisational decision-making are available.'[47]

Most authors dealing with the factors influencing investment decisions come forward with rather simple statements, generally along neo-classical lines. A few representative examples:

'The investor is motivated by reasons of profitability and market access ... Firms undertake direct foreign investment so as to gain access to resources, physical, human, financial and technological; to escape from unfavourable conditions such as saturation of the domestic market, taxation, anti-trust policy, and union militancy; and to overcome tariff barriers.'[48]

Or:

'(The) central mission (of) private enterprise (is) to allocate its capital, manpower, technology, management skills, and other corporate resources so as to maximise economic returns in terms of current earnings as well as asset appreciation.'[49]

These statements, which could be supplemented by countless similar ones, all assume that firms systematically search the world for the most profitable investment opportunities.[50] In practice, this process is rather more complex. They are, nevertheless, correct on one very basic point: the purpose of firms investing in poor countries is not to advance the development of the local economy, it is quite simply to pursue their own goals. This is definitely the first point that the government of a developing country should be very clear about. Failure to understand it – or to accept it – will make all efforts to attract private foreign investment an entirely futile operation.

But this understanding, albeit essential, is not enough to serve as a basis for the formulation of policies. It will be necessary to know more about the investment decision-making process and the factors which play a role in it. And although, as said earlier, no comprehensive theory is as yet available, recent research in this field has provided some useful insights.[51] One of the most significant findings was that the foreign investment decision is not the result of a clear cut sharply delineated process but of a gradual continuous development which takes place in an environment where knowledge is limited and uncertainty a fact of life.[52] The remarkable thing about this is that it is really totally unremarkable as limited knowledge and uncertainty are a common feature to all decisions in life, yet economic theory – and the policies based on it – would seem to have neglected this simple truth by postulating that the firm will continue to invest until marginal benefits equal marginal costs. Of course, such rational behaviour is in practice not followed because of the firm's inability to predict all variables which determine profit. 'Rather, firms pursue several broad goals that are developed through internal organisational processes.'[53] These goals can include maintenance of a market share, both at home and abroad, a certain level of profits and the like. Aharoni has found that a decision to invest abroad is practically always specific and triggered by a strong 'initiating force' rather than by an explicit policy to look for foreign investment opportunities. This initiating force may arise from within the organisation – such as the particular interest of a high-ranking official – but far more often this force is exogenous to it. Usually, therefore, the decision to invest abroad is a response to a specific challenge, which may take various forms:[54]

- an outside proposal, provided it comes from a source that cannot be easily ignored: foreign governments, distributors of the firm's products, clients;
- fear of losing a market;
- the 'bandwagon effect': successful operations abroad of a competitor, or the belief that investment in some area is a 'must';
- strong competition from abroad on the home market: a defensive manoeuvre to fight a competitor on his home ground.

An important qualification should be made at this point. The emerging of an initiating force does not necessarily mean that the foreign investment process will be set in motion. Much depends on the strength of this force and on the social and organisational structure and policies of the firm, previous events in its history, and other problems it is facing.

In this connection, it is interesting to compare Aharoni's findings with a German study which, inter alia, investigated the reasons that had led German firms to invest or conclude cooperation agreements in developing countries.[55] On the basis of a sample of 114 firms, 55 percent of which with actual direct investments in LDC's and 45 percent with licence- or other cooperation agreements, the following picture emerged:

*Table 3.2. Motives of German firms to invest in or conclude cooperation agreements with LDC's*

| *Motive* | *Number of times quoted* | *% of total* |
|---|---|---|
| opening up of new markets | 134 | 28.5 |
| securing of existing markets | 53 | 11.2 |
| incentives provided by German or LDC government | 79 | 16.8 |
| proposals from distributors or clients | 54 | 11.5 |
| locational factors | 48 | 10.2 |
| labour market factors | 45 | 9.6 |
| favourable conditions for sale of equipment or licence | 37 | 7.9 |
| political pressure from LDC's | 20 | 4.3 |
| Total | 470 | 100.0 |

Source: Planungsgruppe Ritter, *op. cit.* (n. 55), Table 7, page 69.

In the German experience at least – and there is no reason to assume that it would be different in the case of other developed countries – factors relating to the market stand out as the prime initiating force. The incentives provided either by German authorities or the host countries come a good second, and this is an important point to note for any government that wishes to attract PFI.

If the initiating force has been strong enough to trigger a decision to study a specific investment proposition abroad, an investigating process is started. Basically, the purpose of this exercise is to minimise the negative effects of uncertainty and limited knowledge.[56] While the investigation covers a multitude of aspects, most of which common to any feasibility study of a particular investment, one issue receives particular attention in the case of investment in a developing country: risk. The risk factors, most commonly cited, are the following:[57]

- political: war, expropriation, revolution, general instability.
- economic: inflation, devaluation, inconvertibility of currency for the purpose of profit transfers and repatriation of capital.
- 'nuisance': lack of adequate basic services, government intervention.

The problem here is that most foreign investors have a tendency to overestimate the risks involved in investing in LDC's due to ignorance, generalisations about LDC's, projections of own national characteristics on other countries and the like. Of course, the information gathered during the investigation process will help to assess risks in proper perspective in as much as ignorance and broad generalisations are reduced. But the fact remains that foreign firms attach great importance to 'political and economic stability' and no developing country will be successful in attracting foreign investment if it is found lacking in this respect.[58]

Aside from political and economic stability there are, of course, a number of other conditions ideally required by a foreign investor before he is willing to commit money and management resources to a particular investment. These are absence of restrictions on remittance of dividends and interest, repatriation of capital, guarantees of compensation in case of expropriation or nationalisation, freedom from double taxation, absence of vexatious government controls, facilities for the employment of foreign staff.

What specific actions then can be undertaken by developing countries that wish to attract private foreign investment, and what can be done by the developed countries?

First and foremost, investors' fears about political instability will have to be laid to rest, as this has time and again proven to be the major impediment to PFI. One might be tempted to say that this is entirely up to the developing country: put your house in order and foreign investment will follow. Unfortunately this is not the case, foreign investors are not easily convinced that such house-cleaning operation by a (new) government in a developing country will be long-lasting. Governments have, in general and therefore in the minds of partially-informed businessmen, a tendency to be overthrown – and their policies with them. A foreign investor would prefer a country that has a proven record of stability over a longer period than the average lifespan of a government and only a few LDC's would fall in this category. The efforts of a developing country to improve the climate for foreign investment, which include such things as stability in the laws and regulations affecting foreign investment,[59] can be supplemented by governmental action at the other end, i.e. by investment guarantee schemes covering political and non-commercial risks sponsored by the developed countries.[60] The Multilateral Investment Guarantee Scheme proposed by the World Bank would, of course, be highly desirable but so far disagreements on its funding have prevented it from coming into being.[61]

A second line of action by developing countries lies in the removal of undue restrictions on profit transfer and repatriation of capital. No foreign investor is going to risk his money if he cannot be reasonably sure that he will be able to dispose of his earnings and retrieve the capital invested.

Thirdly, the flow of private capital can be stimulated by tax concessions although the effects of such concessions are generally overestimated, as found by the Pearson Commission, 'they are generally reported to be of very modest importance in the final investment decision.'[62] Moreover, tax privileges are essentially subsidies which a developing country can ill afford. The issue is further complicated by the fact that a foreign investor in principle is subject to taxation both in his home country and in the country of investment. While there are some developed countries that make partial or full allowance for taxes paid abroad, there are others that do not and in that case the incentives granted by LDC's simply result in higher tax liabilities at home. The size of the 'loss' is, of course, dependent on the tax rates in both countries. Fortunately, there is some progress on this front in the form of tax conventions between developed and developing countries, and 'in the majority of such conventions greater taxing rights are allocated to the developing country for dividends, interest, royalties and technical services.'[63, 64]

A fourth area is the enlargement of information and promotional activities which should be undertaken not only by LDC's themselves but also by agencies in developed countries that wish to stimulate the flow of private foreign investment to the Third World. Ignorance of investment opportunities is widespread, and the Planungsgruppe Ritter even reported that it had found, particularly amoung the medium-sized and smaller

German firms 'eine erstaunliche Unkenntnis über die Möglichkeiten.'[65] Here, again, the main thrust will have to come from the developing countries, several of which are already quite active having set up investment centres at home and in various developed countries.[66]

Finally mention should be made of government sponsored investment corporations in the developed countries – as well as international agencies such as IFC – which perform a useful role in stimulating investment in developing countries principally by acting as a catalyst.[67]

Developing countries that wish to stimulate PFI not only provide incentives, they impose conditions as well. They may, for example, insist on majority local ownership, on '-isation' of management, limit local borrowing, restrict the sectors in which foreign investment is allowed, require the introduction of modern technology as part of the package, and insist on export. From the strict economist's point of view some of these conditions may not make much sense, but that does not necessarily make them irrational. Foreign investment does not only have economic effects on the host country, it has social, cultural and political consequences as well that may be considered undesirable to a developing country. If it therefore imposes certain restrictions, it does no more than exercise its rights as a sovereign state. It is then up to the foreign investor to decide whether he wants to proceed or not, weighing the incentives offered against the conditions imposed.

However strong a case may be made for private foreign investment, in practice the 'foreign investment climate' in most LDC's is deteriorating and this in spite of such declarations as were made at the 1964 UNCTAD meeting. Most governments in developing countries are coming under increasing pressure from xenophobic nationalist quarters. Increased social conflicts and political tensions have accompanied economic growth because it has failed to cope with the problems of population growth, unemployment and the vast inequalities in the distribution of income. In these circumstances, it is not surprising that foreign-owned companies are made a scapegoat and a target of agitation. There is, of course, no easy remedy for this situation. A reversal of present trends – if it comes about – will be a slow and tortuous process. It will require a less emotional and more rational view of private foreign investment and the realisation that the inflow of foreign capital does not necessarily imply a sell-out of national resources. Perhaps the combination of foreign and local participation in a business enterprise – the joint venture – would help to overcome the resentment against investment from the rich countries.

Considerable experience with this type of PFI has already been accumulated over the years. The next section will deal with its specific characteristics.

## 3.3. THE INTERNATIONAL JOINT VENTURE IN DEVELOPING COUNTRIES

### 3.3.1. *Definition*

Since the term 'joint venture' is rather vague and, if loosely interpreted, can imply almost any form of business cooperation, most authors dealing with the subject precede their analysis with a definition. Friedmann and Kalmanoff in their pathbreaking study,[68] though not attempting to formulate a succinct definition, list two elements that distinguish a joint venture from other forms of association: partnership and collaboration for more than a transitory period (excluding pure trading relationships). The form that the partnership may take ranges from 'a long-term construction job' where enterprises combine their equipment, manpower, and finance, to an equity partnership.[69] Tomlinson offers a somewhat sharper formulation: 'the commitment, for more than a very short duration, of funds, facilities, and services by two or more legally separate interests, to an enterprise for their mutual benefit.'[70] Yet another definition is supplied by Van Hilten who published a comprehensive study on the joint venture phenomenon.[71] He defines the joint venture as 'a form of cooperation between several independent business enterprises, possibly including other economic subjects, which takes place in a common, entirely separate enterprise by means of contribution of know-how and participation in the equity capital.'[72]

None of these definitions is entirely satisfactory as they fail to stress the two elements that are the heart and soul of joint venturing: the sharing of risks and the sharing of control. With respect to Van Hilten's definition one has to object to his view that a joint venture necessarily involves the setting up of a new separate enterprise. As Friedmann and Kalmanoff quite rightly point out: 'An existing enterprise may be transformed into a joint venture with the foreign enterprise retaining a controlling interest, while the minority shares are held by the local government or a government-controlled development corporation, a small group of local capitalists, or the public.'[73]

In the context of this study the joint venture is reviewed in terms of a particular form of private foreign investment and a definition used here should therefore apply to the 'joint international business venture'. In this sense the most accurate formulation has been made by Willems: 'A joint international business venture is a business enterprise in which both a foreign and a local enterprise have a share in the management and in the equity capital in such a manner that their participation in management and in financing is relatively important.'[74] Willems clearly identifies the sharing of control and risk (through the 'relatively important' financial stake) while the element of collaboration for 'more than a transitory period' is implicit. Van Hilten has objected to this definition on the grounds that it fails to mention the input of know-how by one of the partners.[75] He has a point, since particularly in developing countries local enterprises often conclude a joint venture with a foreign firm precisely because they want to acquire a specific technology or know-how. On the other hand, an international joint venture without a contribution in know-how is perfectly possible and it would therefore be incorrect to insist on an inclusion in the definition.[76] Moreover, know-how (aside from capital) is not the only contribution a foreign investor may make to a joint venture. There are other things as e.g. access to capital markets in other countries, contacts with importers in the developed world and the like. In the same vein, the local investor as well is contributing more than just capital and management: knowledge of local conditions, access to government officials etc., all of which are rather valuable to a foreign investor.

Having thus accepted Willems' definition as a basis, the next step is to analyse the specific characteristics of the joint venture. This will be done again – as in the case of private foreign investment in general – in terms of its advantages and disadvantages both to the host country (and the domestic partner in the joint venture) and the foreign investor.

### 3.3.2. *Advantages to a developing country*

The advantages of private foreign investment, which were outlined earlier, are typically accentuated if PFI takes the form of a joint venture. Introduction of management skills, transfer of know-how and technology, training of labour, all will benefit the local economy more than in the case of a fully owned foreign subsidiary, for the simple reason that local interests are participating in the enterprise and sharing the benefits. An exception might be made with respect to the inflow of capital inasmuch as in a joint venture – by definition – part of the financing is coming from domestic sources. This potential loss may, however, be partly compensated by the fact that some foreign investors actually prefer local participation and would not have invested without it.

But the joint venture offers a number of additional advantages to a developing country. First and foremost, the joint venture is the most suitable – and perhaps the only – way to solve the ever-present problem of conflict of interest between foreign investor and host country. This is not to say that each and every joint venture will have this salutary effect. Much, if not all, depends on the compatibility of the partners to the deal and the way in which they have regulated their relationship. In a sound set-up the foreign investor will not be able to subordinate the joint venture's interest to those of the foreign enterprise. Obviously, this is one of the main reasons why many corporations from developed countries are reluctant to enter into a joint venture. But the deterrent is apparently not too strong, as witnessed by the rapidly increasing number of joint ventures in developing countries. The best way to eliminate the possibility that the foreign investor subjugates the joint venture's interests to his own is a carefully drafted joint venture agreement. In particular, the question of pricing of inputs procured from the foreign partner (and the output sold to him) should be regulated in detail, as well as standards of quality, delivery terms and conditions of payment.[77]

The second specific advantage of the joint venture lies in the fact that it may help to alleviate the political problems in the host country arising from the presence of strong foreign economic interests on its soil.[78] As related earlier, in many developing countries xenophobic tendencies are increasing. If, however, local capital – private or public – participates in the enterprise, the inflow of PFI becomes politically more palatable. Fears of foreign economic dependency may, of course, be further reduced by imposing additional conditions and restrictions. The most widely applied of these are: insistence on a domestic majority in the equity, exclusion of certain sectors of the economy which are considered 'strategic' (such as banking, trade and commerce, insurance and public utilities), '-isation' of management and the introduction of modern technology. These restrictions are obviously not popular with foreign investors – or even some economists.[79] But they have by now become a fact of life, grudgingly accepted – at least by the business man. And, as Litvak and Maule observe, 'one very significant factor emerges, namely the willingness of foreign investors to stay in these countries providing that profitable opportunities remain.'[80]

It may be tempting to subject this range of conditions and restrictions to an economic analysis, but that would be a meaningless exercise. Not so much because they are 'a fact of life', but rather because they are basically political in character.[81]

Thirdly, the joint venture offers the chance to the local investor to initiate a large project which he would be unable to undertake himself because of inadequate financial resources or limited know-how. In addition, the participation of a foreign partner not only assures equity finance but also improves the creditworthiness of the venture which therefore may find it easier to obtain credits both at home and abroad.

The fourth advantage is commercial in nature. Most enterprises in developing countries have difficulties in exporting. They 'are often deterred from entering world markets by the lack of firm orders, the lack of knowledge of how to obtain orders, the variations in consumer fancies from one year to the next, the problem of meeting exact color and dimension requirements and so on.'[82] The association with a foreign partner provides such knowledge of marketing channels, sales techniques and quality requirements.[83]

### 3.3.3. *Advantages to the foreign investor*

The advantages of the joint venture are fortunately not one-sided. The foreign investor too can derive quite a number of benefits by linking up with a domestic partner, once he has overcome the reluctance against sharing control.

Probably the most important advantage to the foreign investor is the reduction of political risks. As mentioned in the preceding section, the participation of local interests in a business enterprise may go a long way to alleviate political opposition against private foreign investment. From this higher degree of 'acceptability' a number of other advantages flow, such as increased chances of getting government contracts (generally important in developing countries), less government interference, a better image in the domestic market and the like.

The joint venture, however, not only reduces the political risk of the foreign investor, it lessens his financial risks as well, i.e. to the extent that financing is provided by local partners. The corollary of this advantage is obviously that a share of the profits accrues to the local investors. This may be a real disadvantage to those foreign companies that have little problem in raising sufficient funds, and are forced by government regulations to accept domestic partners. But such companies are relatively rare, and most foreign investors do not dispose of unlimited finances. Moreover, as Van Hilten points out, the pooling of resources in a joint venture makes it possible to undertake larger projects and more projects.[84]

The fact of being associated, in a joint venture, with a local partner has certain intrinsic advantages to the foreign investor as well. Not only will his local associate contribute capital and carry a part of the risk, he is moreover highly valuable because of his knowledge of the local market, economic conditions and the political climate. In most cases, he brings land and buildings into the joint venture, knows where to find the required labour force and can help in selecting appropriate candidates for management training programmes.

### 3.3.4. *Disadvantages to a developing country*

The joint venture, as a specific type of private foreign investment, basically has no disadvantages for a developing country beyond those common to all forms of PFI, which were dealt with earlier. Of course, no human institution is perfect and the joint venture can give rise to quite a few problems. It would however, be inaccurate to treat these problem areas as disadvantages per se, and they will be discussed separately.

### 3.3.5. *Disadvantages to the foreign investor*

The disadvantage of the joint venture to any foreign investor is essentially that his freedom of operation is curtailed; he has less flexibility in coordinating his overall interests in such matters as sales planning, financial policy, production programme etc.

### 3.3.6. *Problem areas*

While the joint venture as such may have just one inherent disadvantage – and only for the foreign investor – it is not free from potential problems. In spite of the fact that the joint venture may be the most suitable vehicle to solve the conflict of interest between foreign investor and host country, such conflicts can never be entirely eliminated. To what extent they will impede the operations of the joint venture depends mainly on the compatibility of the partners to the deal. This, in fact, is the crucial issue in any joint venture. No joint venture has a chance to succeed if, from the outset, the partners lack trust in each other or do not get along at a later stage. But even if great care has been taken in the selection of associates,[85] the interests of the partners never entirely coincide. As Friedmann and Kalmanoff point out: 'The basic problems of joint ventures arise from a mixture of harmonies and conflicts of interest.'[86] On the other hand, joint ventures are no special case in this respect, it is a common feature in all economic relationships.

In more concrete terms, the main problem areas relate to such questions as use and distribution of profits (i.e. should profits be reinvested or paid out), pricing, personnel policies, marketing strategies, and expansion programmes.[87] In addition problems may arise due to factors exogenous to the joint venture, such as unwarranted interference by an overanxious government bureaucracy. The best way to avoid conflicts is to deal, as much as possible, with all potential problems at the time the joint venture contract is negotiated. In particular, management responsibilities should be clearly defined and an understanding reached with respect to long-run investment and financing policies. The latter point is, of course, difficult to deal with in a formal agreement as long-run strategies are subject to changes imposed by market conditions etc. Nevertheless, it is an issue the partners should face early so as to avoid problems later. Questions of marketing, pricing policies (with respect to inputs as well as output), technical assistance (know-how and technology), training of local labour and management personnel, on the other hand, should be included in the formal contract.

The problems which a joint venture could face during its life-time may appear awesome. Nevertheless, they are far from being insurmountable as experience so far has demonstrated. Bivens and Lovell, who interviewed 146 executives from developed as well as developing countries for their study *Joint ventures with foreign partners*, summarised their main findings as follows:

> 'Most of these executives have participated in joint ventures with foreign partners. On the basis of their experience, few minimise the dangers and difficulties of such partnerships. They point out the numerous management problems and conflicts of interest that can arise between businessmen with different customs, languages, and methods of doing business. They generally agree, however, that if the partners share objectives and trust, identify the possible problem areas in advance, and carefully negotiate management and ownership arrangements, then the joint venture can survive and prosper.'[88]

In the preceding pages a strong case has been made for private foreign investment–and in particular the joint venture–as a potentially important contribution to the acceleration of economic growth in the Third World. But however strong that case may be, even the staunchest advocate of PFI shall admit that this contribution is limited. The main thrust of the development process has to originate locally. To repeat Nurkse's phrase: 'It all boils down to this: capital is made at home.' What can be expected of private foreign investment is merely that it may help 'to lay the foundations for further growth in the economy and in strengthening the base from which domestic savings and foreign exchange are generated.'[89]

Similar words of caution are in order with respect to the joint venture form of PFI. For many developing countries it is – as yet – an unsuitable vehicle as there is no local business community from which partners could emerge with the necessary minimum of financial resources and skills. To a certain extent the absence of domestic private investors could be compensated by an equity stake of the host government, or local banks, in conjunction with an intensive training programme of indigenous management personnel. But the sort of projects for which this solution would be feasible is restricted, and joint ventures are likely to have a significant impact only in those developing countries where the first steps on the way to industrialisation have been made.

NOTES

1. In this study, for purely stylistic reasons, the terms 'less developed countries', 'developing countries', 'LDC's' or 'Third World' are used interchangeably, and are meant to include all countries of Asia (except Japan, Mainland China, North Korea, North Vietnam), Africa (except South Africa), Latin America, Greece, Portugal, Spain, Turkey, Yugoslavia, Cyprus and Malta.
2. To quote an unusually strong statement from a spokesman of a developing country: '... In no other field of economic theory has so much nonsense been said; in no other field have the enemies of free countries found so much that is vulnerable, and all this is due to our own ignorance and inability to explain the truth. No other myth has been so exaggerated, no statistics so misinterpreted and no truth so distorted by both supporters as well as opponents of foreign capital.' (A. Delfim Neto, 'Foreign capital, logic and development', *ADELA Monthly Bulletin*, October 1971).
3. P.H. Ady, 'Private overseas investment and the developing countries', in P.H. Ady (ed.), *Private foreign investment and the developing world*, Praeger, London, 1971, page 3.
4. Albert O. Hirschman, 'How to divest in Latin America and why,' Princeton University, *Essays in International Finance*, No. 76, November 1969, page 3.
5. In this study only direct investment will be considered, excluding therefore portfolio investment and financing through trade (export credits). It should further be noted that direct investment does not necessarily imply a transfer of Funds. The foreign investor can invest in kind (by shipping equipment or by capitalising fees for know-how and technology etc.), he may invest through borrowing in the domestic capital market and he can build up his equity by reinvesting profits.
6. Harry G. Johnson, *Economic policies towards less developed countries*, Allen & Unwin, London 1967, pages 45–47.
7. Jack Baranson, *Industrial technologies for developing countries*, Praeger, New York and London, 1969, page 26.
8. In certain circumstances, however, the foreign investor may be prepared to take a loss on a particular investment if that is beneficial to his world-wide operations. He may, for example, wish to deny a certain market to a competitor or secure a specific source of raw material.
9. Lester B. Pearson et al., *Partners in development*, Praeger, New York, 1969, pages 100–101.
10. See P. Streeten, 'New approaches to private overseas investment', in P.H. Ady

(ed.), *op. cit.*, pages 53–58; and of the same author, 'Obstacles to private foreign investment in the LDC's', *Columbia Journal of World Business*, May-June 1970.
11. Streeten, in *Col. Journal* (*loc. cit.*), page 33.
12. Charles P. Kindleberger, *American business abroad. Six lectures on direct investment*, Yale University Press, New Haven and London, 1969, page 169.
13. *Ibidem.*
14. *Ibidem.*
15. Cf. Delfim Neto, *loc. cit.*
16. Streeten, in *Col. Journal.*
17. Pearson, *op. cit.*, page 102.
18. Figures computed by the Development Assistance Committee and quoted in P.H. Ady (ed.), *op. cit.*, page 80.
19. *Ibidem.*
20. Pearson, *op. cit.*, page 102.
21. Kindleberger, *op. cit.*, pages 131–132.
22. P.H. Ady (ed.), *op. cit.*, page 27.
23. Jack Baranson, *op. cit.*, page 7.
24. Hirschman, *loc. cit.*
25. *Idem*, page 7.
26. Pearson, *op. cit.*, pages 103–104.
27. Kindleberger, *op. cit.*, page 150; see on this issue also Peter P. Gabriel, 'MNC's in the third world: is conflict unavoidable?', *Harvard Business Review*, July-August 1972.
28. Kindleberger, *op. cit.*, page 152.
29. Christopher Tugendhat, *The multinationals*, Eyre & Spottiswoode, London, 1971, page 30.
30. Tugendhat, *op. cit.*, page 131.
31. *Idem*, page 137.
32. Dr. A. Mozoomdar of the Indian High Commission (London) at a symposium organised by the U.K. Chapter of the Society for International Development in London in 1971, and published by P.H. Ady (*op. cit.*, page 43).
33. To be understood, of course, as defined by Johnson. In this connection it can be noted that P.T. Bauer, reviewing Johnson's book in the *Quarterly Journal of Economics* (August 1968) has suggested that 'modernisation' would be a better term which would avoid the confusion that the term 'industrialisation' may cause.
34. Although PFI may have some effect on governmental policies, its influence in this sphere will necessarily be limited and it can be disregarded for the purposes of this study.
35. Richard E. Caves, 'International corporations: the industrial economics of foreign investment', *Economica*, No. 149, February 1971.
36. For a lively confirmation of this view, see in particular: Bayless Manning, 'Private foreign investment; some dead horses and a live one', in Albert Winsemius and John A. Pincus (eds.), *Methods of industrial development*, OECD, Paris, 1962, pages 260–261.
37. As stated by Kuznets, 'The major capital stock of an industrially advanced nation is not its physical equipment: it is the body of knowledge amassed from and tested by findings and discoveries of empirical science, and the capacity and training to use this knowledge effectively.' Quoted by Ch. Kindleberger in *Economic Development*, McGraw-Hill/Kogakusha, Tokyo, 1958, page 57, from 'Toward a theory of economic growth', in R. Lekachman (ed.), *National policies for economic*

*welfare at home and abroad*, Doubleday and Co., New York, 1953.

38. United Nations, *Foreign investment in developing countries*, New York, 1968, page 30.
39. E.g., Streeten in P.H. Ady (ed.), *op. cit.*, page 62.
40. Peter P. Gabriel, *loc. cit.*
41. *Ibidem.*
42. It is therefore surprising to note that Streeten, who made such a case for a differentiation between the effects of 'any' investment and of PFI specifically, explicitly and without qualification mentions tax revenue and employment creation as advantages for PFI (cf. his article in *Col. Journal*).
43. Caves, *loc. cit.*, page 25.
44. Harry G. Johnson, 'The multinational corporation as a development agent', *Col. J. of World Business*, May/June 1970, page 27. See on this point also Caves, *loc. cit.*
45. These subsidies can take the form of tax allowances, depreciation allowances, tariffs, guaranteed monopoly positions, and the like. An overvalued exchange rate also contains an element of subsidy since it makes both import of equipment and supplies as well as the transfer of dividends cheap. Cf. Charles D. Hyson and Dale R. Weigel, 'Investment in the LDC's: the unresolved debate', *Columbia Journal of World Business*, January/February 1970.
46. Hyson and Weigel, *loc. cit.*
47. *Ibidem.*
48. Isaiah A. Litvak and Christopher J. Maule (eds.), *Foreign investment and international business arrangements: the experience of the host countries*, Praeger, New York, 1970, page 10.
49. Gabriel, *loc. cit.*
50. Hyson and Weigel, *loc. cit.*
51. One of the most important contributions in this field has been made by Yair Aharoni in his book *The foreign investment decision process*, Division of Research, Graduate School of Business Administration, Harvard University, Boston 1966.
52. Hyson and Weigel, *loc. cit.*
53. *Ibidem.*
54. Aharoni, *op. cit.*, pages 54–55.
55. Planungsgruppe Ritter, *Transfer von Technologie in Entwicklungsländer: Empirische Untersuchung zur Kooperation deutscher Industrieunternehmen in Entwicklungsländern*, Forschungsauftrag des Bundesministeriums für wirtschaftliche Zusammenarbeit, Königstein, 1972.
56. The contradiction with what was said earlier, i.e. that firms do not conform to the postulates of neo-classical theory because of limited knowledge and the inability to predict critical variables, is only apparent. In the first instance, these factors prevent a systematic and deliberate world-wide search for investment opportunities. Where a specific investment is concerned, however, the firm obviously seeks all available information to minimise uncertainty.
57. Aharoni, *op. cit.*, page 93.
58. Political and economic stability has always been a major criterion for foreign investors. This is particularly evident when the results of various studies over the post-war period are compared. In 1950, ECAFE found that political stability was the most important element of a 'favourable climate' (quoted in Benjamin Higgins, *Economic development: principles, problems and practices*, Constable and Co.. London, 1959, page 572). Ten years later, the World Bank and the International

Chamber of Commerce, in a joint enquiry, reported that out of 400 industrial firms in 21 developed countries about 61% thought that 'political uncertainty' was the main impediment to the flow of capital to the developing countries, while a further 30% considered it one of the principal obstacles (William Clarke, *Private enterprise in developing countries*, Pergamon Press, Oxford, 1966, pages 34–35). The Pearson Commission listed 'high intrinsic risks' as the first of a series of fundamental reasons why direct foreign investment 'has long been the least dynamic element in the flow of private capital to the developing countries' (Pearson, *op. cit.*, page 99). And finally: the Ritter Report concluded that German investors favoured developing countries 'die eine hohe politische Stabilität aufweisen' and 'deren soziale und finanzielle Verhältnisse verhältnismässig geordnet sind' (Planungsgruppe Ritter, *op. cit.*, page 107).

59. Or, what Aharoni calls 'the creation of a good image' (Aharoni, *op. cit.*, page 223).
60. See on this point, *inter alia:* OECD, *Investing in developing countries*, Paris, 1970, Chapter 1; U.N., *op. cit.*, pages 23–29.
61. In this context mention should be made of another scheme sponsored by the World Bank: the International Centre for Settlement of Investment Disputes. Here too, development has been slow. While the first proposal for an international arbitration machinery was formally made in 1960, it was only in October 1966 that ICSID was established, and it had to wait six more years before the first request for arbitration proceedings was received.
62. Pearson, *op. cit.*, page 108; Aharoni came to the same conclusion (Aharoni, *op. cit.*, pages 234–235).
63. OECD, *op. cit.*, page 17.
64. For more detailed treatment of the effects of taxation, both in developed and developing countries, on private foreign investment see the papers by J.B. Bracewell-Milnes ('Overseas development and British taxation'), A. Mozoomdar ('Overseas investment and Indian taxation') and F. Rampersa ('Overseas investment and fiscal policy in Puerto Rico, Jamaica, and Trinidad and Tobago') in P.H. Ady (ed.), *op. cit.*
65. Planungsgruppe Ritter, *op. cit.*, page 43.
66. OECD, *op. cit.*, page 19.
67. For a detailed analysis of the policies and operations of these institutions, see J.Th. Adolfse, *De Westeuropese Nationale Investeringsbanken voor buitenlandse ontwikkelingsfinanciering*, Stenfert Kroese, Leyden, 1970.
68. Wolfgang G. Friedmann and George Kalmanoff, *Joint international business ventures*, Columbia University Press, New York and London, 1961.
69. Friedmann and Kalmanoff, *op. cit.*, page 6.
70. James W.C. Tomlinson, *The joint venture process in international business: India and Pakistan*, The MIT Press, Cambridge (Mass.) and London, 1970.
71. H.W. van Hilten, *Joint ventures, enkele facetten van de joint business venture*, Kluwer, Deventer, 1968.
72. Van Hilten, *op. cit.*, page 58 (translation supplied).
73. Friedmann and Kalmanoff, *op. cit.*, page 6.
74. H. Willems, *Bedrijfseconomische aspecten van de internationale joint business venture in de ontwikkelingslanden*, Wolters, Groningen, 1963, page 4 (translation supplied). Of course, equity (in the Western sense) does not exist in Yugoslavia, but – as will be explained in the next chapter – 'the risk-capital' put up by the partners to the joint venture between a Yugoslav and foreign enterprise has certain equity features.

75. Van Hilten, *op. cit.*, page 57.
76. It may be noted here that in the Yugoslav case, contributions in know-how by the foreign partner are actively sought (cf. Chapter 4).
77. See, *inter alia*, Van Hilten, *op. cit.*, page XVI.
78. This is far from an issue peculiar to LDC's alone. In such highly developed countries as Canada, Australia and France strong objections against foreign economic imperialism are a popular topic of discussions in parliament and press.
79. Notably Kindleberger, see his *American business abroad (op. cit.)*, pages 163–178.
80. Litvak and Maule, *op. cit.*, page 14.
81. Tomlinson has suggested that there may be a trend in the investment climate in LDC's leading to a relaxation of restrictions. This trend passes through four main stages: unilateral antagonism, mutual suspicion, joint acceptance, and sophisticated integration (Tomlinson, *op. cit.*).
82. Harald B. Malmgren, *Trade for development*, Overseas Development Council, Monograph No. 4, Washington (D.C.), 1971, page 41.
83. It should be added, though, that there is another side to this coin. Quite often the foreign partner imposes restrictions on exports by the joint venture to protect his own market position in certain countries.
84. Van Hilten, *op. cit.*, page 105.
85. See Tomlinson, *op. cit.*, for an exhaustive analysis of this issue.
86. Friedmann and Kalmanoff, *op. cit.*, page 5.
87. A good account of these various problem areas, based on empirical evidence, is given in Karen K. Bivens and Enid B. Lovell, *Joint ventures with foreign partners. An international survey of business opinion and experience*, National Industrial Conference Board, New York, 1966, pages 47–72. See also Friedmann and Kalmanoff, *op. cit.*, Chapters V ('Attitudes and motivations') and VI ('Internal operations of joint ventures').
88. Bivens and Lovell, *op. cit.*, page 1. As will be seen later (Chapter 5), the results achieved by joint ventures in Yugoslavia are encouraging and the experience so far shows that the above quotation applies to the Yugoslav situation as well.
89. Streeten, in *Col. Journal (loc. cit.)*.

# 4. Joint ventures between Yugoslav and foreign enterprises: institutional aspects

## 4.1. INTRODUCTION

At the time the basic principles of the Economic Reform of 1965 were taking shape – a time when many far-reaching and radical changes were discussed, modified, discarded or ultimately adopted – the possibility of allowing private foreign direct investment in Yugoslavia was for the first time seriously put forward. That this suggestion initially raised strong protests, and not only from the side of Marxist dogmatists, is easily understandable. For about 20 years the Yugoslavs had been consciously building a society different from both the capitalist and the Soviet model. The foundations of this system rested to a large extent on the structure of the Yugoslav enterprise. Would not the introduction of foreign direct investment (by which, of course, mainly Western investment was meant) jeopardise the still shaky Yugoslav model? Would it be possible to continue to develop self-management in those enterprises in which foreigners would take an interest? The debate on these questions raged for some considerable time until after the Economic Reform had already been put into effect. Even when the legislation concerned was about to be presented in Parliament (1967), the discussion had not yet lost any of its fervour. In the words of Sukijasovic:

> 'The new investment policy and legislation provoked spirited reactions both inside and outside the country. The principles concerning the socio-economic aspects of joint investment between domestic and foreign enterprises, and of production-financial cooperation between the Yugoslav and foreign economies, which preceded the enactment of the investment legislation, and the preliminary draft laws, were the subject of broad public discussion. Non-governmental institutions and organisations were largely in favour of the adoption of the new laws, although divergent opinions were expressed on particular issues such as the form of business organisation.'[1]

Apart from the socio-philosophical aspects there were other factors as well that caused some reluctance to admit the principle of direct foreign investment. Before World War II, i.e. before the establishment of socialism, what little industry there was in Yugoslavia had been owned mainly by Western European interests, and the same was the case for services and public utilities. The effects of foreign ownership had been far from beneficial to the country.

'Before World War II foreign private capital had invested 4.2 billion dinars (in 1938 $1 = 54 dinars) in Yugoslav manufacturing, mining, banking, trade, transportation and insurance and foreign capital controlled more than one half of the economy excluding agriculture. For example, foreign capital had a 65 percent interest in mining and a 50 percent interest in manufacturing. However, despite this large foreign investment, by the end of the 1930s Yugoslavia's comparative state of economic development vis-à-vis Western Europe had decreased. Her low rate of economic growth can be traced to an infrequency of profit reinvestment, a bilking of fiscal authorities, and a high incidence of bribery.'[2]

Immediately after the war the Yugoslavs had a similar, unsatisfactory experience – this time with their Marxist comrades from the Soviet Union. The USSR had set up in Eastern Europe what were called Joint Stock Companies (JSC). 'The JSC were to promote the economic development of the country and were to serve as gateways through which the Russians would channel capital goods and technical assistance.'[3] In return, the Soviets would receive 50% of the JSC's profits. The Yugoslav experience with these JSC's – fortunately there had been only two – was simply disastrous. The agreements establishing the JSC's had been so loaded in favour of the Russians that the Yugoslavs, even at the time they were still believing in Soviet communism, got rid of them as fast as they could.[4]

In addition, there was the political aspect. The Yugoslavs were well aware that foreign direct investment would be mainly of capitalist origin, and this might have some consequences for the delicately balanced position Yugoslavia had been able to build between the two political blocks.

However, in spite of past experience and the potential difficulties involved, the Yugoslavs decided to press ahead. The main reason was unquestionably the awareness that it would be difficult to realise the principal aims of the Economic Reform without the introduction of modern technology and, perhaps more importantly, modern management methods. The purpose of the Economic Reform, it may be recalled here, was to achieve a 'more rational process of resource allocation – by means of greater deconcentration of economic decisions, of an enhanced role of market forces and the price mechanism, and of an increased integration into world markets.'[5] As was pointed out in the last section of Chapter 2, the basic Yugoslav problems were, and still are, a lack of efficiency in most enterprises, and a lack of modern technology.

'It was felt that foreign private investment might play a useful role in all this. It could bring not only capital for domestic investment as such, but in particular foreign exchange, equipment which is not available in Yugoslavia, fresh technology and improved production processes, new managerial skills and administrative techniques, and knowledge of foreign markets which leads to new outlets and increased exports.'[6]

Of course, even long before the first drafts of the Economic Reform measures with their far-reaching implications were drawn up, did the Yugoslavs try to acquire modern technology. Apart from the normal commercial relationships with foreign firms, there were basically two types of agreements that Yugoslav enterprises had been allowed to enter into. These agreements fall broadly into two categories, in Yugoslav terminology they are labelled:[7]

- Long-term specialisation and cooperation in production.
- Purchase of industrial-property rights.

The first category includes contracts that provide for production and mutual deliveries of parts, assemblies, sub-assemblies and semi-manufactures to be built into a final product; production and mutual deliveries of finished products for the purpose of production specialisation and supplementing the partners' range of products. The value of these mutual deliveries must every year be levelled off for which purpose special accounts are kept with the National Bank.[8] The second category, of course, concerns the purchase of licences, drawings, patents etc.

Whereas the first type of contract by its very nature is not particularly geared to acquisition of modern technology – although the foreign partner quite often does provide technical and other assistance – the purchase of a licence by definition is. It is therefore remarkable to note the virtually unanimous disappointment of Yugoslav writers, academics as well as practical businessmen, with the results of Yugoslavia's extensive buying of foreign licences. As a Yugoslav banker said in an interview with *The Economist*: 'We bought over 1,200 licences before 1967 and found the results disappointing. Our business partners in the West were glad to sell us their licences or help us in some other limited way but had no further interest in the final result.'[9] Similar views were held by those responsible for the country's economic policies. Glickman and Sukijasovic, quoting from an interview given by Edward Kardelj[10] (at the time President of the Federal Assembly) state that 'after seventeen years of experience ... the Yugoslav authorities realised that foreign licensors and business consultants would probably not retain unflagging interest, and thus would not maximise the assistance rendered, without having a substantial investment in the country.'[11] What the Yugoslavs were looking for was not only the purchase of modern technology but the active and continuing participation of technologically advanced foreign enterprises in Yugoslavia's development efforts. This, of course, meant direct investment. Without direct investment the foreign participation would be virtually risk-less and it is precisely the element of risk that guarantees an 'unflagging interest'.

The decision to allow, or rather positively to encourage, foreign private direct investment was obviously a drastic one for a socialist country. And one is struck again by the Yugoslav willingness to experiment, by the pragmatic approach and the open-mindedness. The Yugoslavs were even realistic enough to admit from the beginning that their country's economic development would not be the prime mover for the foreign enterprise: 'The motives of foreigners are their own business. It is up to them to calculate whether they should introduce their capital into Yugoslavia.'[12] No one in Yugoslavia ever doubted that a foreign enterprise would only invest if it saw a possibility for a satisfactory profit. But no matter how pragmatic, there was of course one basic principle that the Yugoslavs were not willing to sacrifice: self-management. Complete foreign ownership and control of a Yugoslav enterprise were therefore out of the question. The only way to combine the principle of self-management with foreign direct private investment was the contractual joint venture, by which resources and risks are shared between the partners.[13]

It is interesting to note at this point that, however important the Yugoslavs considered the possibility of joint ventures with foreign enterprises, the legislation of 1967 first mentioned joint ventures between Yugoslav enterprises. As explained by Radonovic: 'domestic enterprises and their associations are the principal factors responsible for business and financial cooperation based on joint investment ventures regardless of whether these involve domestic enterprises alone, or domestic and foreign firms,'[14] and, 'in the development and elaboration of the socio-economic system to date, especially in the course of the Reform, the need has been particularly acutely felt, *firstly*, to strengthen cooperation and direct integration of domestic enterprises ... and, *secondly*, for the integration of the Yugoslav economy into the world economy and division of labour – through the development of lasting forms of cooperation between domestic and foreign firms in production and finance.'[15]

The emphasis on integration of domestic enterprises may surprise in view of what was said in Chapter 2 with respect to the size of Yugoslav enterprises. The main purpose of the legislation in so far as it related to domestic enterprises was, however, not to create ever bigger industrial giants but rather to encourage a more rational industrial structure through specialisation and the elimination of a waste of resources by creating similar industries in all Republics.

## 4.2. LEGISLATION, RULES AND REGULATIONS

### 4.2.1. *The first laws – basic issues*

It took almost two years since the adoption of the Economic Reform before the discussion on whether to allow private foreign investment had run its course. In March 1967 a policy paper[16] was presented to the Federal Assembly, outlining the basic principles which were to serve as guidelines for the legislation to follow, and in July the legislative proposals were submitted to parliament. The Yugoslavs were clearly aware that the step they were about to take was a momentous one for a socialist country – as demonstrated by the fact that legislative action was preceded by a formal presentation of a policy document to parliament. But they also felt it was a necessary step to take. As Aleksander Grlickov, a member of the Federal Executive Council, stated in the Assembly: 'The degree of development which we have attained demands that we resolutely discard all those methods in economic policy, in the economic system, which have handicapped our development...the initiation of new processes in our socio-economic development, economic policy and economic system represents an essential prerequisite for the successful realisation both of the social and economic aims of the reform and of the processes which will lead to a more rapid reconstruction of our economy and a quicker assertion of new qualities of a modern economy.'[17]

The specific characteristics of the Yugoslav socio-economic system obviously imposed certain restrictions – there could be no question of jeopardising the achievements and the further development of self-management. Private foreign investment would have to take a form that would fit the system. This meant, first and foremost, that fully-owned and controlled subsidiaries of foreign corporations were ruled out. As a matter of fact, only a minority interest is allowed to safeguard Yugoslav control. Moreover, inasmuch as joint-stock companies do not exist in Yugoslavia, the only feasible form of private foreign investment had to be the contractual non-equity joint venture. In the definition of Sukijasovic and Glickman: 'Contractual refers to the co-adventurers' general ability to order their rights and obligations between themselves and toward third parties by means of a negotiated contract. Non-equity alludes to the legal rule that permits either party's rights and obligations to be sold to strangers, who would then replace the seller in the venture, but does not permit the sales transaction to be effected through the transfer of alienable stock certificates.'[18]

There are further restrictions as well, and these derive from the specific rôle which private foreign investment is to play in Yugoslav economic development. It was, of course, hardly to be expected that a socialist country such as Yugoslavia would be prepared to admit capitalist investors just to increase the inflow of financial resources. In fact, the Yugoslav legislation is quite specific on this point. Joint ventures are allowed[19] only if the agreement provides for:

- cooperation aimed at increasing production, productivity and exports;
- introduction and application in a domestic economic organisation of modern techniques, technology and organisation of production and operations;
- contribution to the advancement of scientific research in a domestic economic organisation.

Finally, foreign investment is prohibited in banking, insurance, internal transport, trade, public utilities, and social services (except scientific research).[20]

As mentioned above, the contractual non-equity joint venture is the only form in which private foreign investment is allowed. And while the legislation, as will be seen later, leaves much to be decided by the partners alone, all Yugoslav writers emphasise that the joint venture contract should provide for long-term investment of foreign capital, the pursuance of joint business objectives, and the sharing of risks and profits.[21] This may seem superfluous as a joint venture, by its very nature, implies these features, but the emphasis is understandable in view of the novelty that this form of cooperation represented for the Yugoslavs and their concern about a real, and not token, involvement of the foreign partner.

The legislative action to implement these principles consisted in amending five existing laws rather than in adopting one single comprehensive law dealing with foreign investment.[22] The laws in question are:

- Basic Law on Enterprises
- Law on Assets of Economic Organisations
- Basic Law on Unified Chambers of Economy and Business Cooperation in the Economy
- Law on Institution of Interest Payments on Funds in the Economy
- Basic Law on Contributions and Taxes of Citizens.

For good measure, a small new law was added: the 'Law on Profits Tax of Foreign Persons investing in a Domestic Economic Organisation for the Purpose of Joint Operations'. At first sight, this proliferation of amendments may be confusing; as said in an often quoted OECD statement, 'the legal picture is frankly bewildering and it is not always easy to determine the scope and meaning of the many rules with any degree of precision.'[23] However, the comment is somewhat beside the point. In the first place, Yugoslav legislation in general is unfortunately often difficult to follow and sometimes inconsistent. This is mainly due to the fact that the Yugoslavs had to change their laws quite frequently in line with the change in their socio-economic system and in the process were not always careful to redraft existing laws to be in conformity with the new ones. Secondly, it has been suggested that 'the authorisation for foreign investment was put in this form, rather than in a separate law solely dealing with the subject, so as to demonstrate symbolically that foreigners would not be singled out but would be treated the same as Yugoslavs.'[24] The most plausible explanation, however, is perhaps that the legislation was also intended to facilitate joint ventures between domestic enterprises and that for such purpose the most logical procedure was to make amendments to existing laws. Special provisions applying only to joint ventures with foreign corporations could then simply be added, where required.

But whatever the reasons might have been for the Yugoslavs to choose one legislative method over another, the most important part of the enabling legislation affecting foreigners is found in only nine sections of Article 64 of the Law on Assets of Economic Organisations so in fact, the situation was considerably less bewildering than some observers felt obliged to judge. Moreover, a foreign investor – in any country – will always have to operate within the legal framework of that country, a framework that is inevitably much wider-ranging than what is provided for in a special law dealing with foreign investment. So even now that such special law exists in Yugoslavia – since April 1973 – a foreign investor will be well advised to be informed on what other laws and regulations might affect his operations. A good case in point concerns the Foreign Exchange regime which will be dealt with later in this section.

Rather than an article-by-article analysis of the laws mentioned above, it would seem preferable to proceed by highlighting the main legal issues related to foreign investment as they emerged from the initial legislation. The subsequent changes and modifications will then be discussed separately later on.

The first observation to make, however, is that 'the lawmaker has regulated but the most essential questions, by means of mandatory provisions, leaving enough room to the parties freely to create and shape this form of business cooperation.'[25] What is remarkable, in fact, is not so much what is regulated by law but rather what is left to the partners of the joint venture. The joint venture contract is therefore of particular importance in the Yugoslav situation, and a special section will be devoted to it.

The law also leaves freedom as to the type of joint venture to be established, i.e. the foreign investor and his Yugoslav partner are at liberty to decide whether to set up a new enterprise, whether the joint venture will include the entire existing Yugoslav enterprise, or whether the joint venture will be limited to particular product lines. At the time the initial legislative action was taken (1967), the choice with respect to the latter alternative was further subdivided: the joint venture could be made in a department with or without legal personality. This was of some importance since in the first case the joint venture 'keeps its own books, incurs obligations which can only be satisfied from its own assets, is only responsible for the debt of its Yugoslav parent if a contract between the parent and subsidiary so provides, can contract, sue and be sued, and has its own institutions of self-management.'[26] In theory, a department without legal personality lacks these features but the joint venture contract could expressly provide for them. This happened in most cases, so that for practical purposes the distinction was hardly relevant except for the fact that a department without legal personality did not have its own self-management organs. In any case, since the Constitutional Amendments of 1971, the distinction is no longer even theoretically relevant because all basic departments (OOUR's) of the Yugoslav enterprise have legal personality.

Returning now to the main issues explicitly regulated by the first law, the following are of particular interest. As stated earlier, the foreign partner is only allowed a minority interest. Article 64 i of the Law on Assets of Economic Organisations states that 'the value of the total means invested by foreign contracting parties in the same domestic economic organisation on the basis of a partnership agreement may not exceed the total amount of means invested by domestic economic organisations nor may it equal the total amount of the latter means.'[27] Exceptionally, by a special act of the Federal Assembly a foreign majority participation may be allowed if this is judged to be in the Yugoslav interest. So far, however, such exception has never been granted and it can be safely predicted that it will be given only very rarely. One further comment should be made regarding this Article. The expression 'the value of the total means invested by foreign contracting parties' could give rise to the misunderstanding that 'total means' might include any credits granted to the joint venture by the foreign investor. This is, however, not the case. Only the participations of both sides in the risk-bearing capital of the joint venture are referred to in the Article. The question arises then, of course, what constitutes risk-bearing capital in a non-equity joint venture; the discussion of this issue, however, will be postponed for the moment and left for the section dealing with the joint venture contract.

A second point concerns the nature of the investment (of both partners). Not only cash investments are allowed but also participations in the form of patents, licences, know-how, buildings, land, equipment etc. The only restriction imposed by the law is that the share of the foreign partner[28] in 'non-financial forms' should have been realistically valued. If it is not, registration of the joint venture contract will be denied. It is clear that it is precisely contributions in the form of licences, patents and know-how that are most eagerly sought by the Yugoslavs. Investments in cash only are certainly not encouraged and Glickman and Sukijasovic are undoubtedly right in commenting that 'an investment of cash or (fixed) assets unaccompanied by a corresponding investment of know-how would probably not be acceptable.'[29]

A few Yugoslav commentators attach much importance to the fact that the law allows the foreign investor, specifically by contract, to retain his ownership title to any tangible assets he contributes to the joint venture. 'If he does, he retains the right to veto any sale of such assets by the joint venture, receives any profit on their sale, must repay the venture for any loss suffered on their disposal, and can demand their return when the joint venture dissolves.' (And he must be) 'paid for his assets over a statutorily prescribed period from an amortisation fund of the joint venture.'[30] Apart from the fact that this is, within the Yugoslav context, legally a somewhat confusing construction, it is hard to see what specific advantage such amortisation of this capital would give to the foreign investor, or the Yugoslav partner for that matter. If it was the intention of the lawmaker that joint ventures should be long-run undertakings then it does not make much sense to provide the foreign investor with a possibility to write down his share prematurely. As for the foreign partner's advantages, he cannot be interested to decrease his share starting right at the outset of the joint venture when full profitability has not been reached.

The issue which, of course, was – and still is – of the highest importance to the foreign investor concerns the possibilities for the transfer of his profits and the repatriation of his capital. On both points the law, in principle, is clear: the foreign investor is entitled to transfer his profits (after tax) and to repatriate his capital. There is, however, a catch – both transactions are subject to the provisions of the federal foreign exchange laws and regulations. And, as could be expected, this foreign exchange regime is not as liberal as foreign investors might wish. This subject is important enough to devote a special section to it, suffice it here to say that transfer of profits and repatriation of capital can only be effected out of foreign exchange resources at the free disposition of the joint venture, that is to say that the joint venture itself has to generate the necessary foreign exchange through its exports. Out of its exports it may keep, however, only a certain portion: the so-called retention quota. At the time of the initial legislation this quota, amounting to 7% of export earnings, was the only fund available for profit transfer.

As far as his capital participation is concerned the foreign investor is entitled to sell his interest in a joint venture to a third party. He can do so 'upon any terms he wishes so long as he first offers it, on the same terms, to his Yugoslav partner.'[31] The law specifies that the Yugoslav partner has sixty days within which to respond but it can be assumed that this period can be extended through a special provision in the contract. The foreign investor is free to sell his participation to any other party if no response has been forthcoming within the specified period.

A particularly objectionable provision of the original legislation, as far as the foreign investor was concerned, was the obligation that the foreign contracting party shall be bound to reinvest 20 percent of the means obtained by him by virtue of his share of profits deriving from joint operations, less tax, in the domestic economic organisations in which he has invested means or in another domestic work organisation or to place them on deposit in a bank in Yugoslavia (Article 64o of the Law on Assets of Economic Organisations). Fortunately, this reinvestment requirement subsequently has been abolished, since it acted as a real impediment to an increase in the number of joint ventures which Yugoslavia was trying to achieve. It was moreover not entirely logical, reinvestment in the joint venture itself would imply a proportionate increase in the foreign-held share, unless the Yugoslav partner would reinvest a corresponding amount. In fact, the latter would, for all practical purposes be forced to do so, which might be contrary to its wishes and therefore against the principles of self-management. Investment in another enterprise would necessitate the conclusion of a new joint venture, in which the foreign investor would in all likelihood not be very interested as this might either create a competitor for the first joint venture or involve investment in another line of business to which the foreign investor would have little to contribute by way of technology or know-how. Depositing the 20% in a Yugoslav bank, finally, amounted to a form of blocking of non-resident owned assets,[32] a procedure hardly advisable for a country that wishes to attract foreign capital.

The law did not specify the minimum length of time for which a joint venture would have to be concluded, it only states that it should be 'long-term' and that the period may not be less than the time necessary for the realisation of the objectives of business cooperation. This is rather vague, but a minimum term of five years seems to have generally gained acceptance.

The question of liability has been touched upon briefly before, but it may be useful to look at this matter in more detail, especially since in the words of Dr. Nikola Balog, Yugoslavia's most prominent legal expert in this field, 'the possibility of limited liability now appears for the first time in the Yugoslav legal system.'[33] The Yugoslav law does not normally recognise limited liability companies or enterprises[34] but an exception was made for joint ventures. Article 64c of the Law on Assets of Economic Organisations states: 'Where on the basis of a partnership agreement means have been invested in a separate unit with autonomous accounts, the economic organisation in which means have been invested (i.e. the Yugoslav parent enterprise) shall be liable for obligations by virtue of joint operations *up to the value of the assets of such unit*, unless the contract provides that the economic organisation shall be liable for the obligations even beyond the said value.' Conversely, the joint venture is not liable for obligations incurred by the Yugoslav parent enterprise.[35] As far as the foreign investor is concerned his risk is therefore limited to the amount of his capital participation, a position similar to that in the case of a 'capitalist' subsidiary.

As could be expected, the profits of the foreign investor are subject to tax. The rate was set at 35%, but a lower rate is applicable when a certain portion of the taxable profit is reinvested. The reduction amounts to 15% if at least 25% of the profit is retained, to 30% over the portion between 25 and 50%, and to 50% over the part reinvested over and above 50% of the profit.

A final matter dealt with in detail by the law concerns the validity and registration of the joint venture contract. In order to be valid and enforceable the contract has to be in the form of a written agreement, it has to be ratified by the Workers' Council of the Yugoslav party to the joint venture and it has to be entered in a special register kept at the Federal Secretariat of Economy (now called: The Committee for Energy and Industry). Registration is subject to the fulfilment of a number of conditions which are explicitly laid down in Article 64 k of the Law on

Assets of Economic Organisations. Apart from the obvious conditions, such as that the contract has to conform with Yugoslav laws and that the provisions of the contract should not be contrary to the interests of the country's security or defence, the Article states that registration will be denied:

- if a partnership agreement does not provide for business cooperation aimed at increasing production, productivity and exports, the introduction and application in a domestic economic organisation of modern techniques, technology and organisation of production and operation or if it does not contribute to the advancement of scientific research in a domestic economic organisation;
- if the conditions of business cooperation provided for by a partnership do not correspond to the customary economic conditions under which such cooperation is carried on in international economic relations;
- if the share of a foreign partner in non-financial forms (patents, licences, technology etc.) has been unrealistically evaluated.

The Yugoslav authorities are fairly strict on these three issues and cases are known where registration was denied because one of the conditions was not fulfilled, in particular the first one quoted above which, in effect, makes it very clear that the Yugoslavs will allow only those joint ventures that can be expected to contribute to the country's economic development.

### 4.2.2. *Subsequent changes*

Yugoslav pragmatism and flexibility have already often been evoked in this study so it should come as no surprise that the Yugoslavs have, since 1967, made numerous changes in the laws and regulations concerning private foreign investment. Part of these changes had become necessary by the adoption of the constitutional amendments in 1971 and were therefore conditioned – but the majority of the later modifications were the result of a conscious effort to adapt the rules to the practical requirements of an evolving situation, without, however, endangering the achievements of the self-management system. And while the legislation still contains a few objectionable features (mainly concerning the foreign exchange regime), it is significant to note that virtually all changes were deliberately aimed at further liberalisation. The issue, for the Yugoslavs, was basically a simple one: the existing legal framework apparently did not provide enough incentives to attract foreign investors to the extent hoped for, so it became then a question of liberalising this framework so far that the desired results were obtainable. Inasmuch as the Yugoslavs are still disappointed by the number of joint ventures realised, it can therefore be expected that further changes will be made in the future.

Before outlining the main features of this liberalisation process, some attention should be devoted to the modifications in the legislation that were called for by the constitutional amendments of 1971. It will be remembered (cf. Chapter 3) that the basic novelty of these amendments – which were subsequently incorporated in the 'Law on Assets of Economic Organisations' – consisted in the institution of 'Basic Organisations of Associated Labour' (OOUR's), and the various entities formed by OOUR's. Whereas previously foreign investment could be made into the Yugoslav enterprise as a whole or a unit of it (with or without legal personality), the position now is that the domestic partner to the joint venture contract can be one of the following entities:[36]

- a Basic Organisation of Associated Labour (OOUR);
- an association of OOUR's (which normally constitute a part of an enterprise);
- a 'Working Organisation' (i.e. an enterprise as a whole);
- a 'United Organisation of Associated Labour' (i.e. an association of several enterprises).

Amendment XXII specifically grants the right to conclude a joint venture contract to the OOUR, as it is the basic element of the self-management system. The right to enter into a joint venture agreement by any of the other three entities mentioned above is derived from the right of the OOUR's which together make up the entity, i.e. the OOUR's have delegated, by virtue of the association agreement, their right to the composite entity.

As before, 'foreigners may invest capital in an existing organisation (simple or composite); in an existing or newly-founded unit of an organisation...; or in a new organisation.'[37] In other words, the law leaves freedom as to whether the vehicle of the joint venture agreement is to be an existing entity or one specifically formed for the purpose.

More important, however, than the 'institutional' changes described above – which were triggered by the constitutional amendments (now embodied in the new Constitution) – are the modifications resulting from the growing awareness that more liberal regulations were required if private foreign investment was to have the desired impact on Yugoslav economic development. To illustrate this liberalisation process, the modifications will be dealt with chronologically, so as to bring out the evolution of Yugoslav thinking on the subject. The first of these modifications occurred in December 1969 and affected the possibility of the foreign investor to make remittances abroad. At the time of the initial legislation, the joint venture had only the so-called retention quota at its disposal for profit transfers of the foreign partner. Since this quota amounted to a mere 7% of export earnings, foreign exchange resources available were clearly too limited. Only few joint ventures would be able to generate the very high volume of exports required. It became obvious to the Yugoslav authorities that something had to be done. The solution adopted consisted in amending the law on Foreign Exchange Transactions[38] to the effect that, in addition to the retention quota, the joint venture could dispose of the foreign exchange equivalent to a further 33⅓% of its export earnings for profit transfers of the foreign partner. It should be noted that at this time the foreign exchange funds available for repatriation of capital remained limited to the regular retention quota.

In July 1971 the Federal Assembly adopted a series of amendments of the 'Law on Assets of Economic Organisations' and the 'Law on Foreign Exchange Transactions' which constituted a drastic overhauling of the legislation concerning foreign investment.

First and foremost the obligation of the foreign partner to reinvest 20% of his profit after tax or to deposit this 20% with a Yugoslav bank was abolished.

Secondly, the right of the foreign partner to repatriate his capital was now more clearly defined. Previously, it was only permitted to withdraw from the joint venture if 'the aims of the business cooperation' had been fulfilled (whatever that may have meant) or if the period for which the joint venture agreement had been concluded had ended. The new legislation added two further possibilities.[39]

- if during two consecutive years the joint operations are carried out at a loss or if business results fall considerably short of the results which had been anticipated;
- if one of the parties does not meet its obligations under the agreement.

In addition, the provisions with respect to the foreign exchange available for repatriation of capital were significantly liberalised. As mentioned above, earlier only the retention quota could be used for this purpose. The new regulations added two further sources:

- one third of the foreign currency generated by the joint venture's exports (previously, it will be remembered, this was available only for profit transfer); moreover any part of this 33⅓% not used in any one year can be retained and used later;
- 10% of the annual depreciation charges.

The effect of the new measures was that the joint venture was now allowed to retain more than half of its export earnings for the purpose of capital repatriation.

Thirdly, foreign investors were given an explicit guarantee that changes in the laws governing their investment, occurring after the date the joint venture had been registered, could not lead to a deterioration of their position. Of course, changes in taxes were excluded from this provision. The article in question[40] is important enough to be quoted in full:

'Should after the registration of the agreement on investment of the funds of a foreign person in a domestic economic organisation there be a change in the law governing such an investment, the provisions of the agreement and the law ruling on the day of the registration of the agreement shall be applied to the relationships under this agreement, provided it is more favourable for the contracting parties, or if they do not stipulate specific matters otherwise in accordance with the provisions of the law which has been changed. The provision of paragraph 1 of this Article does not apply to the disbursements of commitments towards the social community.'[41]

Not all amendments to the legislation, however, were of a more liberal nature. In the first place, a floor was now established below which the investment by a foreign party would not be allowed. But the amount was set so low (1.5 million dinars or about U.S. $100,000) as to be practically meaningless. A more important objection to be made against this provision, however, concerns the fact that an amount in absolute terms makes little sense. The foreign participation should rather be related to the size of the overall investment. A provision in this sense would also tie in very well with the second addition of a restrictive character, i.e. that the joint venture will not be registered 'if the total amount of funds under the agreement invested by the contracting parties in a joint venture does not ensure the fulfilment of conditions under point 2 of this paragraph.'[42, 43]

In 1971, the power to tax the profit of the foreign partner passed from the Federation to the Republics. Whereas in the more developed Republics of Serbia, Croatia and Slovenia, the basic tax rate remained at 35%, taxes were considerably reduced in the other Republics. In all cases, reinvestment of profits leads to further reductions.

By lowering their tax rates, compared to those applicable in the comparatively more advanced Republics, the three less developed Republics hope, of course, to increase their relative share of the total of joint ventures. Whether this will be sufficient remains to be seen as tax incentives are normally not enough to attract foreign investment.

While it may have been – as argued above – that the legal situation with respect to joint ventures was not as confused as it may have appeared

*Table 4.1. Tax rates applicable to profits of foreign partner in joint ventures (%)*

| | *Macedonia* | *Montenegro* | *Bosnia & Hercegovina* | *Serbia Croatia Slovenia* |
|---|---|---|---|---|
| Rate payable on paid-out profit | 14 | 14 | 20 | 35 |
| Rate payable on part of the profit reinvested: | | | | |
| up to 25% | 11.2 | 11.9 | 17 | 29.75 |
| 25–50% | 8.4 | 9.8 | 14 | 24.50 |
| above 50% | 5.6 | 7.0 | 10 | 17.50 |

Source: *The International Investment Corporation for Yugoslavia Bulletin*, June 1973.

at first sight to foreign observers, the Yugoslavs nevertheless wisely decided to consolidate the various provisions in a single law: 'Law on Investment of Resources by Foreign Persons in Domestic Organisations of Associated Labour,'[44] which was promulgated in April 1973. In substance, the new law did not contain major changes that would affect the rights and obligations of the foreign partner. Two new points are, however, worth noting.

In the first place, the law stipulates that the workers of the joint venture unit cannot be excluded from the profit sharing – even in the case of a new plant when the initial domestic capital was provided by others. The purpose of this clause is to prevent a situation where the Yugoslav parent enterprise and the foreign partner would exclusively share the profits after paying the workers of the joint venture only their wage. How this provision is to be applied in practice is, as yet, unclear. It is, however, certain that it does not concern the foreign partner who will always retain his share of the profit in accordance with the provisions of the joint venture agreement. The split of the Yugoslav part of the profit amongst the parent enterprise and the joint venture workers will be the subject of an internal agreement between the two.

Secondly, the law reformulated the entire issue of liability to third parties to be in conformity with the constitutional amendments of 1971. The law now makes a clear distinction depending on whether the joint venture takes the form of an OOUR, or an entire enterprise. It is probably correct to assume that the first case comprises the ZOOUR (i.e., a combination of OOUR's within the same enterprise) as well.

If the joint venture includes the entire Yugoslav enterprise (whether this concerns an existing or a newly established one is irrelevant) 'all basic organisations of associated labour, as units thereof, are jointly and severally responsible for the liabilities of the joint venture unless otherwise provided for by the self-management agreement of association.'[45] In other words, it is up to the Yugoslav side to determine whether liability will be restricted to the OOUR's forming part of the joint venture or whether all OOUR's of the enterprise are to be held liable for obligations of the venture. If it is to the former, then this has to be expressly provided for by the (internal) self-management agreement of association. The foreign partner's position is not affected either way.

In the second case, i.e. if the joint venture comprises only a part of an enterprise, i.e. a basic organisation of associated labour,[46] 'this basic organisation is responsible for the liabilities of the joint venture up to the amount of all available assets (basic organisation with limited liability), unless the investment contract provides and the other basic organisations which form part of the same work organisation approve that these basic organisations are also responsible to the extent exceeding the amount of the assets of the basic organisation in which joint venture resources were invested.'[47] Moreover, 'the basic organisation in which the foreign party's resources are invested is not responsible for the liabilities of the work organisation of which it is a part, i.e. the liabilities of the other basic organisations which form part thereof, or which are associated with another organisation or with a union of organisations of associated labour, unless otherwise provided for by the investment contract with the approval of the other basic organisations.'[48] The new formula is clear: in case the joint venture is constituted in only a part of an enterprise it is liable solely for its own obligations – unless expressly otherwise provided for. On the other hand, if an entire enterprise is the object of the joint venture, all constituent parts (OOUR) are held liable – unless, again, they explicitly regulate the issue differently. The foreign observer is inevitably struck by the fact that the legislation nowhere mentions the obligations of the foreign investor in this matter. This is due to the circumstance that the joint venture, in Yugoslav law, remains an exclusively Yugoslav entity. As stated by Sukijasovic, 'since foreign capital is invested in a Yugoslav organisation, it is only this organisation that is liable to third persons. In other words, creditors can only sue the domestic organisation of associated labour in which foreign capital has been invested under the joint venture contract.'[49] The foreign investor, therefore, cannot be sued separately and his liability remains limited to the amount of his participation – unless the joint venture contract would stipulate otherwise, which is, of course, highly unlikely. And, in any case, he is only liable to his Yugoslav partner, and not to the creditor of the joint venture.

The Yugoslav claim that their legislation on joint venturing is rather liberal would seem to be justified. In fact, as said earlier, the law leaves great latitude to the partners to determine their relationship. It is for this very reason that the joint venture contract is of such great importance.

But whereas the general legal framework may not contain any particularly objectionable disincentives, the same can certainly not be said of the foreign exchange and trade regime. A few points relating to this regime have already been touched upon above, but in view of its significance for the ultimate success of the Yugoslav efforts to attract an increasing number of foreign investors, it should be dealt with separately and in more detail.

### 4.2.3. *The foreign exchange and trade regime*

The Yugoslav foreign exchange regime is fairly typical for a developing country: it is characterised by a multitude of rules and regulations, all designed to avoid as far as possible an outflow of precious foreign exchange resources. In view of Yugoslavia's decades' long history of large deficits on the current account and precariously low reserve position – sometimes covering only a few weeks of imports – this is understandable. And while in recent years the situation has altered rather drastically, mainly due to ever increasing workers' remittances from abroad, Yugoslavia has obviously not yet reached the point of making the dinar convertible and liberalising its foreign exchange and trade regime considerably. Nevertheless, as will be argued later, some of the rules affecting joint ventures do not make much sense and should be abolished. Before discussing that subject, however, it may be useful to sketch the foreign exchange legislation in general to provide an overall framework, without which the specific rules affecting joint ventures might be more difficult to understand.[50]

All foreign exchange operations in Yugoslavia must be carried out through the National Bank or an authorised bank. Of the latter there are two categories:[51] fully authorised banks, which must have minimum foreign exchange assets of $2 million equivalent and an annual exchange turn-over of at least $80 million equivalent, may engage in all foreign exchange transactions in Yugoslavia and abroad as well as in foreign credit operations including the granting of guarantees. Limited authorised banks (minimum foreign exchange assets of $400,000 equivalent) may operate only in Yugoslavia and do not have the right to keep foreign exchange accounts abroad or engage in foreign credit operations except through the intermediary of a fully authorised bank.

Foreign trade operations may be effected only by enterprises that are registered for that purpose. Registration is, however, for all practical purposes automatic provided that certain minimal conditions are met. In fact, almost all large industrial producers are registered.

Import licences are required for only about 5% of all imports. The basic classification of all commodities is made according to the manner in which foreign exchange is made available for their importation. There are four of such categories:

- *LB or liberalised goods*, comprising mainly raw materials, foodstuffs and spare parts; in 1971 and 1972 goods imported under the LB regime accounted for about 29% of total imports. Foreign exchange for payments of LB imports from the convertible currency area are made freely available in the appropriate currency; payments for imports from countries with which Yugoslavia has bilateral agreements are made in accordance with the provisions of such agreements.
- *GDK or goods imported under global exchange quotas*, consisting of most consumer goods, certain raw materials and most capital equipment. This category, in 1971 as well as in 1972, represented about 46% of Yugoslavia's imports. GDK imports can be made under several different procedures. For raw materials, the importer receives a global quota which he may use, at his discretion, for the purchase of all goods listed as GDK. Payments for imports of capital goods on the GDK list may be financed from specific allocations,[52] but a considerable portion may be freely financed from the retention quota, depreciation allowances, and credits obtained abroad including suppliers' credits. Enterprises may purchase foreign exchange not exceeding 10% of their annual depreciation charges,[53] one half of which is allocated in convertible and one half in bilateral currency.
- *Goods imported under commodity quotas in physical quantities (RK) or in dinar (DK)*, including mainly agricultural and mineral products, and (surprisingly) machine tools. Imports are subject to maxima established for each commodity and cannot be imported under any other procedure. Allocation of these quota among importers is decided through negotiations by those concerned – if no agreement is reached the Federal Secretariat for Foreign Trade decides. Together imports of the RK and DK lists amounted to 21% of imports both in 1971 and 1972.

There are, in principle, no limitations or controls on exports – except for a few raw materials in short supply (copper) and weapons, narcotic drugs etc. However, fairly stringent rules exist with respect to the use the exporter may make of his foreign currency earnings. While the surrender of the export proceeds to the National Bank is not required, only part remains at the free disposal of the exporter for payments abroad: the so-called retention quota. The remainder may be retained indefinitely in a foreign exchange account with a Yugoslav bank but can be used only to import liberalised raw materials and does not earn interest. The present retention rate – which, incidentally, also applies to receipts from services – is 20% for all export earnings with a few exceptions such as hotels which are entitled to 45%. The retention quota is not transferable to another enterprise (except in the case of a 'business-technical cooperation agreement' between two enterprises) but it can always be sold to authorised banks.

The import of capital is – again, in principle – free: foreign loans and credits may be freely contracted by authorised banks and enterprises.[54] But this freedom is only relative. In the first place, the service of foreign loans (i.e. repayment of principal and payment of interest) has to be effected out of the retention quota and the foreign exchange depreciation allocation. This, of course, severely limits the foreign debt contracting capacity of most enterprises and reduces it practically to zero for those enterprises that have no exports. Moreover, in recent years another limitation has been added to put a stop to the fast-growing foreign indebtedness of the country. Most loans are subject to prior dinar deposit requirements – the deposits are non-interest bearing and are held with the National Bank until full repayment. The percentage of the credit to be so deposited has varied considerably since their introduction in April 1972 depending basically on their term and nature (i.e. financial credit or credit for the import of capital goods), but they have always been high. At one time, for instance, a dinar deposit of 75% was required for all financial credits regardless of maturity. Certain foreign credits, however, have always been specifically exempted from the deposit requirement: these include loans from some international financial agencies (such as the IBRD) and loans contracted on behalf of Federal Authorities. Moreover, and this is of particular interest to this study, loans for investments under a joint venture agreement have been exempted as well.

A new development that should be mentioned, concluding this review of the general framework, concerns the recent establishment of an interbank foreign exchange market. Early 1973, a new way of effecting foreign currency transactions between domestic banks and between the banks and the National Bank was instituted. This is now done at so-called 'Inter-Bank Meetings' which take place twice a week. At these meetings, the 21 authorised banks negotiate and contract between themselves convertible foreign exchange at a price which they agree upon. While the determination of these rates is free in principle, the National Bank announces at the beginning of each meeting its intervention points for each currency thereby effectively establishing floors and ceilings beyond which the Yugoslav dinar should not fall or rise. The importance of this institutionalised foreign exchange market is as yet difficult to judge, but it is viewed by the Yugoslavs as a step to the introduction of the dinar in the international payments system.

Some of the aspects of the foreign exchange and trade regime that are of particular interest to the joint ventures have already been discussed, i.e. the regulations with respect to profit transfers and repatriation of capital. To recapitulate, the joint venture has to generate itself the necessary foreign exchange. For the transfer of profits, the following sources are available: the retention quota plus one third of export earnings. Repatriation of capital can be effected out of these two sources as well, while in addition 10% of the annual depreciation charges can be used for this purpose.

It is probably fair to say that these regulations are the most important obstacles to an expansion of joint ventures. The first – and most legitimate – concern of the foreign investor is that he will be able to repatriate his assets and to take out his profits. Without assurances to this effect, most investors will understandably be reluctant to risk their money. As has been argued in the first chapter, it is entirely reasonable that most countries impose certain limitations as to the nature and extent of foreign investment that they are willing to permit. But once these limitations have been defined, the foreign investor should be allowed to transfer his after-tax profit and to repatriate his capital. Restrictions in these matters discriminate against the foreign investor, as the domestic partner is free to dispose of his profits (and capital) as he pleases. Moreover, again as pointed out in Chapter 1, the whole argument on restrictions on transfers abroad is based on the partial-equilibrium fallacy. A shortage of foreign exchange (which the restrictions are intended to protect) is a weakness of the economy, not of direct investment, and should be remedied on the macroeconomic level.

But there are other considerations which lead to the conclusion that the Yugoslav rules and regulations concerning profit transfer and repatriation of capital are illogical. By requiring that the joint venture generates itself the necessary foreign exchange funds for these purposes, *one effectively limits the possibility to conclude joint ventures to those Yugoslav enterprises that produce goods that can be traded internationally.* This, of course, is unreasonable. Moreover, accepting for a moment the 'balance of payments argument' – even if it is theoretically unjustified – one has to note that a favourable effect on the current account can be achieved not only by an increase in exports but by a decrease in imports as well. In other words, a joint venture that would result in import-substitution,[55] and no exports in view of market conditions, should not be made impossible by virtue of the present restrictions on profit transfer and repatriation of capital.

The main purpose, moreover, of foreign investment should be the introduction of modern industrial and managerial technology in the Yugoslav economy, and joint ventures should be allowed whenever they can be expected to contribute to this target. The acceptance of this criterion poses, of course, practical problems. How is one to judge whether a proposed joint venture is to achieve the desired result? The best solution would probably be a more careful scrutiny than is made at present of the feasibility study that underlies the investment project which will constitute the joint venture. Such studies may be required to contain a section setting forth the expected benefits to the economy. The techniques to estimate these benefits are sufficiently developed at present. Of course, feasibility studies are based on projections and these may fall short of expectations. But to require that projections are fully realised is to eliminate all risk, which is in any case impossible. Moreover, it should not be forgotten that the parties investing in the joint venture Yugoslav as well as foreign, are risking considerable amounts of money and other resources. If anything, feasibility studies therefore tend to be conservative and rather underestimate than overestimate benefits.

One final point should be dealt with in this context, and this concerns bank guarantees for foreign loans, and the repatriation of capital and transfer of profits. This is one instance where the regulations are truly confusing. It will be remembered that debt service of foreign loans can be effected out of the foreign exchange available from the retention quota and depreciation quota. The enterprise (or joint venture) has no other resources in foreign currency that can be used for this purpose. However, the availability of foreign exchange for such debt service may be guaranteed by a Yugoslav bank, i.e. in case the retention and depreciation quotas are not sufficient to meet a due instalment or interest payment the bank (the guarantor) will sell the necessary foreign currency for dinars to the enterprise. Normally, of course, a bank will issue a guarantee only if it is reasonably sure that the enterprise will be able to generate enough exports itself to cover its foreign debt service. But it may happen in a particular year that there is a shortfall in which case the guarantee becomes operative. In other words, Yugoslav banks may unconditionally guarantee the availability of foreign exchange for foreign debt service. The situation is different, however, with respect to profit transfer and repatriation of capital. According to a 'Technical Instruction' of the National Bank, dating from October 1972 and confirmed in April 1973: 'The authorised banks may issue guarantees vouching the transfer of foreign exchange on account of the foreign partner's profit and retransfer of invested capital *if the conditions provided by the law and regulations are fulfilled.* Thus, the authorised banks may not guarantee the profit, transfer of profit or repatriation of capital in case the funds, prescribed as sources from which transfer of profit or repatriation of capital may be effected, are not provided.' Any guarantee of a Yugoslav bank with respect to the availability of foreign exchange for profit transfer and repatriation of capital is therefore conditional and, if fact, practically meaningless. Only in the exceptional case that the joint venture has sufficient claims on foreign exchange resulting from its export earnings but no dinars to buy the foreign currencies does the bank guarantee have any use.

The regulations with respect to bank guarantees are illogical in two respects. In the first place, the possibility of a bank guarantee for foreign debt service effectively makes the legislation on this matter useless, since a guarantee, once issued, is unconditional no matter whether there is foreign exchange available from the quotas or not. Secondly, there is an unjustifiable difference between the security available to a foreign lender (in the form of a bank guarantee) and the lack of such security for the foreign investor in the joint venture. Inasmuch as the latter, in any case, runs considerably higher risks than the former, the present regulations contain a considerable bias against the inflow of risk-sharing capital which Yugoslavia is so actively seeking.

### 4.3. THE JOINT VENTURE CONTRACT

The joint venture, as a specific form of business cooperation, has often been compared to marriage. While the analogy, when pursued too far, could lead to somewhat distracting conclusions, it is undoubtedly true to say that neither marriage nor joint venture stands a chance of success without mutual trust and understanding between the partners. But if these two prerequisites are essential at the time the setting-up of a joint venture is being considered – and, of course, during its life as well –

they do not suffice. Long-term cooperation in a joint venture is an extremely delicate matter, and in particular in the case of joint ventures between Yugoslav and Western enterprises that are rooted in different socio-economic systems. Rather than trying to cope with various problems and difficulties on an ad hoc basis, it is preferable to try and foresee them beforehand, and provide a way to deal with them in the joint venture contract. There is one further reason why the contract is such an important document as far as joint ventures with Yugoslav enterprises are concerned and that is – as mentioned earlier – that the lawmaker deliberately has left ample scope to the partners to determine their relationship.

The issues that normally are dealt with – or should be dealt with – in the contract are discussed below in the order that is usually followed in actual practice. There are, of course, great differences between the various agreements; some of them are carefully drafted and cover all substantial issues while others show important gaps. Unfortunately, it is not possible to quote from existing contracts as they are not published and considered confidential by the partners. In what follows, therefore, only the general principles that are applicable to all contracts can be reviewed.

The outline of a typical contract can be divided into the following headings:

- *general framework*, which includes the preamble in which the intentions of the partners are set forth, a description of the project and the products to be produced, the estimated costs, the legal status of the joint venture;
- *financial plan*, which deals with the investment by the partners and debt-financing;
- *organisational structure*, inter alia dealing with the crucial question of the responsibilities of the management organs of the joint venture;
- *operations*, including provisions with respect to the calculation of profits to be shared;
- *termination*;
- *miscellaneous provisions* (coming into force, arbitration, future amendments to the contract etc.).

Quite often, the joint venture agreement is supplemented by contracts dealing with such matters as technical assistance, licences, marketing abroad and the like. Inasmuch as these agreements are similar to those in use all over the world and do not offer particular features that are relevant only to the Yugoslav case, they will not be reviewed here.

Prior to the discussion of the subject matter of the contract, some attention should be given to a specific aspect of the Yugoslav joint venture agreement. In the section dealing with legislation it was noted that, given the Yugoslav socio-economic system, the only feasible form that private foreign investment could take was the contractual non-equity joint venture, and Sukijasovic and Glickman were quoted on the meaning of the terms contractual and non-equity.

The contractual joint venture is, of course, not a specifically Yugoslav concept. According to Friedmann,[56] this form of cooperation 'has gained increasing importance in recent years and may well become the predominant form of joint exploitation of natural resources in the years to come.'[57] Friedmann does not offer a specific definition, but he describes the contractual joint venture as 'a continuing cooperative venture, a partnership in which the foreign investor and the host country share the cost of the investment, the risks and the long-term development plans.'[58] In contrast to the usual type of international joint venture 'in which the partners hold equity shares...the contractual joint venture is much closer to the joint venture as known in U.S. law...defined as a special combination of one or more persons, where in some specific venture, a profit is jointly sought without any actual partnership or corporate designation.'[59] The latter part of this description, however, is not correct in the Yugoslav case. Without any doubt, partnership is one of the main elements in a joint venture between a Yugoslav and a foreign enterprise. This point is emphasised in the definition given by Sukijasovic: 'Under Yugoslav foreign investment legislation, a joint investment contract is a written agreement entered into by a foreign juristic or natural person and a domestic economic work organisation whereby they undertake to pool for a long run their assets within the enterprise of the domestic partner or within a domestic enterprise to be set up in the future, for the purpose of doing business together and achieving joint business objectives which provides that profits and risks will be jointly divided.'[60] The above, while perhaps susceptible to improvement, is adequate since it clearly brings out the distinctive elements of the Yugoslav joint venture contract: the sharing of risks and profits, and the pursuance of joint objectives in a partnership situation.

There remains, however, one point to be clarified – if clarification is at all possible – and that concerns the nature of the foreign capital participation in Yugoslav joint venture. Since the Yugoslav system does not know the joint-stock company, evidently this participation does not take the form of shares. The expressions 'share capital' or 'equity capital' which are commonly used when referring to the participation of the partners are therefore confusing. It is also not correct to compare the Yugoslav joint venture to a 'partnership' in the sense of the U.K. Partnership Act (1890) since in such form of business venture each partner individually may act on behalf of the firm and, moreover, all partners are in principle liable for the firm's obligations with all their assets.[61] In fact, it would seem that the concept created by the Yugoslav foreign investment legislation is a unique one that has no equivalent in the Western world. But in view of the fact that the rights and obligations of the foreign partner – and the Yugoslav partner for that matter – are fairly clearly established by the law, this lack of a proper legal definition of the participation of the partners to the joint venture should not give rise to any particular worries. It is therefore probably best to avoid the issue altogether and to speak simply of 'risk capital', and, for lack of a better one, this expression will henceforth be used in this study.

#### 4.3.1. *The general framework of the contract*

The major issues to be dealt with in this section of the contract concern, in the first place, the objectives to be reached under the agreement. Normally speaking these are mentioned in the preamble and while the preamble as such carries no legal weight it is nevertheless desirable to put these objectives on record since 'by recording the aims guidance is provided for the future arrangements of the partners in establishing their business policy.'[62] The second point to be dealt with is a description of the project and of the products to be manufactured. In order to avoid that the agreement becomes an unwieldy document, the description should be concise and the details are best handled in an annex to the contract itself. There should further be a provision allowing for adaptations in the product-mix if this becomes desirable in view of changed market conditions.

Thirdly, the contract should contain an estimate of the investment cost – both for fixed assets and working capital. This is of importance since the financing plan for the joint venture will have to be based on this estimate.[63] Ideally, therefore, the project should be the subject of a feasibility study – preferably carried out by both partners, or by an independent consultant. In the latter case, it would be desirable that the partners record their agreement with the conclusions and recommendations of the study. In some instances, the feasibility study has been made an integral part of the agreement by annexing it to the contract, and this procedure has much to say for it.

Fourthly, the contract should be explicit on the legal status of the joint venture: is it to include the entire enterprise, an OOUR – or a combination of several OOUR's – or is a new enterprise to be formed? In this context, the liability issue should also be regulated (cf. the section on legislation).

It has become increasingly common to conclude this part of the agreement with a few articles defining the meaning of expressions used in the contract. This is a sound practice since quite a number of – especially – financial terms are understood differently in the West and Yugoslavia and problems of misunderstanding can be avoided by working with agreed-upon definitions.

### 4.3.2. *The financial plan*

The drawing-up of a financial plan is a difficult matter for any investment project – involving decisions concerning a debt/equity ratio, the determination of working capital requirements, negotiation of loans, to name just a few points – but becomes really complicated in the case of a joint venture since usually a portion of each partner's capital participation is contributed in kind, and that entails an agreed-upon evaluation of the assets concerned.

The difficulties involved in this process of costing and financing a joint venture project are best illustrated by a practical but fictitious example: e.g. the production of particle boards.[64] A Yugoslav forestry and wood-processing enterprise has, after some preliminary investigations, come to the conclusion that it might be a profitable operation to put the large quantities of waste from its sawmills to good use by manufacturing particle boards. Since the enterprise does not have the know-how required it has decided to implement the project in the form of a joint venture with a foreign partner. The foreign partner selected not only has the know-how to design the manufacturing facilities, but, in addition, has developed a particle board with special qualities (weather resistant, for instance) for which there is both in Yugoslavia and abroad a large unsatisfied demand. Having agreed in principle to set up a joint venture for the production and marketing of particle boards, the partners proceed with the preparation of a cost estimate and a financial plan.[65]

The Yugoslav enterprise has land available and it proposes to include the value of this land in its capital contribution, the remainder of which will be in cash. The foreign partner is willing to capitalise its licence fee and the charges for design work and for supervision of construction. In addition, since part of the machinery to be imported is manufactured in his own plants, the foreign partner is prepared to capitalise the value of this equipment as well. The rest of his capital contribution will be in cash. The remaining financial requirements of the project will have to be met by loans in foreign exchange and in dinars.

The above procedure and financial structure are fairly typical: the broad outlines of the financial plan are often established before a final cost estimate is available and the investment of both partners is usually made partly in cash and partly in kind. A not uncommon alternative is that the partners decide at the outset on a particular debt/equity ratio, and a relation between the foreign and Yugoslav share in the risk-capital.

The next step is to reach an agreement about the value to be put on the various contributions in kind. In practice, this is usually one of the most difficult phases of the negotiating process, particularly since there are no objective criteria to measure the value of intangibles such as licences etc. Assuming that agreement has been reached and that for other items price quotations have been obtained from equipment suppliers and construction companies (for the buildings to be erected), the cost of the investment in fixed assets can be established. To this figure the net requirements for working capital should be added to obtain the total amount required for the project. In the case of the particle board joint-venture the total investment cost might look as follows:

*Table 4.2. Investment cost particle board joint venture project (in million dinars)*

| *Cost category* | *Local currency* | *Foreign exchange* | *Total* |
|---|---|---|---|
| *Fixed assets* | | | |
| Land | 10 | – | 10 |
| Buildings | 25 | – | 25 |
| Equipment (CIF): | | | |
| Yugoslav origin | 10 | – | 10 |
| Foreign origin, supplied by partner | – | 10 | 10 |
| Foreign origin, procured from others | – | 70 | 70 |
| Design, erection and supervision of construction | – | 5 | 5 |
| Contingencies | 5 | 5 | 10 |
| Licence fee | – | 20 | 20 |
| Subtotal | 50 | 110 | 160 |
| Net working capital | 40 | – | 40 |
| Grand total | 90 | 110 | 200 |

Having established a final cost estimate, the partners are now in a position to firm up a financial plan for the joint venture. At this stage a decision has to be taken with respect to the division between risk-capital and borrowed resources (the debt/equity ratio), and the share of each partner in the risk-capital. Let it be assumed here that the partners decide to finance half of the total outlays with risk-capital and half with loans, and that a maximum participation of the foreign partner in the risk-capital is agreed upon (i.e. a 51/49 ratio). This would lead to the following financial structure for the joint venture.

*Table 4.3. Financing particle board joint venture project (in million dinars)*

| *Source of funds* | *Local currency* | *Foreign exchange* | *Total* |
|---|---|---|---|
| *Risk-capital* | | | |
| Yugoslav partner | | | |
| in kind | 10 | – | 10 |
| in cash | 41 | – | 41 |
| Foreign partner | | | |
| in kind | – | 35 | 35 |
| in cash | – | 14 | 14 |
| Subtotal risk-capital | 51 | 49 | 100 |
| *Loans* | | | |
| Local currency | 39 | – | 39 |
| Foreign currency | – | 61 | 61 |
| Subtotal loans | 39 | 61 | 100 |
| Grand total | 90 | 110 | 200 |

At first sight, the above financial plan does not differ very much from any other investment operation anywhere in the world: the project is financed by the usual combination of capital contributions by the partners and long-term debt. There is, however, one basic difference and this lies, of course, in the nature of the capital participations. It has been explained earlier that these participations are not 'equity' in the Western sense of the word, but that they are nevertheless to be considered as risk-capital. While the legal definition of such risk-capital might give rise to rather complicated problems for the Western lawyer, it would seem that the Yugoslavs have found a practical solution which can satisfy both sides. In the first place, as said above, the law clearly defines the rights and obligations of both partners with respect to their capital contributions – there can be no misunderstanding on this point. Secondly, as far as what might be called the 'accounting-aspect' is concerned, the problem has simply been solved by the invention of the 'Nominal Capital Account'. This account records the capital contributions of the partners – and their reinvestment of profits – and the proportionate share of each partner in the account serves as a basis for the distribution of profits. In most of the joint ventures concluded so far, the Capital Account has been denominated in foreign currency, i.e. including the share of the Yugoslav partner. The principal purpose of this arrangement was, obviously, to eliminate the exchange risk of the foreign investor. At the time of writing, there have been no serious objections of the Yugoslav authorities against this practice. It is, however, entirely possible that in future it may no longer be allowed. In that case, the question of the foreign partner's exchange risk will have to be dealt with. This will undoubtedly be difficult; it can hardly be expected that the Yugoslav authorities will permit conversion at the rate in force on the day the contribution was paid in nor can forward cover be obtained for a period extending to several years. For those joint ventures where the Capital Account has been denominated in dinars, the foreign investor would seem to have agreed to carry the risk as conversion upon termination of the joint venture – i.e. the moment of capital repatriation – is made at the rate in force at that time.

It may be added here that in both cases the profit transfer of the foreign partner is effected at the rate prevailing at the day of conversion, which means that return on capital of the foreign partner is not only subject to normal business risks but to a foreign exchange risk as well. In other words, while the joint venture may have achieved the desired profit level in terms of dinars, the foreign partner may receive less in his own currency due to a devaluation of the dinar intervening in the time between the moment the capital was paid in and the profit distributed.

A slight complication may arise when the foreign investor wishes to retain the right of ownership over specific assets-in-kind invested by him in the joint venture – a possibility which the law explicitly has provided for. In that case, the contract should, of course, contain a number of clauses spelling out in detail the use to which the asset may be put, maintenance and repair conditions etc. The foreign partner may transfer abroad the depreciation charged annually against the asset, which will result in a corresponding decrease in his share in the risk-capital. As far as could be ascertained, there have been no instances in practice where the foreign partner has made use of this possibility to retain ownership. In view of the fact that it does not offer any real advantages, this is hardly surprising.

The financial plan is, of course, drawn up before the actual implementation of the project has begun. And in spite of the fact that in most cases a contingency allowance is provided for to cover price increases, the possibility that further cost overruns occur should be reckoned with. The joint venture contract should therefore spell out in detail how this matter will be dealt with. Usually the partners agree to increase their capital contribution by the required amount, while keeping their proportionate share constant. Another possibility might be that one, or both, undertake to raise additional loans – or that the funds required are put up in a combination of a capital increase and credits. The financial plan should be supplemented by a detailed table setting out the timing of project cost outlays; of course, this table is subject to changes (notably in case of cost overruns and of delays in the implementation of the project), but it is highly desirable that the partners have an idea beforehand when the various funds (capital and loans) have to be disbursed so that the necessary arrangements can be made in time.

A last point to be dealt with in the section concerned with financing relates to reinvestment of profits, and capital increases. Since unilateral action by one of the partners would upset the agreed-upon ratio between the respective participations, the joint venture contract should prescribe the procedures to be followed on this point.

There are further observations to be made with respect to the financial structure of the Yugoslav joint venture. In the first place, the capital contribution of the foreign partner should include not only the capitalised value of assets-in-kind (equipment, licences etc.) but an amount in cash as well. There are, as of the time of writing, no specific rules or regulations on this point but there is no doubt that the Yugoslav authorities are reluctant to register a joint venture contract unless it provides for a cash contribution of the foreign partner. This is an entirely reasonable attitude to take. Of course, the purpose of the joint venture legislation is to introduce modern technology and modern management methods in Yugoslavia and joint venture contracts that are unsatisfactory in this respect will certainly not be registered. On the other hand, it is clear that the risk of the foreign partner, and consequently his interest in the success of the joint venture, will be less if his contribution consists only in the capitalised value of his licence, or even his equipment (albeit in that case to a lesser extent). A substantial participation in cash, however, can be expected to lead to real involvement and that is what the Yugoslavs are looking for.

A second point concerns the debt/'equity' ratio. Here, again, there are no rules or regulations, and in general the Yugoslavs do not seem to be particularly concerned about this matter – perhaps because of the Yugoslav practice to finance new enterprises entirely by long-term debt.

Recently, however, there have been unofficial reactions against the excessive amount of foreign debt incurred by some joint ventures. It will be remembered that foreign loans contracted by joint ventures have always been exempted from deposit requirements and it is felt that this has led to a number of 'fake' joint ventures where the foreign loan financing is disproportionately large in relation to the foreign equity investment, i.e. that certain joint ventures have been established solely for the purpose of circumventing the deposit requirement. It is therefore not unlikely that in the near future joint ventures will be obliged to achieve a certain minimum debt/equity ratio and that a minimum (relative) share of the foreign partner in the capital account may be required. Provided that some flexibility is maintained, so that the specific requirements of individual projects may be taken into account, this would be a desirable development.

### 4.3.3. *Organisational structure*

While the partners may wish to devote some attention in the joint venture contract to the organisational structure of the enterprise in terms of departments and divisions, by far the most important subject to be dealt with under this heading is the delineation of decision-making authority between the management organs of the joint venture. It is probably hardly necessary to emphasise that the Yugoslav self-management system makes this delineation a complicated matter. On the one hand, it is obviously impossible to tinker with the basic principles of self-management, on the other the Yugoslavs themselves are convinced that a real joint venture entails the participation of the foreign partner in the decision-making process. This is explicitly confirmed by the law on foreign investment which further prescribes that this participation is exercised through a committee consisting of representatives of both partners:

> 'The investment contract may also provide for the foreign party to exercise its rights, which will be determined by an agreement with the domestic organisations of associated labour, through a joint body (business board).
>
> The investment contract stipulates the method of setting up the joint body, its powers and modus operandi.'[66]

Here, again, the legislation is liberal and provides only the general institutional framework within which the partners are free to reach agreement with respect to decision-making within the joint venture.

The joint venture, thus, has normally three management organs:

- the workers' council;

- the business board;
- the director, or general manager.

The *workers' council* remains the supreme decision-making body, as provided for in the Constitution, but it may delegate – and this done through the joint venture contract – a number of its powers to the business board. There are, however, certain rights of the workers' council that cannot be transferred. These concern:
- modification of the statutes or adoption of new statutes;
- determination of labour relations;
- approval of annual balance sheet and income statement, and long-term investment and financing plans;
- appointment and dismissal of the director.

While these rights are inalienable, the partners are free to agree that the business boards submit proposals to the workers' council with respect to decisions to be taken by the council. This is, in fact, the procedure arranged for in most joint venture contracts. Initiatives emanating from the workers' council are likely to be limited to questions relating to labour relations. It would appear, therefore, that the rôle of the council in the managing of the joint venture is rather limited. While this may be true, one should note that in the case of the purely Yugoslav enterprise the situation is not very different. As was pointed out in Chapter 3, most decisions of the council are based on proposals drafted either by the 'management board' or its sub-committees, or by the director and his staff from the specialised departments of the enterprise (planning, finance etc.). Only on rare occasions does the council itself take the initiative to propose specific action. Furthermore, as noted by Sukijasovic, 'even in cases when the contract explicitly specified which questions may only be decided by the workers' council on the proposal of the business board, the decision of the workers' council need not conform to the proposal of the business board, nor does it need any subsequent approval by it.'[67] One should add, however, that most contracts provide for a conciliation procedure for the event that a disagreement arises between workers' council and business board. Finally, it can be argued – although this is perhaps too legalistic a point to make – that the approval by the council of the joint venture contract (by virtue of which decision-making powers are vested in the business board) is a voluntary act of self-management of the council.[68]

Notwithstanding the above-mentioned inalienable rights of the workers' council, it is probably justified to say that the *business board* is the management organ that runs the joint venture. Its composition, powers and operating procedures should therefore be regulated in the contract with great care and in as much detail as possible. As far as the composition of the board is concerned, there are two alternatives: the board may consist of a varying number of representatives of the partners according to their share in the Capital Account or it may be composed on a parity basis.[69] It would seem that in most cases the second alternative is adopted:

'Contracts concluded to date reflect great similarities in respect of the composition of the business board. Business boards are composed on the principle of equal representation, and not proportionately to the size of the participating interest of the partners. The equal composition vests the foreign partner with equality even though the size of his investment has to be less than that of the domestic enterprise. The fact of registration of contracts providing for equal representation business boards reflects the implicit attitude (of the Yugoslav authorities) that such a practice is considered to be permitted, which provides a way for equalising the position of the foreign partner.'[70]

This, of course, gives extraordinary safeguards to the foreign investor, and the Yugoslav arrangement is probably unique. Even with a participation in the Capital Account as low as 10%, the foreign partner may still obtain equal representation in the business board. Obviously under no circumstances can the foreigner have a greater participation on the board than the Yugoslav side, and even in the case that there are two foreign partners in a three-partner venture, the combined representation cannot exceed that of the Yugoslav interest.[71]

The operating procedures of the board – including the important issue of voting – can freely be agreed upon by the partners: 'Neither statute nor practice has definitely indicated any limitations on party control of the joint venture internal decision-making process. Thus, the parties are theoretically autonomous when deciding the quorum and voting requirements of the joint operation board.'[72] Usually, representatives to the board are nominated by each partner for a fixed period and the chairmanship rotates between the partners. The number of nominees for each partner, in the majority of cases, ranges between one and three.[73] Different arrangements are possible with respect to voting procedures: the partners may agree that on all issues presented to the board for decisions a unanimous vote is required, or that all questions are decided by a majority vote. Alternatively, the contract may stipulate that only certain issues (which are, of course, to be defined in the contract) are subject to a unanimous vote while the remainder are to be settled by a majority vote. Since in most joint ventures, the partners have equal representation on the board, the question is academic in those cases since it can safely be assumed that the representatives of each partner will vote 'en bloc'. This means in practice veto power for either partner, and the distinct possibility of stalemates. It is therefore advisable that the contract contains provisions to deal with a tied vote. A not uncommon practice is to refer, in such case, the matter under dispute to the general managers of the 'parent' enterprises who should then work out a compromise.[74]

Even more important than composition and operating procedures are the powers of the business board, and its relation to the workers' council. There are several approaches to deal with this matter. Sukijasovic, who had the opportunity to investigate a substantial number of contracts, has found that 'until now the competence of the joint business board has in practice largely been regulated in three ways: 1. the contract only enumerates questions which fall within the competence of the board; 2. the contract specifies which questions fall within the exclusive competence of the workers' council and which within that of the business board, providing at the same time that the board can submit proposals to the workers' council as to how to solve individual questions falling within the latter's competence; 3. the contract specifies three sets of questions: those decided exclusively by the workers' council, regardless of whether or not any proposal has been submitted by the business board, those decided by the workers' council on the proposal of the board, and those falling exclusively within the competence of the business board.'[75]

Generally speaking, the following questions are dealt with by the business board:[76]

- implementation of the investment project, i.e. construction or modernisation of production facilities, purchase and installation of machinery and equipment, trial runs and start-up operations;
- organisation of production and of the labour force (number of jobs by skills, job descriptions etc.);
- determination of technical standards, production volume and product mix, quality requirements;
- determination of commercial policy, including price policy, marketing policy in Yugoslavia and abroad, market research;
- drawing-up of the annual financial statements (which will have to be approved by the workers' council);
- preparation of annual and long-term plans (which, again, are subject to approval of the workers' council);
- determination of depreciation charges (for which minimum percentages are laid down by law);
- allocations to the Reserve Fund above the legally required minimum;
- setting the terms and conditions for the employment of senior executive personnel (N.B. the director has to be appointed by the workers'

council but the business board may be entitled to propose a candidate);
- distribution of net income and personal incomes (workers' salaries and wages). It should be noted that the powers of the business board are limited to the making of proposals and that decisions are taken by the workers' council.

The last point requires additional comments. As was explained in previous chapters, under the Yugoslav system of self-management wages and salaries in theory do not exist: the workers only share in the profits of the enterprise and labour is not – again, in theory – a cost category. In practice, however, workers' remuneration consists of two parts, a fixed and a variable part. The first one is determined in advance and paid out weekly or monthly, the second depends on the results achieved by the enterprise and is paid out whenever these results are figured out. The important issue here is the determination of the point in the 'accounting process' at which profits are realised, in other words what proportion – if not all – of the workers' remuneration is considered as costs? This should obviously be settled in the contract, but this issue is better discussed in the next section where all questions concerning the accounts of the joint venture will be dealt with in detail.

The *director* of the joint venture – regardless of whether the joint venture is a part of an enterprise or constituted by the enterprise as a whole – must be a Yugoslav citizen. He is appointed by the workers' council, but the business board may propose suitable candidates and, in addition, may establish professional qualifications for the job. The partners are free to provide for foreign specialists to be appointed to particular posts, save for the position of chief accountant who has to be a Yugoslav citizen as well.[77] In some cases, the foreign partner makes one of its executives available as deputy director, who is then responsible for technical questions. This functional distribution of offices has a certain logic. Normally speaking in most business operations, the director 'does not necessarily possess expertise on all aspects of production and delegates these responsibilities to an expert.'[78] Since it is the foreign partner who is providing the technology, know-how and licences to the joint-venture, it is desirable that responsibility for these questions rests with one of its representatives who has the necessary experience. The director, who represents the joint venture before the law ex officio, should be well familiar with the local business climate, all rules and regulations, have contacts with local banks, suppliers, customers etc. and is therefore best a citizen of the country in which the joint venture has to operate.

Within this context, two further contributions of the foreign partner should be mentioned. In most joint ventures specialists, seconded by the foreign partner, are temporarily assigned to the joint venture to assist in the implementation of the project, to supervise the installation of equipment, to conduct trial runs and other tests, and to train Yugoslav workers to operate the new machines. Quite often this training takes the form of a special programme whereby Yugoslav workers and technicians are sent abroad to receive instruction in the plants of the foreign partner. While such programmes are obviously also in the interest of the foreign partner inasmuch as they contribute to the success of the joint venture, they are of great benefit to the Yugoslavs. There is no better method of mastering new skills than practical training in optimal learning conditions.

#### 4.3.4. *Operations*

There are three sets of issues that should be dealt with in this section of the joint venture contract, i.e. those relating to technical, commercial and financial questions.

It was mentioned earlier that usually the foreign partner's risk-capital contribution consists partly of the capitalised value of machinery and equipment. The contract should therefore contain provisions whereby the foreign partner undertakes to ensure that this equipment will meet certain technical and other requirements.[79] Further technical issues concern the rôle to be played by the foreign partner in the design and construction of the manufacturing facilities, the assembly and installation of the required machinery and equipment, trial runs and start-up operations, and quality control. It depends on the specifics of each individual case whether these matters should be regulated in the joint venture agreement itself or whether they are better dealt with in separate agreements annexed to the contract.

As far as the commercial issues are concerned, there is often a conflict of interests between the two partners: 'A common complaint of local partners of joint ventures is that the foreign partner wants the Joint Company to supply only the market of the host country and perhaps those of a few neighbouring soft-currency countries, while it services other profitable world markets from its wholly-owned facilities located elsewhere. On the other hand, it would be unreasonable to expect an international company to compete with itself through its overseas affiliates.'[80] However, given the fact that the Yugoslav foreign exchange regime permits profit transfer and repatriation of capital only out of export earnings generated by the joint venture itself, it is definitely also in the interest of the foreign partner to assist the joint venture in marketing at least a certain minimum of its output abroad. The Yugoslav enterprises, during negotiations, usually try to obtain guarantees from their foreign partners in this respect, but generally are not able to achieve more than that the foreign party will help on a 'best effort' basis. The situation is, of course, different in those cases where the foreign partner has entered into a joint venture agreement with the deliberate purpose of supplementing his own output with part of the production of the joint venture. In other words, the capacity of the foreign partner's manufacturing facilities may not be sufficient to meet the demand for his products and, in order not to lose his market share, he draws on the production of the joint venture. Contracts of this type, therefore, tend to contain a clause giving the foreign partner a *right* to a certain percentage of the joint venture's output instead of the usual provision *obliging* him to use his best efforts in achieving the amount of exports necessary to meet the need for foreign exchange of the joint venture.

Both technical and commercial issues are not very different in the Yugoslav case from any other joint venture in a developing country – the same can, however, not be said of the financial aspects of the Yugoslav joint venture's operations. From the review in the previous chapter of the Yugoslav system of accounting, it will have become clear that these aspects merit special attention in the joint venture contract. In particular, it is of the greatest importance to determine unequivocally at which point 'distributable profits' arise. The law on foreign investment is not particularly enlightening in this aspect. Article 7 states that: 'The investment contract may provide for the foreign party to be entitled to participate in the net income earned by the joint venture operation, ... (and that the) contract shall also stipulate the duration, terms and conditions of such a participation.' Obviously, the foreign partner is entitled to a share in the profit, and – obviously – the way this share is computed should be regulated in the contract. The difficulty, however, arises from the fact that Net Income and profits, in the Western sense, are different concepts. As was explained in the section on accounting principles, Net Income excludes labour costs but includes repayment of credits (which is a so-called contractual obligation). Whereas the foreign partner might be very willing to accept that Net Income is divided between the partners before charging labour costs – which would mean that these would come out of the Yugoslav partner's share – he will be less inclined to agree that loan repayments are charged to the Income Statement. In the same vein, the Yugoslav side is unlikely to accept that the remuneration of the joint venture's workers is paid for exclusively out of its profit share. For this reason it is an absolute necessity that the joint venture contract contains an agreed-upon model of a Balance Sheet and Income Statement. Such models will properly define 'profit' and the basis for sharing the profit between the partners. The necessity for agreed-upon formulae, however, exists for various cost-categories as well. The first of these concerns the purchase by the joint venture of supplies (raw materials, semi-finished goods, services etc.) from one or both of the partners. In some contracts it is explicitly provided for that these deals are conducted on an 'arm's-length' basis (i.e. at normal market prices) while in others a 'cost-plus' formula is used. The pricing of these inputs can become a particularly tricky issue if the joint venture includes a non-industrial partner such as a bank or an international financial agency. For the non-industrial partner only the joint venture itself is a source of profits whereas the industrial partners have room for manoeuvre between maximising their own profits and those of the joint-venture so as to arrive at an optimal combination. Of course, the interests of the industrial partners themselves are not likely to be identical either on this issue and it is therefore mandatory that the joint venture contract includes a clear definition with respect to the pricing of the inputs involved.

A second cost category which requires elaboration in the contract concerns depreciation charges. Yugoslav legislation prescribes only minimum depreciation rates and every Yugoslav enterprise – and joint venture – is perfectly free to set higher rates. The partners will have therefore to decide what depreciation charges are to be applied. Here again, the interests of the partners may differ: one of them may wish to keep these charges as low as possible so as to increase profits while the other may prefer to build up the financial strength of the joint venture by high depreciation allowances.

Finally the matter of workers' remuneration will have to be dealt with. Usually the business board is authorised in the contract to propose 'wage' levels for all jobs to the workers' council, these levels to be reviewed each year. Of course, the final decision remains with the workers' council. The amount involved is then considered as a cost for the purpose of the Income Statement. Any additional payments – bonuses etc. – to the workers will be met out of the share in the profit of the Yugoslav partner. Of course, the contract may provide that the foreign party makes a contribution to these bonuses as well, but this is normally not the case. In this context mention should also be made of allocations to the Common Consumption Fund – the fund which finances such things as workers' housing, recreational facilities etc. In quite a number of cases the foreign partner has agreed that allocations to this Fund are made before profits are determined, i.e. such allocations to be regarded as costs. Usual practice is, however, to fix a limit which such allocations may not exceed, e.g. by setting an absolute amount or by establishing a percentage of, say, total revenue.

Allocations to the Reserve Fund of the joint venture are, in practically all cases, made before the determination of profit, i.e. borne by all partners.

The Income Statement of a typical joint venture will therefore be in the following form.

*Table 4.4. Income Statement Yugoslav joint venture*

1. Sales
2. Other revenues
3. Inventory changes
4. *Total Income* (1 + 2 + 3)
5. Cost of materials
6. Cost of services
7. Depreciation
8. Business expenses
9. Net Income [4 − (5 + 6 + 7 + 8)]
10. Legal and contractual obligations (except repayment of credits)
11. Workers' remuneration
12. Allocations to Reserve Fund and Collective Consumption Fund
13. Profit [9 − (10 + 11 + 12)]

In principle the profit is available for distribution between the partners in the ratio agreed-upon in the contract. Of course, the actual disbursement of the amounts due to each partner can take place only if sufficient liquid funds are available, and loan repayments have a prior claim on these funds. But it is incorrect, as has happened in the case of a number of contracts, to include loan instalments in the Income Statement as a cost item. Meeting these payments – as well as any other payment due – is a cash-flow problem which is totally unrelated to the profits of the enterprise.

The tax payable by the foreign partner over his profit is normally deducted immediately and paid directly to the Internal Revenue by the joint venture itself. The Yugoslav partner usually assumes the obligation, out of his profit share, for the tax on the Business Fund which has been replaced by the obligatory loan to the Fund for Developing Regions. Having met these obligations the partners are free to dispose of their profit share as they see fit. They may decide to reinvest part (or all) of their share in the joint venture but since unilateral action on this point would change the respective percentual participations in the Capital Account, any reinvestment should be subject to agreement between the partners.

The procedures to be followed for the transfer abroad of the foreign partner's profit are usually spelled out in a special clause. In practically all cases the rate of exchange to be applied is the official Yugoslav rate in force on the day of conversion.

The joint venture agreement should, of course, also establish the procedures to be followed in case the accounting period ends in a loss. The most usual arrangement is that the shortfall shall be met in the first instance from the Reserve Fund, and, if this is not sufficient, by a write-down of the shares of the partners in the Capital Account. Some contracts further provide that no profits will be distributed until the capital participations have again reached the original level.

Apart from a model of the Income Statement, the joint venture agreement should include a model of a Balance Sheet as well, in particular since the Capital Account, and the respective share of the partners therein, forms the basis for the sharing of profits. In general, such model resembles closely a Western-type Balance Sheet and it is therefore not necessary to reproduce the model here. The only notable difference is that fixed assets are usually presented 'gross' and that accumulated depreciation is shown separately under the liabilities.

A final question to be settled under this section of the contract concerns the auditing of the joint ventures accounts. Present practice has been to neglect this issue, and the foreign partners concerned are relying on the Social Accounting Service and their right 'to have access to the accounts showing the joint venture income' (Article 13 of the law on Foreign Investment). It is, however, not unlikely that in the near future auditing firms will be allowed in Yugoslavia – possibly taking the form of joint ventures between Western auditing companies and Yugoslav firms – and if that comes about it would be desirable to have the joint ventures accounts audited by such firms.

### 4.3.5. *Termination*

The law leaves the partners free to determine the duration of the joint venture agreement – it requires only that the contract 'as a rule, (is) a long-term arrangement' and that, if a specific period is agreed upon, this period 'is not shorter than the time needed for the realisation of joint business objectives.'[81] Once a period is fixed, 'the investment contract cannot be cancelled by the consent of the parties concerned prior to expiry of its agreed term.'[82] However, the law permits that the contract may provide for prior cancellation: 1. in case one of the parties fails to fulfil its contractual obligations, and 2. if the joint venture incurs losses in two consecutive years or if the business results are considerably worse than projected.[83] As far as the minimum period is concerned for which a contract may be concluded, experience so far indicates that 'the lower limit of the duration of contracted co-operation is ... a five-year period.'[84] In view of the somewhat vague wording of the law in respect of the grounds for cancellation prior to the expiry of the term of the agreement it may be 'useful that in concluding their contract the partners elucidate the elements warranting repudiation of the contract. Thus, they may indicate the size of the loss in the event of which the contract may be repudiated, or the minimum of profit that justifies (a continuation of) the contract.'[85] It would seem, however, that in practice very few agreements contain such a clause which may make it difficult to determine whether in fact profits achieved are 'considerably worse than projected'.

When the joint venture is concluded for a fixed period, in most contracts provision is made for extension either by tacit consent (i.e. one of the partners has to inform the other(s) that it wishes, in fact, to terminate the agreement) or by stipulating the procedure according to which the agreement may be prolonged. As far as the foreign partner is concerned, there is another way by which he may terminate his participation in the joint venture: 'With the consent of the domestic organisation of associated labour in which its joint venture resources are invested and of the other parties to the contract, the foreign party may transfer its rights and obligations under the investment contract to another foreign individual or corporate body or another domestic organisation of associated labour, unless otherwise provided for by the investment contract.'[86] In such case, the Yugoslav partner has the right of first refusal, a right which has to be exercised within a period of sixty days following the date of receipt of the offer.[87]

In the event of termination of the joint venture agreement the foreign partner, of course, will wish to repatriate his share in the risk-capital and this involves the evaluation of such share.[88] The law does not provide any guidelines as to how this evaluation should be carried out, it only confirms the right of the foreign partner to repatriate his participation: 'The foreign party is entitled to the transfer of resources, i.e. the residual resources invested in a joint venture if the investment contract is terminated through accomplishment of its business objectives, i.e. on expiry of the term of the contract, if the investment contract is annulled for the reasons provided for by this law, or if the investment contract provides that the foreign party is entitled partially to withdraw the resources invested during the term of the investment contract. The transfer of resources specified in paragraph 1 of this Article is effected in conformity with the existing regulations on foreign exchange operations.'[89] It can therefore safely be assumed that it is up to the partners to agree in the contract on the criteria and procedures to be adhered to for the evaluation of the share of the foreign partner. This is confirmed by Sukijasovic, 'in the event of the termination of the contract, the contracting parties mutually decide whether the capital contributed by the foreign contracting party is to be reckoned at the nominal value stipulated in the contract or at its market value.'[90] He seems, however, to be mistaken in his assumption that 'most joint venture contracts entered into to date provide that the foreign contracting party should receive back his capital in its nominal amount.'[91] In actual fact – and this applies in particular to the most recent contracts – rather complicated formulae have been adopted to determine the 'market value' of the foreign partner's share. To settle on market value rather than on the nominal value would also appear to be the more logical arrangement. Except in the case of termination on account of losses (viz. a disappointing profitability) or of non-performance by one of the partners, the joint venture is a profit-making going concern which would imply that the stake of the partners in the joint venture has increased in value beyond the nominal amounts of the initial paid-in participations. Similarly, if the joint venture agreement is cancelled because of losses or low profits, the risk-capital is probably worth less than the 'nominal value'. In both cases, therefore, determination of the market value of the respective shares would seem to be a reasonable and justifiable procedure.

The arrangements provided for in existing contracts differ from case to case, but are generally variations on one of two possibilities. In the first one the partners divide, in proportion to their part in the Capital Account, the 'total value' of the joint venture. The usual procedure in this case is that the partners try to reach agreement on what this total value amounts to and that, if agreement is impossible, the matter is left to an independent expert. The contract often further states that in determining the total value the same criteria are to be used as were applied at the time of the evaluation of the initial contributions in kind. This formula might prove to be unworkable – so many different concepts of 'total value' are possible that even an independent expert's judgement may be contested by all parties concerned.

The second method – which would seem to find increasing application –

is much to be preferred. It generally consists of the arithmetic medium of two amounts: the first amount is constituted by the net worth of the joint venture and the second amount by a multiple of the average profits achieved by the joint venture over the past x years. The use of this formula, of course, necessitates a definition of net worth (i.e. total assets less total liabilities) and for this purpose an agreed-upon model of a Balance Sheet should be included in the contract. As far as the second amount is concerned, the multiple ranges from three to seven times and the number of years over which the average profit is calculated varies between three and five. The advantage of this second method is principally that it is based on clearly defined concepts about which there can be no further disagreement or misunderstanding. Moreover, the parties will not lose any time in trying to determine the joint venture's 'total value' – let alone that an independent expert will not have to be called in.

The contract should also define the terms and conditions according to which the foreign partner's share is to be transferred abroad. The amount involved will in most cases be too large to permit payment in a single lump sum and normally joint venture agreements provide for a period over which the capital repatriation takes place. Such period usually ranges between two and five years, and repayments are made in equal instalments. During the repayment period the foreign partner is paid interest over the outstanding amount at a rate which varies considerably from case to case.

It will be remembered that foreign exchange regulations allow for 53% of the joint venture's foreign currency receipts (plus 5% of the annual depreciation charge) to be utilised for capital repatriation, but that no bank guarantees may be granted for this purpose. Loans, on the other hand, may be guaranteed with respect to foreign exchange availability. It has therefore become common practice that joint venture contracts provide for a conversion of the foreign partner's capital stake at the date of termination into a loan. The advantage for the foreign partner, is, obviously, that such loan can be guaranteed by a Yugoslav bank, in which case he has no further worries about whether or not over the period of repayment the Yugoslav partner will dispose of sufficient foreign exchange. Of course, such bank guarantee will only be given if the bank expects the foreign currency receipts of the Yugoslav side to be sufficient for the purpose, and it should be noted that for debt service only the retention quota is available (normally 20% of export earnings). However, once given the guarantee is irrevocable. The Yugoslav authorities have implicitly given their approval of this method of repatriation by exempting in January 1974 from payment of dinar deposits those foreign loans which resulted from the conversion of foreign capital participations upon the termination of a joint venture agreement.

### 4.3.6. *Miscellaneous provisions*

Among the various miscellaneous provisions which form part of any joint venture agreement, two should be singled out in the Yugoslav case, i.e. those relating to the coming into force of the agreement and those concerning the settlement of disputes.

With respect to the coming into force, the partners may at their discretion stipulate all conditions that they deem necessary, but there are two that are indispensable: the joint venture agreement will have to be formally approved by the workers' council(s) of the Yugoslav partner(s) and it will have to be registered by the Federal Secretariat for Economy. It should be noted that, according to the law, the contract when registered becomes valid as from the date of signing.

Disputes arising with respect to the interpretation or implementation of the joint venture agreement 'shall be settled by the appropriate Yugoslav economic court unless provided by the investment contract or by separate consent in a written form that these disputes shall be settled by a selected court (of arbitration) set up within the Chamber of Economy of Yugoslavia, by the Foreign Trade Arbitration Court of the Chamber of Economy of Yugoslavia, by a special court of arbitration appointed by the parties in accordance with the contract, or by a foreign court of arbitration' (Article 21 of the Law on Foreign Investment). The law, therefore, leaves the parties various options to choose from. Yugoslav legislation allows, moreover, for the enforcement of arbitral awards in Yugoslavia provided that certain conditions are met.

NOTES

1. Miodrag Sukijasovic, 'Foreign investment in Yugoslavia', in Isaiah A. Litvak and Christopher J. Maule (eds.), *Foreign investment and international business arrangements: the experience of host countries*, Praeger, New York, 1970, page 388.
2. Branko Horvat, 'Yugoslav system of self-management and the import of foreign private capital', in Wolfgang G. Friedmann and Leo Mates, *Joint business ventures of Yugoslav enterprises and foreign firms*, Institute of International Politics and Economy, Belgrade, 1968, page 83.
3. Marshall I. Goldman, *Soviet foreign aid*, Praeger, New York, 1961, pages 13-14.
4. Cf. Goldman, *op. cit.*, page 14 ff.
5. OECD, *Economic Survey*, *Yugoslavia*, November 1969, page 5.
6. OECD, *Foreign Investment in Yugoslavia*, 1970, page 7.

7. See *inter alia*, S. Miloskovic, 'Cooperation between the Yugoslav and foreign economies', *Yugoslav Survey*, May 1970; and Milan Pavicevic, 'Transfer of foreign technology and the Yugoslav economy', *Yugoslav Survey*, No. 2, May 1973.
8. Pavicevic, *loc. cit.*, page 72.
9. *The Economist*, January 6, 1973, page 21.
10. *Borba*, March 19, 1967.
11. Richard B. Glickman and Miodrag Sukijasovic, 'Yugoslav worker-management and its effect on foreign investment', *Harvard International Law Journal*, Vol. 12, No. 2, Spring 1971, page 261.
12. Miodrag Sukijasovic, *Yugoslav foreign investment legislation at work: experiences so far*, Institute of International Politics and Economics, Belgrade, 1970 (2nd edition), page 13.
13. The Yugoslav legislation will be dealt with in section 4.2 of this chapter, whereas the characteristics of the contractual joint venture will be treated in the section on the joint venture contract.
14. Milija Radonovic, 'Joint investment by domestic enterprises, and business and financial cooperation between Yugoslav and foreign firms', *Yugoslav Survey*, No. 1, February 1968, page 44.
15. Radovanic, *loc. cit.*, page 43 (emphasis supplied).
16. 'Theses on the socio-economic aspects of joint investments by domestic enterprises and production-financial cooperation between the Yugoslav and foreign economies'.
17. Statement reproduced in *Joint investment and production – technical cooperation of Yugoslav economic organisations and foreign firms*, Federal Chamber of Economy, Belgrade, 1967, pages 5-10.
18. Miodrag Sukijasovic and Richard B. Glickman, 'Yugoslav joint ventures: some legal problems', *Florida State University Slavic Papers*, Volume 3, 1969, page 35.
19. Article 64 k of the 'Law on Assets of Economic Organisation'.
20. Article 64 l of the 'Law on Assets of Economic Organisation'.
21. Cf., *inter alia*, Nikola Balog, 'Legal relations concerning foreign investment in domestic economic organizations', in Federal Chamber of Economy, *op. cit.*, page 15; K. Stojkovic, *Foreign capital investment in Yugoslav enterprises*, published by the Yugoslav Export and Credit Bank, Belgrade, 1972, page 13.
22. Although in 1973 such law was drawn up (this law will be dealt with later on).
23. OECD Committee on Invisible Transactions, *Foreign investment in Yugoslavia*, Paris, 1970, page 8.
24. Glickman and Sukijasovic, in *Harvard International Law Journal (loc. cit.)*, page 286.
25. *The legal system of foreign capital investments in Yugoslav enterprises*, Yugoslav Chamber of Economy and Institute of Comparative Law, Belgrade, 1972, page 37.
26. Glickman and Sukijasovic, in *Florida State University Slavic Papers (loc. cit.)*, page 36.
27. All legal texts, unless otherwise specified, are quoted from the version published by the Federal Chamber of Economy, Belgrade, 1967.
28. Strangely enough only the foreign partner is mentioned in the law, although the Yugoslav party's contribution normally consists for a large part of investment in kind (fixed assets).
29. Glickman and Sukijasovic, in *Florida State University Slavic Papers (loc. cit.)*, page 38.
30. *Ibidem.*
31. *Idem*, page 40.

32. OECD, *Foreign investment... (op. cit.)*, page 22.
33. Balog, *loc. cit.*, page 23.
34. *Ibidem.*
35. Sukijasovic, *Yugoslav foreign investment legislation... (op. cit.)*, page 49.
36. Cf. Miodrag Sukijasovic, 'Investment of foreign capital in the Yugoslav economy', *Yugoslav Survey*, Vol. XIV, No. 4, November 1973, page 43.
37. *Ibidem.*
38. *Official Gazette*, No. 55, 1971.
39. Article 66 b of the 'Law on Assets of Economic Organisation,' published in the *Official Gazette*, No. 34, 1971.
40. *Idem*, Article 73 b.
41. The last sentence refers to taxes.
42. *Idem*, Article 69.2. b.
43. These conditions refer to the results to be achieved by the joint venture, such as an increase in production, productivity and exports, the introduction of modern technology etc.
44. *Official Gazette*, No. 22 of April 19, 1973. An (unofficial) translation of the law is reproduced in the Annex.
45. 'Law on Investment of Resources by Foreign Persons in Domestic Organisations of Associated Labour', Article 14, paragraph 1.
46. Or, presumably, a combination thereof forming only a part of an enterprise.
47. 'Law on Investment of Resources...', Article 14, paragraph 2.
48. *Idem*, Article 14, paragraph 3.
49. Sukijasovic, in *Yugoslav Survey (loc. cit.)*, page 49.
50. The following general review of the Yugoslav foreign trade and foreign exchange regime is based on the chapter about Yugoslavia in the *27th Annual Report on Exchange Restrictions* of the International Monetary Fund, Washington, 1973, pages 536-543.
51. There is, in addition, a third category which comprises 'authorised exchange offices' but these may only deal in foreign bank notes and travellers' cheques.
52. These specific allocations are limited mainly to large investment projections, the amounts are determined by the Federal Assembly.
53. For certain industrial sectors this percentage is higher, e.g. 67% for producers of copper and 50% for a number of basic metal and chemical industries.
54. With the exception that no consumer goods may be imported on deferred payment terms and that no foreign financial credits may be taken up with a grace period of less than two years.
55. Unless, of course, such import substitution can only be achieved because of high effective protection measures.
56. Wolfgang G. Friedmann, 'The contractual joint venture', *Columbia Journal of World Business*, Vol. VII, No. 1, Jan./Feb. 1972.
57. Friedmann, *loc. cit.*, page 58.
58. *Ibidem.*
59. *Ibidem.*
60. Sukijasovic, *Foreign investment legislation... (op. cit.)*, pages 32-33.
61. Cf. Michael Greener, *The Penguin Dictionary of Commerce*, Penguin Books, London, 1970, pages 235/236. It should be noted here that the Limited Partnership Act of 1907 created the possibility of limited liability for certain partners in a partnership. The general partners, however, remain fully liable. Moreover, limited partners cannot dispose of their share or withdraw it, take part in the management

or bind the firm. The concept of partners with limited liability is therefore even less relevant to the Yugoslav case.

62. Institute of Comparative Law, *Foreign investment in Yugoslavia: legal problems*, published by the Yugoslav Chamber of Economy, Belgrade, 1972, page 47.
63. The determination of the costs of the investment is, of course, intimately linked with the valuation of the assets-in-kind that are contributed to the joint venture by both partners – this issue will be dealt with in more detail in the section on the financial plan.
64. It so happens that there exists in Yugoslavia a joint venture for the manufacture of particle boards. However the data and figures on which the example is based are not derived from this operation but are taken from the OECD publication *Manual of industrial project analysis in developing countries*, Annex to Volume I, 'Industrial profiles', Paris, 1968, pages 209-219 (Particle Boards). The OECD data are supplemented by purely fictitious figures for licences etc. Moreover, since the OECD data cost estimates date from 1968, the example is entirely hypothetical.
65. In view of the nature of the proposed project, the partners agree that the joint venture should take the form of an OOUR (with limited liability) within the framework of the Yugoslav parent enterprise.
66. Article 9, 'Law on Investment of Resources by Foreign Persons in Domestic Organisations of Associated Labour.'
67. Sukijasovic, in *Yugoslav Survey (loc. cit.)*, page 50.
68. Cf. Stojkovic, *op. cit.*, pages 31-32.
69. Cf. Institut za Spoljnu Trgovinu, *Model of a contract for joint foreign capital investment in Yugoslav companies*, Belgrade, 1970, pages 56-57.
70. Institute of Comparative Law, *op. cit.*, page 55.
71. Glickman and Sukijasovic, in *Harvard International Law Journal (loc. cit.)*, page 295, note 177.
72. *Idem*, page 296.
73. *Ibidem.*
74. Some contracts provide for arbitration by court even on disagreements over policy decisions. The most original way of dealing with a stalemate is the one noted by the Institute of Comparative Law in a particular (unnamed) contract: 'The proposal of one of the parties is to be adopted even if the other party should oppose it in the business board. But if the so proposed transaction should result in a loss, this will be borne by the party whose representatives in the business board had proposed it. On the other hand, if the transaction should result in a profit, this will be divided according to the contract clause on division of profits. However, such a practice can be repeated only a fixed number of times, following which the contract is repudiated' (Institute of Comparative Law, *op. cit.*, page 56). While the originality of this trouvaille is beyond doubt, the same cannot be said for its practicality. One can easily imagine the difficulties in determining the causes of a loss.
75. Sukijasovic, in *Yugoslav Survey (loc. cit.)*, page 50.
76 Cf., *inter alia*, Stojkovic, *op. cit.*, pages 30-31; and Institut za Spoljnu Trgovinu, *op. cit.*, pages 55-56.
77. Institute of Comparative Law, *op. cit.*, page 58.
78. UNIDO, *Manual on the establishment of industrial joint venture agreements in developing countries*, U.N., New York, 1971, p. 23.
79. UNIDO, *op. cit.*, page 46.
80. *Idem*, page 29.
81. 'Law on Investment of Resources by Foreign Persons in Domestic Organisations of

Associated Labour', Article 6.

82. *Idem*, Article 11.
83. *Ibidem*.
84. Institut za Spoljnu Trgovinu, *op. cit.*, page 63.
85. Institute of Comparative Law, *op. cit.*, page 65.
86. 'Law on Investment of Resources by Foreign Persons in Domestic Organisations of Associated Labour', Article 46.
87. *Idem*, Article 16.
88. In case the foreign partner has retained title to specific fixed assets (e.g. equipment), these assets will simply be shipped back and the question of evaluation does not arise.
89. Article 19 of the 'Law on Investment of Resources...'
90. Sukijasovic, in *Yugoslav Survey (loc. cit.)*, page 45.
91. *Ibidem*.

# 5. Joint ventures between Yugoslav and foreign enterprises: the experience so far

## 5.1. INTRODUCTION

Since the adoption of the first legislation in July 1967 more than seven years have passed – a period which would seem to be long enough to arrive at an assessment of results. Yet, the experience accumulated is far from conclusive. It took a long time before the drive to attract private foreign investment gathered some momentum and the number of joint ventures contracted has remained well below the – admittedly high – Yugoslav expectations. Moreover, the great majority of ventures has, at this time of writing, only one or at most two years of operational experience which is too short to arrive at a firm judgement about success or failure. It may nevertheless be of some use to take stock of the present situation and to arrive at a few tentative conclusions notably with respect to possible improvements in the investment climate. This effort is none the easier since the situation in Yugoslavia – as has been often noted in this study – keeps evolving and any conclusions reached at this stage risk to be overtaken by events having occurred in the meantime.

## 5.2. JOINT VENTURE AGREEMENTS REGISTERED UP TO 31–1–1974[1]

### 5.2.1. *Registered contracts by year*

By the end of January 1974, 97 contracts were operational. Since a number of registered contracts were additional agreements concerning earlier concluded joint ventures, the total number of joint ventures is somewhat lower, i.e. 90. Eight other approved and registered contracts are no longer valid, four of these were not implemented at all while the remaining four were terminated shortly after registration.[2] Although perhaps not too much significance should be attached to the fact, it is somewhat discouraging to note that the first contract registered was among those cancelled prematurely.

As shown by Table 5.1, the adoption of the legislation allowing private foreign investment in Yugoslav enterprises hardly caused a stampede of foreign investors rushing in to take advantage of this opportunity. No contracts were registered in 1967, and not more than five in 1968, of which only three are still in existence. In the following years, the pace increased rather slowly to reach 26 agreements in 1972 which so far is still the top year both in terms of agreements concluded and amounts of foreign capital invested.

*Table 5.1. Yugoslavia: joint venture contracts by year of registration*

| Year | Number of contracts | Risk-capital investment | | | | |
|---|---|---|---|---|---|---|
| | | Yugoslav share | | Foreign share | | |
| | | Million dinars | Percentage of total | Million dinars | Percentage of total | Total |
| 1968 | 3 | 677.6 | 77 | 202.8 | 23 | 880.4 |
| 1969 | 8 | 799.2 | 71 | 319.6 | 29 | 1,118.8 |
| 1970 | 12 | 1,044.7 | 79 | 279.0 | 21 | 1,323.7 |
| 1971 | 17 | 814.3 | 73 | 295.6 | 27 | 1,109.9 |
| 1972 | 26 | 4,662.3 | 88 | 616.3 | 12 | 5,278.6 |
| 1973 | 25 | 2,631.2 | 85 | 482.1 | 15 | 3,113.3 |
| 1974 (1 month) | 6 | 169.6 | 83 | 35.6 | 17 | 205.2 |
| Total | 97 | 10,798.9 | 83 | 2,231.0 | 17 | 13,029.9 |

Source: Computed from OECD, *Foreign investment in Yugoslavia (1974)*, Annex I.

Foreign investment in Yugoslavia thus reached 2,231 million dinars or $137.3 million, at present exchange rates.[3] The total capital inflow generated by these joint ventures is, of course, higher – and this point is generally overlooked – because of the fact that the financing of joint ventures in many cases involves foreign loans as well. Inasmuch as can be assumed that such loans would not have been made but for the joint venture(s) concerned, they should be included in the total amount of foreign capital inflow. Unfortunately no data are available on the foreign loans contracted in connection with joint ventures, and to arrive at a reasonable estimate is a hazardous exercise. Nevertheless – if the sample of 15 foreign investors surveyed in the next section (see Table 5.12) would be representative on this score as well – one could tentatively guess that foreign lending to joint ventures is of the same order as foreign risk-capital participation, i.e. roughly 2 billion dinars.

A total of 90 joint ventures, achieved over a period of some seven years, is not particularly impressive. Assuming that the number of Yugoslav enterprises has not significantly decreased since 1970 (cf. Table 1.9), this would imply that less than 4% has been involved in a joint venture. From the angle of the inflow of capital – although it should be recalled that the Yugoslavs have never considered this one of the main reasons for encouraging private foreign investment – the performance is much better. The average capital transfer to Yugoslav enterprises between the years 1967 and 1972 (the last year for which this information is available) amounted to about $185 million.[4] Averaged out over the period 1968–1973 the inflow of foreign risk-capital alone was about $23 million, and if that amount is doubled to take into account joint venture-linked foreign credits, the total inflow generated by joint ventures represents about 25% of the overall capital transfers to Yugoslav enterprises.

### 5.2.2. *Registered contracts by industrial sector*

In one respect the experience with joint ventures has probably been successful: private foreign investment has concentrated on high-technology industries. It may be recalled here that the main reason why Yugoslavia decided to allow joint ventures with foreign enterprises was the expectation that this would lead to the introduction of modern industrial know-how. With a few exceptions, practically all joint ventures were set up to manufacture products that before were either beyond Yugoslavia's capabilities or – at least – would have taken a considerably longer time to develop. More than a third of the foreign capital inflow has gone into the automotive industry, and 16% into chemicals and chemical products. The range of new products introduced by joint ventures further includes such items as telecommunications equipment, roller bearings, radial tyres, machine tools, industrial equipment, special types of board, contact lenses etc.

The investment in the automotive industry is not only the largest as far as the total amount is concerned, but also in terms of investment per contract, almost three times the average. This, of course, is hardly surprising in view of the capital-intensive nature of this type of industry. Investment per individual joint venture has also been high – twice the average size – in the rubber industry because of a few large projects for the production of radial tyres.

*Table 5.2. Yugoslavia: joint venture contracts by sector*

| Sector | Number of contracts | Foreign investment: Total (mln. dinars) | Foreign investment: Average per j.v. | Percentage of total foreign investment |
|---|---|---|---|---|
| 1. Automotive industry | 13 | 784.7 | 60.4 | 35.2 |
| 2. Chemicals and chemical products | 14 | 365.4 | 16.1 | 16.4 |
| 3. Metallurgy and metal processing | 9 | 183.5 | 20.4 | 8.2 |
| 4. Rubber products | 4 | 182.4 | 45.6 | 8.2 |
| 5. Electrical products and equipment | 13 | 149.2 | 11.5 | 6.7 |
| 6. Construction and building materials | 7 | 137.2 | 19.6 | 6.1 |
| 7. Paper and board | 7 | 134.1 | 19.1 | 6.0 |
| 8. Machinery and industrial equipment | 5 | 51.9 | 10.4 | 2.3 |
| 9. Textiles and clothing | 6 | 41.1 | 6.8 | 1.8 |
| 10. Food, beverages and tobacco | 6 | 22.0 | 3.6 | 1.0 |
| 11. Tourism | 3 | 18.8 | 6.3 | 0.8 |
| 12. Other | 10 | 160.6 | 16.6 | 7.2 |
| Total | 97 | 2,231.0 | 23.0 | 100.0 |

Source: Computed from OECD (1974), *op. cit.*, Annex I.

### 5.2.3. *Foreign investment by size of participation*

The 90 joint ventures registered so far show a great variety as far as foreign investment is concerned, both in terms of absolute amounts and percentage participations in the risk-capital. The smallest sum invested was only 642,400 dinars – this was before a minimum of 1.5 million dinars was set – and the largest investment put up by a single partner (FIAT) amounted to 275 million dinars. Participations in the risk-capital range from a minimal 2.1% to the legally permissible maximum of 49.9%. Up to the end of January 1974 no foreign investor had obtained permission to acquire a majority interest.

More than half of all joint ventures has a foreign investment below 10 million dinars (about $615,000) and only in five instances the foreign investment amounts to 100 million or more.

*Table 5.3. Yugoslavia: foreign investment by amount of participation*

| *Amount per joint venture (mln. dinars)* | *Number of joint ventures* |
|---|---|
| below 1 | 5 |
| 1–2 | 12 |
| 2–5 | 13 |
| 5–10 | 17 |
| 10–25 | 17 |
| 25–50 | 15 |
| 50–100 | 6 |
| over 100 | 5 |
| | 90 |

Source: OECD (1974), *op. cit.*, Annex I.

*Table 5.4. Yugoslavia: distribution of percentage shares of foreign investors in risk-capital of joint ventures*

| *Percentage share* | *Number of joint ventures* |
|---|---|
| 0–10.0 | 10 |
| 10.1–20.0 | 13 |
| 20.1–30.0 | 13 |
| 30.1–40.0 | 18 |
| 40.1–48.9 | 8 |
| over 49.0 | 28 |
| | 90 |

Source: OECD (1974), *op. cit.*, Annex I.

In a rather large number of cases – about 30% of the total – the foreign investment is at the legal maximum; the majority of these, however, concern joint ventures of a smaller size. The weighted average of the foreigners' share amounts to 17% (cf. Table 5.1), but this figure is somewhat unduly influenced by one enormous project (a rolling mill) that by itself accounts for 20% of the total (Yugoslav plus foreign) investment in all joint ventures registered sofar. Foreign participation in this one joint venture amounts to 2.1% of the risk-capital. If this project is eliminated from the computation, the average foreign participation in the remaining 89 joint ventures rises to 21%. This may still seem on the low side, but in a sizeable number of joint ventures the existing plant has been put up as the share of the Yugoslav partner while the foreign participation (plus a much smaller amount of Yugoslav cash) has gone to meet the additional investment which mostly is considerably less than the value of the existing manufacturing facilities.

### 5.2.4. *Yugoslavia: foreign investment by Republic and Autonomous Province*

The large differences in economic development between Yugoslavia's constituent Republics and Autonomous Provinces have been highlighted in Chapter 2. Clearly the Yugoslavs would have preferred that foreign investors would have helped to eliminate these differences by investing in the lesser developed regions. This, however, has not been the case. Foreign companies have shown a marked preference for those Republics with a more developed industrial sector and a better infrastructure. Lower workers' remuneration and tax incentives have failed to attract foreign investors to the country's poorer regions.

The main beneficiaries of foreign investment have been Slovenia – Yugoslavia's most developed Republic – with 35.3% and Serbia with 32.5%, the latter in particular because of the sizeable investment (275 million dinars) made by FIAT in the Zavodi Crevena Zastava automobile plant. Yugoslavia's lesser developed regions (Bosnia and Hercegovina,

*Table 5.5. Yugoslavia: foreign investment by Republic and Autonomous Province*

| *Republic (resp. Autonomous Province)* | *Foreign investment* | | *Number of joint ventures* |
|---|---|---|---|
| | *Mln. dinars* | *% of total* | |
| Slovenia | 788.4 | 35.3 | 31 |
| Serbia proper | 726.2 | 32.6 | 17 |
| Croatia | 283.4 | 12.7 | 22 |
| Bosnia and Hercegovina | 169.0 | 7.6 | 10 |
| Montenegro | 138.1 | 6.2 | 2 |
| Macedonia | 98.8 | 4.4 | 4 |
| Vojvodina | 15.4 | 0.7 | 2 |
| Kosovo | 11.7 | 0.5 | 2 |
| Total | 2,231.0 | 100.0 | 90 |

Source: Computed from OECD (1974), *op. cit.*, Annex I.

Kosovo, Macedonia and Montenegro) together account for only 18.7% of the total amount, slightly more than half of the share of Slovenia alone.

### 5.2.5. *Origin of foreign investment*

Not surprisingly, Yugoslavia's main partners in foreign trade are also its principal partners in foreign private investment: Italy, F.R. Germany, USA and France. The nine countries of the EEC together account for 57.4% of the total amount invested.

*Table 5.6. Yugoslavia: countries of origin of foreign industrial partners*

| *Country* | *Amount invested (mln. dinars)* | *Percentage of total foreign investment* | *Number of* foreign investors* |
|---|---|---|---|
| Italy | 491.6 | 22.0 | 24 |
| F.R. Germany | 462.1 | 20.7 | 20 |
| USA | 233.8 | 10.5 | 10 |
| France | 215.7 | 9.7 | 5 |
| DDR | 138.3 | 6.2 | 1 |
| Austria | 123.6 | 5.5 | 4 |
| Switzerland | 112.2 | 5.0 | 8 |
| Sweden | 94.5 | 4.2 | 2 |
| Czechoslovakia | 59.0 | 2.6 | 1 |
| Belgium | 52.6 | 2.4 | 4 |
| U.K. | 29.9 | 1.3 | 5 |
| Netherlands | 25.5 | 1.1 | 1 |
| Lichtenstein | 20.9 | 0.9 | 4 |
| Canada | 8.4 | 0.4 | 1 |
| San Marino | 6.1 | 0.3 | 1 |
| Denmark | 4.4 | 0.2 | 2 |
| Total | 2,071.5 | 93.0 | 93 |

Source: Computed from OECD (1974), *op. cit.*, Annex I.

* Number not identical to the number of registered countries since in some cases there are several industrial partners to the same contract.

The remaining 159.5 million dinars – 7.0% of the total – of the foreign risk-capital inflow have been made available by the International Finance Corporation and the International Investment Corporation for Yugoslavia S.A.

As shown in Table 5.6 practically all foreign investment is of Western origin. In only two instances have joint ventures been concluded with firms from COMECON countries: DDR and Czechoslovakia. Although there

**is nothing in the legislation or in any other governmental directives that could be interpreted as a discouragement of joint ventures with countries from the Eastern bloc, it is nevertheless understandable that Yugoslav firms look mainly in the West for industrial partners as modern industrial, and managerial know-how happens to be more developed in capitalist countries. Still, one cannot fail to notice that the Soviet Union is conspicuously absent from the list.**

## 5.3. A SURVEY OF FOREIGN INVESTORS' EXPERIENCE

### 5.3.1. *Selected data about a sample of foreign investors*

The experience that the 90odd foreign industrial partners to existing joint ventures have accumulated could provide useful knowledge both for other foreign firms that consider investing in Yugoslavia and for the Yugoslavs themselves, particularly with respect to the possible elimination of certain obstacles to foreign investment in the present legislation and regulations affecting joint ventures. Of course, as said earlier, only a limited number of joint ventures have been operational for a period of at least two years. Yet, potentially interesting experience undoubtedly has been gained and in order to get some insight in this experience a questionnaire has been sent (end-1973) to the 60 industrial foreign firms that had concluded joint venture contracts before mid-1972 and that could, therefore, be expected to have been engaged in 'actual' operations for about one year. The response to the questionnaire has been somewhat disappointing, only 15, or 25%, replied. The reason for this reluctance to provide data on business operations was quite obviously – and understandably – a fear of informing competitors. To protect the interest of those firms that did respond, their names and all further information that could lead to their identification will be withheld.

The 15 firms concerned can be said to constitute a fairly representative sample of the total (60), albeit that on average their investment in Yugoslavia is higher than the general average: while in terms of number of joint ventures they represent 25% of the total, the amount invested by them accounts for 31% of the total. However, the average share of the firms in the sample in the risk-capital of the joint venture amounts to 22% against 23% for the entire group of 60, which would imply that the average size of the projects included in the sample is higher than the overall average. As far as countries of origin are concerned the sample includes four firms from Italy and F.R. Germany – Yugoslavia's main joint venturing partners – and one each from seven other different countries. In addition, the joint ventures, in which the 15 firms are partners, cover a wide range of industrial activity: chemicals, automotive industry, electrical equipment, paper, metal processing and tyres.

Obviously, the results of the analysis of the answers to the questionnaire by the 15 foreign investors included in the sample will have to be interpreted with caution. It is not suggested here that in this way a complete picture of the sum total of the experiences of all foreign firms involved in Yugoslav joint ventures can be obtained. On the other hand, in view of the fact that the sample is representative in many respects, the experiences of the firms concerned are probably fairly indicative.

### 5.3.2. *Investment decision and selection of the Yugoslav partner*

The rather modest number of joint ventures concluded – especially in the earlier years covered by the survey – obviously implies a reluctance of foreign firms to invest in Yugoslavia. It would therefore be interesting to find out what specific reasons have led those foreign firms that did invest to take the risk. In the questionnaire a choice of eight possible reasons was given plus a ninth category for 'other'. Respondents were requested

*Table 5.7. Yugoslavia: rating of foreign investors' reasons to invest*

| *Reason to invest* | *Points obtained* | *Percentage of total number of points* |
|---|---|---|
| 1. To maintain an existing (local) market | 32 | 26.5 |
| 2. To make a profitable use of licences, patents, know-how | 29 | 24.0 |
| 3. To develop a new (local) market | 27 | 22.3 |
| 4. To use Yugoslavia as a base for exports to Eastern Europe | 21 | 17.4 |
| 5. To obtain raw materials | 5 | 4.2 |
| 6. To take advantage of low labour costs | 2 | 1.6 |
| 7. To overcome tariff barriers | 2 | 1.6 |
| 8. To take advantage of favourable labour relations | 1 | 0.8 |
| 9. Other (reason specified: proximity to important Western European markets) | 2 | 1.6 |
| Total | 121 | 100.0 |

to mark their various reasons for investing 1, 2, 3, 4 in order of importance. According 4 points for the most important reason, 3 for the second most important, etc., a score could be established for each of the nine categories. For easier comparison, the score for each category is also expressed, in Table 5.7, in terms of a percentage of the total number of points for all nine categories together.

It is quite clear from the table that – at least for the 15 respondents – factors relating to the market (be it in Yugoslavia itself or abroad) constitute the main motivation to invest in Yugoslavia. Together, the categories concerned (Nos. 1, 3, 4, and 9) account for more than two-thirds over the total number of points. This confirms the findings of the Planungsgruppe Ritter (cf. Table 1.4), which concluded that for German firms investing abroad the market potential was the prime initiating force.

The second principal motive to invest in Yugoslavia is the desire to sell technology and industrial know-how in the form of licences, patents etc. Ten respondents, or two-thirds of the total, marked this category as of special interest. The importance of this issue to foreign investors coincides perfectly with Yugoslav wishes to acquire up-to-date industrial know-how, and it might be advisable to stress this point in any publicity efforts to attract more foreign investment.

It would seem that the remaining possible reasons for investing in Yugoslavia are of minor importance, in particular the relatively low wages and the – on the whole – favourable labour climate do not appear to be of special interest.

Respondents were also requested to list the reasons for choosing a particular partner. In a third of the cases the foreign investor was approached by the Yugoslav side, and in a further third the joint venture developed out of a previous association. In the remaining five instances,

*Table 5.8. Yugoslavia: foreign investors' reasons for choosing a particular Yugoslav joint venture partner*

| *Reason* | *Number of times quoted* |
|---|---|
| Previous association | 5 |
| Approach by Yugoslav firm | 5 |
| Availability of production facilities and/or other resources on Yugoslav side | 5 |
| Other | – |

the foreign party was looking for additional productional facilities and/or other resources which it was lacking itself.

For many foreign investors the Yugoslav self-management system is either an unknown quantity or a cause for more or less serious misgivings. Of course, given the fact that the foreign firms approached had decided to invest in Yugoslavia, it could not be expected that they would have been unduly frightened by Yugoslavia's unique social system. But still, it is encouraging to note that none of the 15 respondents felt seriously apprehensive and that a majority had no apprehensions at all.

*Table 5.9. Yugoslavia: foreign investors' attitude towards self-management*

| *Degree of apprehension* | *Number of times quoted* |
|---|---|
| Seriously apprehensive | – |
| Moderately apprehensive | 7 |
| Not apprehensive | 8 |

As far as the formal set-up of the 15 joint ventures is concerned, one notes that in only one case a new enterprise was formed. In all other instances the investment either took place in an entire existing Yugoslav firm or a division thereof.

*Table 5.10. Yugoslavia: formal set-up of joint ventures included in the sample*

| *Set-up* | *Number* |
|---|---|
| New enterprise | 1 |
| Entire (existing) enterprise | 4 |
| Division(s) with legal personality | 7 |
| Division(s) without legal personality | 3 |

The last category, of course, was only relevant at the time the joint venture contracts were concluded. Since the constitutional amendments of 1971 all basic divisions of a Yugoslav enterprise have legal personality.

In general the negotiation of a joint venture agreement with a Yugoslav firm is a long, drawn-out process. None of the 15 respondents had been able to complete all arrangements within three months and in seven instances it took more than one year. One should be careful not to put the blame for this inordinately slow process entirely on Yugoslav shoulders. It is just as often the foreign investor who holds back in the hope of obtaining additional advantages. Mostly, however, it is simply a matter of both parties trying to get a feel of each other and negotiating a weatherproof agreement.

*Table 5.11. Yugoslavia: time needed from first contact to conclusion of contract for joint ventures included in the sample*

| *Time needed* | *Number* |
|---|---|
| 0–3 months | – |
| 3–6 months | 2 |
| 6–9 months | 3 |
| 9–12 months | 3 |
| More than one year | 7 |

### 5.3.3. *Financing*

The financial structure of joint ventures between Yugoslav and foreign enterprises would appear to be a function of their size. Small and medium-sized joint ventures tend to be financed almost exclusively by risk-capital, and only the relatively larger projects involve loan financing.

*Table 5.12. Yugoslavia: financial structure of joint ventures included in the sample*

| *Size of project (mln. U.S. $)* | *Number of joint ventures* | *Risk-capital* | | *Loans* | |
|---|---|---|---|---|---|
| | | *Yugoslav* | *Foreign* | *Yugoslav* | *Foreign* |
| | | *percentage* | | | |
| under 1 mln. | 3 | 62 | 38 | – | – |
| 1–5 mln. | 7 | 56 | 41 | 2 | 1 |
| over 5 mln. | 5 | 58 | 14 | 10 | 18 |
| Weighted average | 15 | 58 | 17 | 9 | 16 |

It is interesting to note that the Yugoslav participation in the form of risk-capital remains fairly constant in all categories, while the foreign share drops sharply with the increasing size of the total project.

The individual financial plans of the 15 joint ventures, of course, differ a great deal. Yet, it is remarkable that in only five instances loan financing was included, long-term debt exceeded risk-capital only in a single case (68:32).

The relationship between Yugoslav and foreign risk-capital varied considerably: from a low foreign share of 6% to the legal maximum of 49%. In general, the foreign participation would tend to diminish with the increasing size of the project – although even in one of the larger projects the foreign party held 49% of the risk-capital.

*Table 5.13. Yugoslavia: risk-capital structure of joint ventures included in the sample*

| *Foreign percentage share* | *Number of joint ventures* |
|---|---|
| up to 10.0 | 1 |
| 10.1–20.0 | 1 |
| 20.1–30.0 | 4 |
| 30.1–40.0 | 2 |
| 40.1–48.9 | 4 |
| 49.0 and over | 3 |

*Table 5.14. Yugoslavia: structure of foreign risk-capital participation in joint ventures included in the sample*

| | *Risk-capital participation (in %)* | | |
|---|---|---|---|
| *Foreign investor* | *Machinery and equipment* | *Licences, patents, know-how* | *Cash* |
| Number 1 | – | 50 | 50 |
| 2 | 100 | – | – |
| 3 | – | 10 | 90 |
| 4 | – | – | 100 |
| 5 | 80 | 10 | 10 |
| 6 | – | 30 | 70 |
| 7 | – | – | 100 |
| 8 | 80 | 20 | – |
| 9 | – | 70 | 30 |
| 10 | – | 80 | 20 |
| 11 | – | – | 100 |
| 12 | – | 17 | 83 |
| 13 | 57 | 43 | – |
| 14 | 10 | 15 | 75 |
| Weighted average | 7 | 19 | 74 |

Earlier mention was made of the fact that the Yugoslav legislation permits the foreign partner to invest part of his risk-capital contribution in kind, i.e. in the form of machinery and equipment or the capitalised value of licences, patents, know-how etc. A considerable number of foreign partners appear to have made use of this opportunity. In only three cases out of 14 – one respondent did not answer a question on this subject – the foreign participation consisted entirely of a cash contribution, while in three instances no cash was invested at all.

It is worthwhile to note that 10 out of 14 foreign investors opted for the possibility to capitalise the value of their intangible industrial property as part of their risk-capital contribution. Not surprisingly, these were the 10 that listed the opportunity to do so as one of the motives leading to the investment decision (cf. Table 5.7).

### 5.3.4. *Secondment of foreign staff*

Apart from their representatives on the joint venture's business boards, the foreign investors put remarkably few of their own staff at the disposal of the joint venture. The fifteen foreign firms involved seconded together

*Table 5.15. Yugoslavia: foreign personnel seconded to the joint ventures included in the sample*

| *Foreign investor* | | *Deputy general manager* | *Other management staff* | *Commercial staff* | *Technical staff* |
|---|---|---|---|---|---|
| Number | 1 | – | – | – | 2 |
| | 2 | – | – | – | – |
| | 3 | – | – | 1 | – |
| | 4 | – | – | – | – |
| | 5 | – | – | – | – |
| | 6 | – | – | 1 | – |
| | 7 | 1 | 1 | – | 7 |
| | 8 | – | – | – | – |
| | 9 | – | – | – | – |
| | 10 | – | 1 | 1 | – |
| | 11 | 1 | – | – | 1 |
| | 12 | 1 | 1 | – | – |
| | 13 | – | – | – | – |
| | 14 | – | – | – | – |
| | 15 | – | – | – | – |
| Total | | 3 | 3 | 3 | 10 |

a total of 19 people, 10 of which are technicians most of whom are employed in Yugoslavia on a temporary basis only. Apparently – and this is an encouraging sign – the confidence of the foreign firms in their Yugoslav partners was large enough to trust them with the day-to-day running of the joint venture. Only three foreign partners made use of their right to appoint a Deputy General Manager, and none has bothered to place one of its financial specialists in the joint venture to keep a running check on accounting procedures and practices.

### 5.3.5. *Foreign investors' evaluation of performance*

Respondents were asked to evaluate the performance of the joint venture in which they are participating in terms of: 1. the return on their risk-capital investment, and 2. the rate of growth of sales – performance to be rated as A (more than satisfactory), B (satisfactory), or C (less than satisfactory). In view of their relatively short operating experience, three foreign investors declined to answer a question on this subject.

*Table 5.16. Yugoslavia: foreign investors' evaluation of performance of joint ventures included in the sample*

| *Performance in terms of:* | *Foreign investor* | | | | | | | | | | | | | | |
|---|---|---|---|---|---|---|---|---|---|---|---|---|---|---|---|
| | *1* | *2* | *3* | *4* | *5* | *6* | *7* | *8* | *9* | *10* | *11* | *12* | *13* | *14* | *15* |
| Return on investment | C | B | B | B | B | A | C | – | – | C | B | B | – | B | B |
| Rate of growth of sales | C | A | B | B | A | A | C | – | – | A | C | B | – | B | B |

Note: A = more than satisfactory
B = satisfactory
C = less than satisfactory
– = no information provided.

As far as the return on investment is concerned, only three out of twelve respondents reported a less than satisfactory result, which is not an excessively high proportion. On average, the foreign investors included in the sample would appear to be satisfied on this score.

The growth performance of the joint ventures involved rates an even better evaluation. While – again – there are three respondents that declare themselves to be less than satisfied, four others report a more than satisfactory performance.

International joint ventures often face problems, ranging from minor irritations to major misunderstanding, due to the different cultural and socio-economic background of the partners. However, the differences in business approach between the foreign and Yugoslav parties to the joint ventures included in the survey have, on the whole, not given rise to major difficulties. Only two out of fourteen respondents – one foreign investor did not answer the question on this subject – had experienced serious problems for this reason. As could be expected, the two foreign firms concerned were those that were less than satisfied with respect to both the return on their investment and the growth performance of the joint venture. The two remaining foreign investors (nos. 10 and 11) that rated only one of the performance categories as less than satisfactory reported only minor problems (no. 11) or no problems (no. 10).

*Table 5.17. Yugoslavia: foreign investors' evaluation of problems arising from a difference in business approach*

| | *Foreign investor* | | | | | | | | | | | | | | |
|---|---|---|---|---|---|---|---|---|---|---|---|---|---|---|---|
| | *1* | *2* | *3* | *4* | *5* | *6* | *7* | *8* | *9* | *10* | *11* | *12* | *13* | *14* | *15* |
| No problems | | × | | × | | × | | – | | × | | | | | |
| Minor problems | | | × | | × | | | – | × | | × | × | × | × | × |
| Serious problems | × | | | | | | × | – | | | | | | | |

On the basis of the data presented in Table 5.17, it would seem that the difficulties, arising from differences in business approach, should not be exaggerated as is sometimes done in the West. Experience has shown that Yugoslav and foreign firms can cooperate profitably. Misgivings on this point are inspired by ignorance about the Yugoslav socio-economic system rather than based on facts. This, of course, does not mean that on a number of specific issues joint venture partners may not find themselves in disagreement. In fact – as shown by Table 5.17 – there is not a single area of business policy or operations where some foreign investors did not report at least minor problems. Moreover, with one exception, all respondents that provided information on this subject had experienced minor difficulties of one kind or another. Yet, one should not be tempted to conclude that joint ventures with Yugoslav enterprises inherently pose more serious problems than international joint ventures in any other country.[5] For one thing, Yugoslav legislation on joint venturing (except for the foreign exchange regime) is considerably more liberal than in many other countries and, moreover, the governmental attitude is one of positive encouragement instead of reluctant acceptance as is so often the case.

*Table 5.18. Yugoslavia: foreign investors' evaluation of problems in specific areas of business policy and operations*

| Problem area | Foreign investor | | | | | | | | | | | | | | |
|---|---|---|---|---|---|---|---|---|---|---|---|---|---|---|---|
| | *1* | *2* | *3* | *4* | *5* | *6* | *7* | *8* | *9* | *10* | *11* | *12* | *13* | *14* | *15* |
| Export to third markets | – | a | a | a | a | | C | – | – | a | a | a | – | a | B |
| Marketing strategy | – | a | B | a | a | a | B | – | – | a | B | B | – | a | a |
| Planning | – | a | C | a | a | a | B | – | a | B | B | B | B | a | a |
| Expansion | – | a | – | a | a | a | C | – | – | B | a | B | – | a | B |
| Reinvestment policy | – | a | – | a | a | a | B | – | – | B | a | a | – | a | B |
| Pricing | – | a | a | B | B | a | B | – | a | B | C | C | – | B | B |
| Dividend policy | – | a | B | a | a | a | – | – | – | C | a | a | – | a | a |
| Fees, royalties | C | a | a | a | a | B | a | – | B | a | a | a | a | B | B |
| Accounting | – | a | C | a | B | B | C | – | – | B | C | a | – | C | C |
| Personnel policy | – | a | C | a | a | a | B | – | B | a | B | B | – | a | a |
| Workers' salaries | – | a | B | a | a | a | B | – | a | a | a | B | – | a | a |
| Allocation to Common Cons. Fund | – | a | B | a | a | a | a | – | – | a | a | a | – | a | a |

Note: a = no problems
B = minor problems
C = serious problems
– = no information provided.

The major problem areas would seem to be pricing and, particularly, accounting. The first is a common problem to all international joint ventures, but the second probably more typical for the Yugoslav case. The financial statements of the Yugoslav enterprise differ from those used in the West (cf. Chapter 2) and it is therefore of the highest importance that the partners include in the joint venture contract an agreed-upon detailed Income Statement and Balance Sheet. Failure to do so will result later in serious misunderstandings.

Relatively few difficulties are apparent in what one would have expected to be major problem areas: i.e. those relating to personnel policy and workers' remuneration. Only one respondent signalled serious problems in the field of personnel policy, while the others had experienced either minor or no problems. Foreign investors clearly do not feel that the influence exercised in these areas by the workers' councils is unduly harmful to their interests. This is confirmed by Table 5.19.

No respondent rated the influence of the workers' council as severely restrictive, while a large majority (10 out of 14) judged it to be neutral, and two others even appreciated its contribution as constructive. Of the

*Table 5.19. Yugoslavia: foreign investors' evaluation of the influence of the workers' council on the operations of the joint venture*

| | *Foreign investor* | | | | | | | | | | | | | | |
|---|---|---|---|---|---|---|---|---|---|---|---|---|---|---|---|
| | *1* | *2* | *3* | *4* | *5* | *6* | *7* | *8* | *9* | *10* | *11* | *12* | *13* | *14* | *15* |
| Severely restrictive | | | | | | | | – | | | | | | | |
| Restrictive | | | × | | | ×* | | – | | | | | | | |
| Neutral | × | | | × | | | × | – | × | × | × | × | × | × | × |
| Constructive | | × | | | × | | | – | | | | | | | |

* Time-consuming.

two foreign investors that had negative views about the workers' council, one commented (no. 6) that its main complaint was that deliberations were time-consuming. The evaluation given by the other (no. 3) is not surprising in view of the fact that it reported problems in all areas where the workers' council may exert its influence (cf. Table 5.18).

### 5.3.6. *Foreign views on Yugoslav legislation and regulations concerning joint ventures*

Foreign investors were finally asked to state what changes in the present Yugoslav laws and regulations would further improve the investment climate and attract more foreign investment. As could be expected, most suggestions concerned the foreign exchange regime. The restrictions on the free transfer of profit and repatriation of capital are generally considered a definite impediment, although one respondent was prepared to admit that 'from the Yugoslav point of view they may appear justified'. But even this foreign investor felt 'that any restrictions on money transfers to the foreign investor are undesirable'. Another respondent suggested that 'a National Bank guarantee for repatriation of invested cash capital, subject to normal business risk' would be a considerable improvement. Further comments underlined the desirability of liberalising foreign trade regulations by lowering import duties, greater flexibility in customs formalities, etc. No objections were raised against the provision of the law that foreign investors may acquire a minority interest only. Contrary to what is sometimes thought[6] this rule is not considered to be a serious obstacle. One should note, however, that this is the view of foreign investors that themselves accepted this provision and that it is difficult to ascertain whether or not other potential investors are deterred by it.

In only one instance irritation about the workings of the self-management system was voiced: 'The lack of incentives (i.e. for the foreign investor) has little to do with the laws and regulations, but lies rather in the organisational and decision-making structure of the Yugoslav enterprise, which does not permit the setting of clear targets.' This comment, not surprisingly, came from one of the two respondents that had reported serious problems due to the difference in business approach between Yugoslav and foreign firms. Given the fact that most other foreign partners did not see a serious obstacle here, it may be that in this one case a somewhat more flexible mental attitude and a better understanding of the peculiarities of the Yugoslav social system would be in order.

## 5.4. THE INTERNATIONAL INVESTMENT CORPORATION FOR YUGOSLAVIA S.A.

### 5.4.1. *Background*

A little more than a year after the adoption of 1967 joint venture legislation, the idea arose in Yugoslav banking circles that it might be useful to establish a special institution to promote joint ventures between Yugoslav and foreign enterprises. The more perceptive Yugoslav bankers – and government officials, for that matter – were well aware of the fact that, particularly on the side of Western enterprises, there would be a strong initial reluctance to overcome. For most foreign investors Yugoslavia and its socio-economic system was uncharted territory, moreover Yugoslav legislation was complicated and often difficult to understand, and accounting and business practices were presumed to be a cause for misunderstanding. Finally, Yugoslav banks had – obviously – no experience in joint venture financing.

While the initiative to establish some kind of 'broking' institution originated in Yugoslavia, it was only after contact had been made with the International Finance Corporation of the World Bank Group that the idea started to take shape. In November 1968, IFC and a group of Yugoslav banks began actively working together to define the broad outlines of what precise form the new institution should take. It was felt that the range of activities should be broader than the mere rendering of advisory and consulting services, and that, in fact, the institution should have a strong financial basis to have a significant impact. Consultations with European bankers in the first half of 1969 made it clear that there was sufficient interest in a type of specialised 'merchant bank', or 'investment company', to proceed with definite proposals to interested parties. The objectives of the new institution were defined as follows:

- to assist Yugoslav and foreign private enterprises in forming joint ventures;
- to help identify and select projects;
- to assist in the drawing up of financial plans and arrange financing;
- to invest its own capital in the joint ventures it promotes;
- to provide advisory and consulting services;
- to borrow funds and issue debentures and make loans to clients with joint ventures or prospects for joint ventures;
- to underwrite capital requirements, issue stand-bys and provide guarantees;
- to revolve its portfolio by selling its investments to third parties;
- to collect and distribute information affecting the flow of capital into Yugoslav joint ventures;
- to invest in subsidiaries and affiliated institutions with similar objectives.

The corporation was to be a private profit-making institution deriving its income from fees for advisory and consulting services, underwritings etc. and from the employment of its capital and borrowed funds. A memorandum outlining the above principles was discussed with a large number of American and European banks, which resulted in pledges to participate. Negotiations with interested banks, in a few months, were brought to a successful conclusion and in December 1969 the 'International Investment for Corporation for Yugoslavia' was formally established. For tax and other reasons the corporation was registered in Luxemburg, while its head office was to be located in London. The latter choice was inspired by two principal reasons. In the first place, there was uncertainty whether a financial institution such as IICY could legally be located in Yugoslavia, moreover it was felt that it would be desirable to emphasize IICY's international character by locating it outside Yugoslavia. Secondly, London was – and remains – Europe's major financial centre and IICY's physical presence there might facilitate its fund-raising activities.

### 5.4.2. *Capital structure*

The initial authorised capital of IICY was \$12 million, an amount raised to \$15 million in August 1971. The subscribed capital presently amounts to \$13.5 million of which half has been paid-in. The remaining \$6.75 million can be called at any time by a majority vote of the Board of Directors.

IICY's promotors have been very successful in attiacting, from the beginning, a wide grouping of shareholders. The list reads as an Almanac de Gotha of the international banking community. Apart from IFC itself and the 13 most important Yugoslav banks, practically all major Austrian, Dutch, French, German and Italian banks are shareholders. The list further includes Japanese, Kuwaiti, Swedish, Swiss, British and American financial institutions. The obvious purpose was to provide IICY with an easier access to the financial resources and business contacts of the major banks in those countries which could be expected to supply partners for Yugoslav joint ventures. IICY has certainly taken advantage of this opportunity although perhaps not to the extent originally hoped for. The shareholder banks – with a few exceptions – have generally shown some reluctance to extend credits to Yugoslav joint ventures. On many occasions IICY therefore had to resort to the Euro-currency-market, borrowing itself for on-lending to the joint venture. The cost to the final beneficiary of this type of credit is, however, on the high side and floating interest rates introduce an element of insecurity that most borrowers would like to do without. Moreover, in order to remain competitive IICY will have to offer finance on terms and conditions that are at least as good as, and preferably better than, the terms and conditions that Yugoslav banks are able to grant to their customers which are participating in a joint venture. The increasing activity of the Yugoslav banks on the international financial markets and their growing ability to secure good terms constitute a real danger to IICY's rôle as a financial intermediary.

### 5.4.3. *Operations*

In the first four years since its establishment, i.e. up to the end of 1973, IICY has assisted in the setting up of 20 joint ventures or about 22% of the total number registered by that date. In addition, it helped organise one 'industrial-cooperation' agreement which is expected to develop into a joint venture at a later stage. The total investment costs of these 21 operations amounted to slightly more than $500 million, of which foreign financing provided 53% in loans and risk-capital. IICY itself took part in the financing of 14 of these joint ventures for a total of $16 million equivalent, of which $10.5 million in loans and $5.5 million in risk-capital. IICY has achieved a fairly good balance both in terms of geographical spread over the various Republics and of sectoral distribution. Special attention is given to potential joint venture projects in Yugoslavia's less developed regions.

### 5.4.4. *Prospects*

After a somewhat hesitant start – due, of course, to the fact that it had to find its place as a new and highly specialised institution – IICY is now a going concern with sufficient expertise and experience to play a useful rôle in the further development of Yugoslav joint ventures. But while its prospects for the short and medium term are undoubtedly good, there can be some doubt about its future in the long run. In the first place, Yugoslav banks, which initially had no experience in the field of joint venture promotion and financing, are now increasing their activities – and expertise. Inasmuch as these banks charge little or no fees to their clients for the advisory services involved, they will come to constitute a formidable competition for IICY which – not having the range of sources of income of a normal bank – will have to continue to demand relatively high fees for its services in order to remain profitable. Secondly, as mentioned above, Yugoslav banks are becoming increasingly adept at raising foreign financing at terms which IICY will have difficulty to improve on. The initial advantages of IICY over Yugoslav banks with respect to both consulting expertise and money-raising may therefore tend to disappear, and given the fact that its services are more expensive than those of Yugoslav banks IICY may price itself out of the market.

NOTES

1. The register of joint ventures, which used to be open to public inspection, was declared confidential as of 31st January 1974, and no information about joint ventures concluded since that date is being made available.
2. OECD, *Foreign investment in Yugoslavia (1974)*, Paris, 1974, page 56.
3. Conversion based on an exchange rate of U.S. $1 = 16.25 dinars, as per OECD (1974), *op. cit*. It should be noted that since the adoption of the foreign investment legislation the Yugoslav dinar has devalued from 12.5 to 16.25 to the U.S. dollar. The actual amount of foreign exchange invested is therefore higher than the $139.3 million cited above. The correct figure is impossible to compute since the actual rates of conversion for each individual transfer are not known. It is therefore preferable to use only the Yugoslav dinar as reference.
4. IMF, *International financial statistics*, July 1974.
5. For a good survey of the difficulties that may arise in international joint ventures, see, *inter alia*, K.K. Bivens and E.B. Lovell, *Joint ventures with foreign partners. An international survey of business opinion and experience*, National Industrial Conference Board, New York, 1966, *passim*.
6. See, *inter alia*, OECD (1974), *op. cit.*, page 18.

# 6. Summary and conclusions

## 6.1. INTRODUCTION

The purpose of this study was twofold: in the first place to highlight some aspects of the Yugoslav socio-economic system – on the macro- as well as the enterprise level – and, secondly, to analyse the most important issues relating to joint ventures between Yugoslav and foreign enterprises.

The emerging picture is, of course, far from complete. In particular the treatment of that complex, far-reaching system known as self-management has been sketchy and eclectic. Several major problem areas of Yugoslavia's labour-managed market economy have not even been touched upon – such as unemployment and emigration, agriculture, the balance of payments – nor has justice been done to the sociological and philosophical background of the system. In addition, several interesting theoretical issues (e.g. the investment decision of the labour-managed firm) have been passed over rather rapidly. The aim pursued in the first part of this study was, however, not so much to provide a comprehensive analysis, but rather to lay a basis for a better understanding of Yugoslavia's socio-economic system by focusing on its historical development as well as on those features that make it unique. Without such basic understanding, the analysis of joint ventures between Yugoslav and foreign enterprises would be meaningless.

But also this analysis, as presented here, is necessarily incomplete. To begin with, the experience gained with joint venturing in Yugoslavia is still very limited as most joint ventures have barely reached the operational stage. Moreover, each joint venture is a case of its own and generalisations cannot adequately cover the broad spectrum of possibilities and problems. The reason, then, nevertheless, to attempt an analysis is basically – as was said at the beginning of Chapter 5 – that it might be useful to take stock of the situation at present and to make a few suggestions which could help to improve the climate for joint ventures in Yugoslavia.

In this final chapter the main findings of the study will be summarised, then some preliminary conclusions will be drawn, and lastly a few thoughts will be advanced with respect to the possible evolution of joint venturing in Yugoslavia.

## 6.2. YUGOSLAVIA: A LABOUR-MANAGED MARKET ECONOMY

The analysis of the Yugoslav socio-economic system has been conducted along three lines of approach: a historical one, a theoretical one and a confrontation of the 'pure' theoretical system (as developed by Vanek) with the 'real' system.

### 6.2.1. *History*

The historical evolution of the Yugoslav system has been a highly complex process that went along in leaps and bounds with occasionally strong counteracting forces leading to diversions from the general trend. Nevertheless, three distinct stages can be identified in the development of the system.

- the centrally-planned economy, which was a carbon copy of the Soviet system, lasting from the end of the war to the early fifties, say 1952;
- the phase of decentralisation, from 1952 to 1965, essentially a period of transition, leading to:
- the self-management system, from 1965 onwards.

The first period can be characterised as one compulsive effort to build an economy modelled on the Soviet example. Most remarkable about this was that the Yugoslavs genuinely believed in all things Russian, nobody forced them to follow the Soviet line as was the case in the satellite states. The accusation of revisionism and anti-Sovietism, in early 1948, came therefore as a rude shock. At first, the Yugoslavs tried to prove that they were really following the correct policies, but slowly the awareness grew that the Russians were not so much concerned with economic policies but with politics. The target was Yugoslavia's political independence and this was something the Yugoslavs were not prepared to give up. As a result, they not only began to question Russian politics but Soviet Marxism as well. This led to a critique of centralised decision-making and dominance of the state bureaucracy. Based on Marx's notion of the withering away of the state, Yugoslav thinkers (Kardelj and Djilas) came forward with the idea of a classless society grounded in popular participation in all fields and workers' management of the factories.

In the early fifties this theory gained acceptance and by 1952 the process of decentralisation of the economy and workers' participation in the management of enterprises started in earnest. 'State capitalism' was formally abolished and the planning system was liberalised. This rather radical departure from communist orthodoxy can, in part, be explained by the philosophical rejection of the Soviet system and the subsequent rethinking of Marxism. But there is another factor that undoubtedly played a major rôle: Yugoslavia's historical and central background. Yugoslavia became a unified country really only after World War II and its turbulent long history had led to cultural, religious and political differences between its constituent parts. These deep-rooted differences were perhaps not the prime cause of the decentralisation process, but they certainly contributed greatly to the momentum the process achieved. This is not to say that the decentralisation and the increasing reliance on the market as the guiding force of the economy proceeded smoothly. The economic problems in the early sixties led to intense debates and only towards the end of 1964 could victory be claimed by the defenders of the new system.

The Economic Reform of 1965 finally established the 'labour-managed market economy.' Enterprises, managed by the workers, were given the ultimate responsibility for production and investment decisions, in which they would be guided by the market. The plan, from an instrument of coercion as in the Soviet system, had now become an instrument of cooperation. Subsequent legislation and regulations all had one purpose: further to strengthen self-management, which will remain the cornerstone of the Yugoslav socio-economic system as long as the Yugoslavs are free to choose their own course.

### 6.2.2. *Theory*

While the self-management system is virtually the only recent effort to develop a new socio-economic organisation of human society, it has attracted surprisingly little theoretical interest. Of course, much has been written by the Yugoslavs themselves, but with the exception of Horvat very little has been produced that could qualify as pure theoretical analysis. The principal authors in the West to study the theory of the labour-managed market economy were Ward, Domar and Vanek.

In 1958 Ward published an article in the *American Economic Review* on 'The firm in Illyria: market syndicalism', and this hypothetical Illyria resembled Yugoslavia very closely in its socio-economic structure. Ward argued that the Illyrian, labour-managed firm would have a maximising principle different from that of the capitalist firm: the latter maximises profit, whereas the labour-managed firm behaves rationally if it maximises income per worker. Ward's analysis was rather limited, he examined the Illyrian firm only under conditions of perfect competition and he assumed that only one commodity is produced.

Eight years later, in 1966, Domar's study on 'The Soviet collective farm as a producer cooperative' appeared. While Domar did not specifically mean to analyse the Yugoslav system, the assumptions on which his model was built were very close to Ward's. Domar's analysis was much broader in scope, however. His production function not only included several factors but several products as well and he introduced further a supply curve for labour. He followed Ward – as indeed all Western authors have done – in assuming that the labour-managed firm would maximise income per worker. Domar's principal conclusion was that 'judged by strictly economic criteria' the labour-managed firm was less efficient than the capitalist one.

This conclusion came under attack from Horvat, a Yugoslav economist. His principal objection against Domar was directed against the assumptions that the labour-managed firm maximises income per worker. He argued that the Yugoslav enterprise sets each year a target for 'income per worker', which is used as an accounting device for cost calculation and resource allocation. This income may later be adjusted by way of a bonus at the end of the year. In those circumstances, it would be rational for the Yugoslav firm to maximise total profits over and above the target sum of income per worker. He concluded that therefore there was no difference in maximising principle – and hence efficiency between the Yugoslav and the capitalist firm.

The first to attempt a comprehensive theory of the Yugoslav system was Vanek with his *General theory of labor-managed market economies* (1970). While Ward and Domar only dealt with a few aspects of microeconomic theory, Vanek developed a complete theory of the firm in the labour-managed system covering not just the short run and perfect competition, but the long run and market imperfections as well. In addition, he dealt with macroeconomic theory and such issues as economic policy and planning.

Vanek's theoretical analysis led him to conclude that the labour-managed market economy is more efficient than the 'capitalist' system. In particular, because there would be no conflicts of interest between management and workers. He further maintained that the labour-managed market economy effectively guarantees full employment, that the equilibrium size of the labour-managed firm is smaller than that of the capitalist firm, that there would be less inflationary pressures than in the capitalist economies, that income distribution patterns would be more egalitarian.

### 6.2.3. *The 'real' system*

In a companion volume to his *General Theory*, *The participatory economy* (1971), Vanek claims that the Yugoslav economy is, in fact, performing in accordance with his theoretical conclusions. The economic realities of Yugoslavia were found, however, to be rather different, while the 'efficiency' issue is difficult to solve – in theory as well as in practice – there are no definite indications to enable a conclusion to be drawn as to Yugoslavia's superiority (or inferiority for that matter) to the capitalist economies. However, as far as employment, inflation, and the size of enterprises are concerned, Vanek's theoretical postulations proved to be far from Yugoslav reality. With respect to income distribution, the available data indicate that Yugoslavia is not markedly more egalitarian than the Netherlands.

The juxtaposition of Vanek's theory and Yugoslav practice has highlighted some important aspects of the system, but there are, of course, other issues that had to be dealt with. The first of these concerns the financing of investments. In this field, the most remarkable phenomenon is the rôle that banks have come to play. In spite of a growing importance of self-financing by enterprises, the banks in Yugoslavia are extremely powerful and this had led to a re-thinking of the banks' position in the self-management system. In 1971 a law was adopted to give enterprises a larger say in the banks' operations but the question remains how effective this law will be in practice. The lack of capital market in Yugoslavia – which is legally perfectly possible – has the effect that there is no alternative to banks as a source of external financing.

A second specific aspect of the Yugoslav system is that the Federal Government's responsibilities have been so far reduced that it proved to be impossible to develop a balanced set of economic policy tools appropriate to deal with the problems of a decentralised system. Yugoslavia has to rely almost exclusively on monetary policy and the result has been that corrective measures were often applied too forcefully and thereby invariably overshot the mark.

Regional differences in economic development are a third characteristic that deserves mention. In spite of vigorous efforts, the gap between the (relatively) rich and poor areas has continued to widen. The basic problem here is that assistance is almost exclusively envisaged in terms of transfers of funds, and that little attention is paid to the much wider aspects of economic development.

Whatever its problems may be, Yugoslavia nevertheless has had an outstanding record in economic growth, which justifies a certain optimism about its future.

A study of Yugoslavia cannot ignore the problems that have arisen with the implementation of the self-management system. The Yugoslavs themselves are the first to admit that much is left to be desired. The main criticism is focused on the necessary power of the technocrats and the corresponding loss of influence of the workers' council. Among the measures for improvement, the most far-reaching has been to divide enterprises into so-called 'basic organisations of associated labour' which are endowed with sizeable powers and autonomy.

Western scholars have also voiced criticism about the working of the system in practice. In particular, the French sociologist Albert Meister has stated that self-management is a thing of the past in the sense that it is no longer a living reality in Yugoslavia and, moreover, that it is no longer necessary. Meister's thesis is mainly built on the premise that the Yugoslavs have been wrong to reduce the rôle of the State.

Chapter 1 is concluded with a brief review of Yugoslavia's development targets. These are: a continuing development of the self-management system and fast economic growth, particularly in the less developed regions. To help achieve these goals Yugoslavia seeks an increasing participation in world trade and cooperation with industrial partners from the developed countries.

## 6.3. THE YUGOSLAV ENTERPRISE

While the Yugoslav enterprise functions in many respects like its capitalist counterpart, there are important differences. These fall into two principal categories: those of an institutional and those of an operational nature. To the first belong such questions as the legal structure of the Yugoslav enterprise, the implementation of the self-management system at the enterprise level, and accounting principles. The second category includes Yugoslav practices with respect to planning, distribution of income and financing.

### 6.3.1. *Legal structure*

The means of production are, in the Yugoslav system, not owned by the State or by individuals but by the Yugoslav people as a whole. Legally speaking this is perhaps a vague concept, which even Yugoslav scholars find difficult to define. What is clear, however, is that the workers of an enterprise – i.e. an integrated set of means of production – are free to manage these assets subject only to a few constraints which partly are intended to prevent the running down of the enterprise and partly set the framework within which self-management is to be exercised.

The Yugoslav enterprise is, since 1971, divided into 'Basic Organisations of Associated Labour' (OOUR). An OOUR is defined as a group of workers who produce a product or a service which has a recognisable value and is capable of fetching a price on the market. OOUR's have a large degree of autonomy and can even dissociate themselves from an enterprise. In practice, most enterprises have been carrying on as before, the only difference being that relations between the various divisions (i.e. OOUR's) are now the subject of formal contractual agreements.

Yugoslav enterprises are independent, legal entities, that can enter into contractual relationships without any interference of the State.

### 6.3.2. *Self-management*

The major organs of self-management at the enterprise level are:

- The workers' council, which is the supreme decision-making unit; the council is elected by universal, direct and secret ballot, all workers (with the exception of the director of the enterprise) are eligible for the council.
- The management board, elected by the workers' council, to which the council usually delegates the responsibility for the day-to-day operations of the enterprise.
- The director, who is the chief executive, appointed by the workers' council to which he is answerable. The director executes the decisions of the council and the management board and represents the enterprise in its contractual relationships.

### 6.3.3. *Accounting principles*

The financial statements of the Yugoslav enterprise are – just as in the case of a capitalist enterprise – the balance sheet and the income statement. There are, however, some important differences with the accounts of a Western firm. The most significant of these concern the income statement. Since the workers of the Yugoslav enterprise are considered to be its managers, their reward is not a wage but a sharing of the profit. Personal incomes of the workers are therefore legally not regarded as a cost item, and consequently do not appear on the income statement as costs. Secondly, there is no profit tax. The only taxes levied at the enterprise level are taxes on personal income payments. The consequence is that legislation does not prescribe maximum depreciation charges as in the West, but minimum levels to prevent artificial increases in profit (and paying out of personal incomes). A third difference is that repayment of loans is often carried on the income statement as a cost, since according to Yugoslav law all debt obligations have a legal claim to funds prior to allocations to personal incomes. It goes without saying that, even in the Yugoslav context, this practice is incorrect.

The only major difference with a Western balance sheet is that the Yugoslav enterprise is obliged to present three sub-balances of assets and liabilities respectively those related to the means of production (the so-called Business Fund), the reserves, and the Collective Consumption Fund (which contains the investments earmarked for the collective use of the workers, i.e. medical facilities, schools, housing). It should further be noted that in the Yugoslav system share capital does not exist, the 'equity' of a Yugoslav enterprise consists exclusively of retained earnings. A newly established Yugoslav enterprise is therefore practically entirely financed by debt.

### 6.3.4. *Planning*

Planning in the Yugoslav enterprise serves a dual purpose. In the first place it is the basic instrument to determine business policy. Secondly, it is an exercise of the workers' right to self-management through their participation in the planning process.

Usually plans are drawn up for a multi-year period (3-5 years), for the year ahead, and for monthly operations. The major elements of the plans are forecasts of production, needs for raw materials and other inputs, investments, sales, staffing, and financing requirements.

### 6.3.5. *Determination of personal incomes*

Although the entire income of the workers should logically be determined by the results achieved over the year, in practice the income consists of two parts: a fixed part which is paid out at weekly or monthly intervals according to a pay scale, and a variable part which depends on profits made. The workers' council plays an important rôle in this matter.

### 6.3.6. *Financing*

Just as in the case of its capitalist counterpart, the need for funds of the

Yugoslav enterprise is determined by its investments as required increases in working capital. The investment decision should theoretically be determined by different criteria as the maximising principle is assumed to be – by Western authors, it should be noted – the maximalisation of income per worker. This principle is, however, never applied. The investment decision is the result of the planning process. Based on its views about market developments, the availability of raw materials and other inputs, technological developments etc. the Yugoslav enterprise establishes its plan and thereby, implicitly, the investments required to implement the plan. Any investment which, after a more detailed appraisal, will not yield a profit is abandoned.

As far as sources of funds are concerned, the self-management system of course has a built-in bias against self-financing through retained earnings.

## 6.4. PRIVATE FOREIGN INVESTMENT IN A DEVELOPING ECONOMY

Before going into the subject matter of the second part of this study – joint ventures between Yugoslav and foreign enterprises – some attention should be given to direct private foreign investment (PFI), and joint ventures in general, in a developing economy.

PFI is a much misunderstood issue, basically because it is often considered in the framework of the 'aid' picture. Of course, PFI is not development aid, but a commercial operation undertaken in the expectation of profit. This is not to say that PFI cannot be beneficial to LDC's: if it is made under the right conditions PFI can make an important contribution to economic growth.

### 6.4.1. *The case against private foreign investment*

The arguments against PFI can be grouped together into a few major categories.

Firstly, it is said that since PFI leads to a net outflow of foreign exchange, it is detrimental to the host country. The basic flaw in this argument is that it considers only the effects of PFI on the balance of payments rather than on the economy as a whole. If there is a net overall benefit, PFI is advantageous for a developing country in spite of the outflow of foreign exchange.

Secondly, it is argued that PFI results in high profits for the foreign investor and that LDC's would be better off relying on bonds or fixed-interest loans. This argument, however, cannot be supported by the available data.

Thirdly, PFI is said to impose the wrong – i.e. capital-intensive – technologies on LDC's. Theoretically this is plausible, but in practice substitution of production factors is possible only in a very limited number of cases. For most production processes there is only one combination of production factors that is technically and economically justified.

Fourthly, PFI is criticised because of its effect on local entrepreneurship. Curiously, some critics condemn PFI for interfering too much, while others accuse it of interfering too little. Whoever may be right, the solution should not be to reject PFI but to develop policies which stimulate local entrepreneurs while at the same time institute appropriate controls over PFI.

Finally, it is argued that foreign investors' interests do not coincide with the interests of the host countries and that, in case of conflicts, the host country is likely to be harmed. This is, in fact, a serious possibility but in practice giving rise to less difficulties than could be expected.

### 6.4.2. *Advantages of private foreign investment*

The principal advantages of PFI are: the introduction of management skills, the transfer of technology and know-how, the training of local labour, productivity spill-overs, and the transfer of capital. With respect to the latter, it should be noted that the amounts involved are relatively small. In 1970, PFI accounted for about 4% of gross investment in the LDC's.

On balance, it would seem fair to conclude that the advantages of PFI outweigh the disadvantages. Of course, whether a particular foreign investment will, in fact, be of benefit to the host country depends on the specific circumstances of the case.

### 6.4.3. *Incentives for private foreign investment*

In order to provide the right incentives to attract PFI, host countries would be well advised to be aware of the factors that play a rôle in the investment decision-making process of foreign firms. So far no comprehensive theory on foreign investment has been developed, yet recent research has provided some light (Aharoni, Planungsgruppe Ritter). Major impediments to PFI are political instability, restrictions on profit transfer and repatriation of capital, tax concessions and lack of information about investment opportunities.

### 6.4.4. *The international joint venture in developing countries*

The foreign investment climate in most LDC's is deteriorating. It is possible that a combination of foreign and local participations in a business enterprise – the joint venture – would help to overcome the growing resentment against PFI. The two basic elements of the joint venture are the sharing of control and of risk.

The advantages of PFI are typically accentuated if it takes the form of a joint venture, for the simple reason that local interests are participating in the enterprise and sharing the benefits. Additional benefits to the host country are that the joint venture is the most suitable way to solve the potential conflict of interest between the foreign investor and the host country, that the joint venture may help to alleviate the local political problems arising from the presence of foreign economic interests, and that the foreign partner's connection and expertise can help exports.

As far as the foreign investor is concerned, the major advantage of association with local interests in a joint venture is the reduction of political risk and a better local image. His disadvantage is that his freedom of operation is curtailed.

Of course, a joint venture may encounter serious problems. The best way to limit those problems is to ensure the compatibility of the two partners. Secondly, the joint venture contract should clearly define such matters as: management responsibilities, long-run investment and financing policies, pricing, personnel policies and marketing. Experience with joint ventures so far has demonstrated that in most cases problems are surmountable and that they can make a contribution to economic growth.

## 6.5. JOINT VENTURES BETWEEN YUGOSLAV AND FOREIGN ENTERPRISES: INSTITUTIONAL ASPECTS

At the time of the Economic Reform of 1965, which led to many radical changes, the possibility of allowing private foreign investment in Yugoslavia was for the first time seriously considered. The suggestion initially raised strong protests, not only from Marxist dogmatists but also from those who feared for the effect of PFI on the self-management system. Moreover, Yugoslavia had had a rather disastrous experience with foreign investment in the pre-war period and with Soviet-Yugoslav joint ventures. The willingness to experiment prevailed, however, again, and in 1967 the first legislation on joint ventures was adopted.

### 6.5.1. *Legislation*

Since the Yugoslavs were not prepared to jeopardise the achievements and further development of the self-management system, PFI would have to take a form that would fit the system. This meant that fully-owned subsidiaries of foreign firms were ruled out – in fact, only a minority interest was allowed to safeguard Yugoslav control. Moreover, as joint-stock companies are impossible under the Yugoslav system, the only feasible form of PFI was the contractual non-equity joint venture. No foreign investment was permitted in banking, insurance, internal transport, trade, public utilities, and social services. To make sure that PFI would contribute to Yugoslavia's economic development the legislation further stipulated that joint ventures were only allowed if the joint venture agreement provided for increased production and exports, (and/or) the introduction of modern technology and management techniques, (and/or) scientific research.

There were two additional restrictions, the first one obliging the foreign investor to reinvest in Yugoslavia 20% of his profits after tax (set at 35%) and the second allowing transfer of profits and repatriation of capital only if the foreign exchange resources at the free disposition of the joint venture were sufficient. In particular the latter provision was particularly restrictive. At the time of the initial legislation the joint venture – as indeed all Yugoslav enterprises – could freely dispose of only a certain proportion of the foreign exchange generated by its exports (the so-called retention quota), and this proportion amounted to 7%.

It quickly became clear that more liberal regulations were required if PFI was to have the desired impact on Yugoslav economic development. At the end of 1969, the Law on Foreign Exchange Transactions was amended to the effect that, in addition to the retention quota, the joint venture could dispose of a further one-third of its export earnings for profit transfers of the foreign partner. In 1971, the obligation of the foreign partner to reinvest 20% of his profit after tax was abolished. At the same time, the additional one-third of export earnings was now also made available for capital repatriation (and not only for the transfer of profits) to which further were added 10% of the annual depreciation charges. In 1973, the various regulations on foreign investment were consolidated into a single law, which also provided a better definition of liability.

The major objection against the Yugoslav legislation remains that the joint venture has to generate itself the necessary foreign exchange for profit transfer and capital repatriation. This effectively limits the possibility to conclude joint ventures to those Yugoslav enterprises that produce goods that can be traded internationally. A further inequity is that a Yugoslav bank may guarantee the availability of foreign exchange for the service of foreign debt but not for profit transfer and repatriation of capital. This introduces a considerable bias against the inflow of risk capital which Yugoslavia is actively seeking.

In spite of the various restrictions on PFI, the Yugoslav regulation is remarkably liberal. The partners to the joint venture are left free to determine their contractual relationship, and for that reason the joint venture agreement is, in Yugoslavia, of particular importance.

### 6.5.2. *The joint venture contract*

The joint venture contract should contain a description of the project involved, and of the products to be manufactured, an estimate of the investment cost – both for fixed assets and working capital – and a financial plan setting out in detail how the partners' capital shares are to be paid in and providing for the cover of cost overruns. Further issues to be dealt with concern the organisational structure and the decision-making process, and technical, commercial and financial questions relating to the operations of the joint venture. As far as the organisational structure is concerned, the joint venture – which is a Yugoslav enterprise – will have, of course, the usual self-management bodies: workers' council, management board, and director. The workers' council may, however, delegate most of its authority (except certain inalienable rights) to the management board which for all practical purposes runs the joint venture. The foreign investor may obtain equal representation and voting power in the board, although he has only a minority interest.

In view of the particularities of the Yugoslav accounting system, it is advisable that the agreement contains detailed models of a balance sheet and income statement. Such models will properly define profits and the basis for sharing the profit between the partners. Finally, the partners should agree on a procedure to determine the capital share of the foreign partner in case of termination.

## 6.6. THE EXPERIENCE SO FAR

Although more than seven years have passed since the adoption of the first legislation in 1967, the experience is far from conclusive. The number of joint ventures concluded has remained below expectations and the great majority of joint ventures have only a few years of operational experiences. Yet it may be useful to review what has been achieved so far.

At the end of January 1974, 90 joint ventures had been established.

Foreign risk capital invested amounted to $137 million equivalent which represented 17% of the total capital (of these joint ventures). The automotive industry accounted for 35% of total foreign investment, followed by chemicals and chemical products with 16%. In about a third of all cases, the foreign investment was at the legal maximum of 49.9% – most of these, however, concern joint ventures of a smaller size. The main beneficiaries of foreign investment have been Slovenia (Yugoslavia's most developed Republic) with 35% of the total amount, and Serbia with about one-third. The lesser developed regions (Bosnia and Hercegovina, Kosovo, Macedonia and Montenegro) together received only slightly more than half of the share of Slovenia alone. Italy, F.R. Germany, USA and France are Yugoslavia's principal partners; the nine Common Market countries account for 51.4% of the total amount involved.

A survey was conducted among the 60 foreign investors that had entered into a joint venture by mid-1972 and could therefore be expected to have operational experience. Although only 15 firms replied (25%), they can be said to constitute a fairly representative sample of the total as far as country of origin and type of industrial activity are concerned. For the 15 respondents factors relating to the market (be it in Yugoslavia itself or abroad) provided the main motivation to invest in Yugoslavia. The second principal motive was the desire to sell technology and know-how.

The self-management system did not appear to frighten these firms unduly, and the influence of the workers' council was never regarded as severely restrictive. Some foreign investors even appreciated its contribution as constructive.

In general the joint venture incorporated either an entire existing enterprise or a division thereof. In only one case, a new enterprise was established. Negotiations, on the whole, took a long time, in seven instances even more than a year.

With respect to financing, the relationship between Yugoslav and foreign risk capital varied considerably; from a low foreign share of 6% to the legal maximum of 49.9%. In general, the foreign participation tended to diminish with the increasing size of the project. Ten foreign investors opted for the possibility to capitalise the value of their know-how as part of their capital contribution.

Only 3 out of 12 respondents – the remainder did not answer this question – reported that the return on investment and the rate of growth of sales were less than satisfactory. On average, foreign investors would appear to be satisfied on both scores.

As could be expected, all foreign firms reported at least some minor problems but only in a few cases difficulties were considered to be serious.

The major problem areas were pricing and, particularly, accounting. Relatively few difficulties were apparent in the field of personnel policy and workers' remuneration.

Most respondents stated that restrictions on profit transfer and capital repatriation were the main impediment to an increase in the number of joint ventures, the fact that only a minority interest is allowed was not considered to be a major obstacle.

## 6.7. CONCLUDING OBSERVATIONS

### 6.7.1. *General evaluation*

A final and definite judgement about the Yugoslav joint venturing experience would be premature at this stage. Nevertheless, it would appear that the odds on eventual success are shorter than those on failure. The number of joint ventures is increasing year by year and those that are already in existence do seem – if the experience of the 15 foreign firms of the sample is anything to go by – to operate reasonably well. It is, of course, easy to claim with hindsight that the initially disappointing achievements should have been expected. On both the Yugoslav and the foreign side there was a large measure of ignorance about each other's ways. For most Western investors Yugoslavia was – and for some, unfortunately, still seems to be – a communist state with all the negative connotations that this concept evokes in the mind of a capitalist entrepreneur. And even for some of those that were aware of the fact that Yugoslavia had developed its own socio-economic system, the idea of self-management by workers was far from appealing. As far as the Yugoslavs are concerned, ignorance about the other side was probably not so basic but included a certain amount of naivety about the mentality and behaviour of foreign investors. It was generally expected that by opening up the country for profitable (foreign) investment, Western enterprises would without much prodding rush in to take advantage of the opportunity. Except for the creation of the International Investment Corporation for Yugoslavia S.A. very little promotional work was done and it is probably fair to say that on this score the efforts are still too limited. To give just one example: there is no publication available which explains to potential foreign investors succinctly and comprehensively the rules and regulations concerning joint ventures and the basic features of the self-management system. Information is handed out piecemeal and often couched in terminology which is difficult to understand for the Western entrepreneur.

Apart from ignorance and fears of all things communist on the side of capitalist enterprises, the slow momentum may be explained by specific disincentives contained in the legislation concerning joint ventures. As was seen in Chapter 4, some of these have been removed in the meantime, but others remain. If Yugoslavia intends to continue its policy of encouraging private foreign investment, it would be desirable to consider the elimination of those disincentives that are impeding the further development of joint ventures. These – plus a few other problem areas – will be reviewed in the next section.

### 6.7.2. *Problems*

The major obstacle against a substantial expansion of foreign private investment in Yugoslavia is undoubtedly the restrictive nature of the foreign exchange regime (cf. Chapter 4). Present rules and regulations, in practice, mean that only joint ventures which will export a very high proportion of their output to hard currency areas are permitted. Of course, the Yugoslav authorities are perfectly justified in trying to promote exports but it makes little sense to single out joint ventures for special – and unfavourable – treatment on this score. Not only is the present policy inconsistent with the desire to promote joint ventures, it rests on fallacious arguments as well. It may be useful to repeat what has been said on this matter in more detail in Chapter 4. In the first place, a favourable effect on the balance of payments can be achieved not only by an increase in exports but by a decrease in imports as well. Joint venture projects that would result in import-substitution but that, in view of market conditions, cannot be expected to export are presently ruled out. Secondly, one should not view the economic benefits of a venture from the balance of payments angle alone. What matters is its overall effect on the economy. Thirdly, restrictions on profit transfer and capital repatriation constitute a discrimination against the foreign investor, as the Yugoslav joint venture partner is free to dispose of his profits (and capital contribution upon termination of the contract) as he thinks fit.

Moreover, it is quite obvious that the amounts involved are relatively so small that they will have little effect on the overall balance of payments position. To liberalise the transfer of the foreign partner's share in the profits and the liquidation proceeds of the joint venture would involve little cost to the Yugoslav economy, but might result in a significant expansion of private foreign investment as it would remove a major risk which many potential foreign investors are not prepared to accept. If complete liberalisation, for one reason or another, would at present not be a viable proposition then, as a first step, at least bank guarantees with respect to foreign exchange availability for profit transfer and capital repatriation should be permitted – just as they are for foreign loans.

The rule that foreign investors are not allowed to have a majority interest in the risk capital of the joint venture is often considered to be another impediment to the expansion of private foreign investment. The importance of this restriction is, however, often greatly exaggerated. While it is undoubtedly true that for a number of foreign firms it is a matter of principle not to accept a minority holding, it has been the experience of the present author that this is the exception rather than the rule. Of the countless Western firms that have made inquiries at IICY about investment opportunities in Yugoslavia, only a few abandoned their interest upon learning that they would not be able to acquire a majority holding.[1] Moreover, as has been often pointed out in this study, the Yugoslav joint venture legislation leaves so much freedom to the partners themselves that the foreign investor may negotiate sufficient safeguards to protect his interests.

The decision to allow only a minority foreign interest is basically a political one and should be respected as such. On economic grounds there would seem to be little against it, except for the fact that it may perhaps slightly retard the expansion of private foreign investment.

Perhaps the most difficult issue concerning private foreign investment in Yugoslavia is the question of whether joint ventures are compatible with the self-management system – in particular in view of the fact that foreign investors may be given the right to share control on an equal basis with the domestic partner; a right which normally is exercised by the Yugoslav workers alone. Of course, this is primarily a problem for the Yugoslavs themselves. As far as the foreign investor is concerned, his only worry is that the joint venture's operations are proceeding without undue problems. As long as this is the case, questions of a philosophical and political nature are irrelevant to him. In fact, it would seem that foreign investors do not experience serious difficulties on account of the self-management system in Yugoslav enterprises. Of the 15 firms surveyed in the sample only two judged the differences in business approach to be an obstacle to smooth operations and two others thought the influence of the workers' council to be restrictive. This finding is confirmed by the recent OECD report about foreign investment in Yugoslavia which states that 'in practice self-management does not appear to have given rise to any difficulties in the joint ventures which exist today.'[2]

If, in general, foreign investors have no complaints about the functioning of the system because it does not interfere with business operations, one could have expected that there would have been more reservations on the Yugoslav side. And while some criticism has been voiced, it is remarkable how limited it has been. The major objection concerned the fact that foreign investors often exercise an influence out of proportion with their participation in the joint venture's risk capital.[3] It is even more remarkable that this type of criticism has come under strong attack from Yugoslav writers. One of them even remarked that complaints about undue interference by the foreign partner were raised either by people having ideological objections against foreign investment in general or by those that are incapable of adapting themselves to the requirements of a modern economy.[4]

At this stage, there is not enough information available to assess whether or not the functioning of the self-management system in joint ventures is less satisfactory – to the Yugoslavs – than in the average Yugoslav enterprise. It would require a special study on this subject to have a basis for judgement.

A factor which could, in a small but important way, contribute to an improvement in the investment climate would be the introduction of competent, independent auditing firms. So far audits are carried out exclusively by the SDK (the Official Social Accounting Service) but its performance is not considered satisfactory – not only by foreign investors but by many Yugoslavs as well. It has already been explained that the Yugoslav accounting system poses serious problems of understanding for the Western financial specialist and while the partners may agree in the joint venture contract upon model financial statements, there will always remain a large area where financial records and bookings of the joint venture will continue to be mysterious to the foreign partner. Even if there exists complete mutual confidence between the joint venture partners, it would still be desirable that the foreign party could be sure that all records are properly audited. At present, this is not the case. SDK audits are not intended to arrive at a judgement about the enterprise's financial position but are simply a check whether all relevant legal accounting prescriptions have been followed.

It would appear that the joint venture form would be a very appropriate vehicle for independent auditing firms to be established in Yugoslavia, since such firms will by necessity have to offer a combination of modern Western accounting expertise and a detailed knowledge of local rules and regulations.

### 6.7.3. *Prospects*

The fact that joint venturing between Yugoslav and foreign enterprises had a slow start should not be a reason for undue pessimism about further prospects. Of course, quite a lot will depend on factors beyond anybody's control such as the economic climate both in Yugoslavia and Europe, and political developments.

When discussing Yugoslavia's future one can hardly avoid the question of what will happen to the country when President Tito eventually disappears from the scene. This question is almost an obsession in the minds of many Western observers, leading to the most unlikely speculations. And inasmuch as political uncertainty is an obstacle to foreign investment, the matter should be given some brief attention here.

Notwithstanding the dire predictions of political upheaval, the most probable outcome is that nothing drastic will happen. The battle over the succession of President Tito has already been fought and the issue was solved, in typical Yugoslav fashion, by the institution of a collective Presidium in which all Republics and Autonomous Provinces are represented. This is not to say, of course, that no political problems will arise. Yugoslavia has had its share of these and will continue to have problems – just as any other country. It would be wrong, however, to assume that without Tito problems will become so acute as to threaten the country and its socio-economic system. But even in the unlikely event that Yugoslavia – perhaps under pressure from the Soviet Union – would revert to some degree to a centralised economy of the Soviet model, this would not mean that joint venturing between Yugoslav and foreign enterprises would have no future. During the last few years there has been an increasing interest in this type of industrial cooperation with the West in most COMECON countries, and Hungary, Poland and Romania have adopted legislation specifically allowing joint ventures with capitalist firms. It is therefore hard to see how an aligning of the Yugoslav economic system on that of its Eastern neighbours would negatively affect the future of joint ventures.

Leaving speculation aside, there are three factors which would justify a certain amount of optimism.

In the first place, apart from some cancelled joint venture contracts there have been very few failures and the proportion of projects that have given satisfaction to the partners is relatively high.[5] Secondly, Yugoslavia will ultimately – just as other countries in a similar situation – have to change from export of its labour force to import of capital. Finally, the Yugoslavs are genuinely interested in increasing cooperation with foreign enterprises and their pragmatism and flexibility can be expected to result in a continuing liberalisation of the rules and regulations governing joint ventures.

NOTES

1. The law on foreign investment, however, leaves open the possibility that in exceptional cases the foreign partner may have a majority holding, but this requires a special act of the Federal Assembly (art. 4). So far this permission has not been granted nor applied for.
2. OECD, *Foreign investment in Yugoslavia (1974)*, Paris, 1974, page 23.
3. Cf. 'Jugoslawische Selbstverwaltung und Auslandskapital', *Wirtschaftlicher Dienst Südosteuropa*, No. 5/6, May/June 1973, page 87ff.
4. *Ibidem.*
5. This point is demonstrated by the case of Dow Chemical, which on the basis of its experience with a rather modest first joint venture, recently decided to conclude a joint venture with INA (Yugoslavia's major oil company) for the establishment of a $600 million petrochemical complex (cf. *The Economist*, March 15, 1975).

# Annex

LAW ON INVESTMENT OF RESOURCES BY FOREIGN PERSONS IN DOMESTIC ORGANISATIONS OF ASSOCIATED LABOUR*

## *Article 1*

Foreign persons may invest their resources in a domestic organization of associated labour in order to realize joint business objectives at joint risk (joint venture).
In the context of this Law, a domestic organization of associated labour is considered to be a basic organization of associated labour, a union of basic organization of associated labour, a work organization or a compound organization of associated labour.

## *Article 2*

Relations between the contracting parties to the joint venture are stipulated by a contract.
The contract must be made in writing.
A contract which is not made in writing has no legal validity.

## *Article 3*

Contracts on investment of resources by foreign persons in a joint venture (investment contract) cannot be concluded in the following fields of activity: banking, insurance, domestic transport, trading, communal and similar services and social services with the exception of the field of scientific research work.
As an exception, the Federal Executive Council may permit in certain cases domestic organizations of associated labour to conclude investment contracts specified in para 1, of this Article, if it is felt that this will contribute to a more rapid development of the economic sector or activity in question.

## *Article 4*

The value of total resources invested by the foreign parties to the investment contract

* Unofficial translation (supplied by the International Investment Corporation for Yugoslavia S.A.) from the *Official Gazette of SFRY*, No. 22, April 19, 1973, pp. 742–745.

in any one domestic organization of associated labour may neither exceed nor equal those invested by the domestic organization of associated labour.
In exceptional cases, if there is a special interest in developing a particular economic sector or activity, determined by an act of the Federal Assembly, the investment contract may provide for the value of total resources invested by the foreign parties in a domestic organization of associated labour to be higher than the total resources invested by domestic organizations of associated labour.

*Article 5*

The investment contract may neither provide for the foreign party to have rights other than those of the domestic organization of associated labour, nor rights exceeding those of the domestic organization of associated labour.

*Article 6*

The investment of resources by the foreign party in a domestic organization of associated labour is, as a rule, a long-term arrangement.
The investment contract may also provide for the foreign party to invest its resources in a domestic organization of associated labour for a specific period of time, providing that this is not shorter than the time needed for the realization of joint business objectives.

*Article 7*

The investment contract may provide for the foreign party to be entitled to participate in the net income earned by the joint venture operation.
If the investment contract provides for the participation of the foreign party in the net income earned by the joint venture operation, such a contract shall also stipulate the duration, terms and conditions of such a participation.
The right to participate in the net income from the joint venture operation may be excercised by the foreign party only for as long as it is participating with its own resources in the joint venture operation.

*Article 8*

The investment contract makes provision out of the net income for resources which are to be allocated for personal incomes, the collective consumption fund and the expansion of the asset base of the domestic organization of associated labour, in which the foreign party has invested its resources and thus acquired the right of participating in the income realized by the joint venture operation. This allocation shall be relative to the contribution of the domestic organization of associated labour in the creation of the net income.

*Article 9*

The investment contract may also provide for the foreign party to exercise its rights,

which will be determined by an agreement with the domestic organization of associated labour, through a joint body (business board).
The investment contract stipulates the method of setting-up the joint body, its powers and modus operandi.

*Article 10*

The investment contract may provide for the right of the foreign party to the repatriation of individual items invested in the joint venture.

*Article 11*

The investment contract cannot be cancelled by the consent of the parties concerned prior to expiry of its agreed term.
As an exception to the provision of para 1, of this Article, the investment contract may provide for cancellation:
1. if the joint venture incurs losses in two consecutive years, or if the business results are considerably worse than projected;
2. if the other party fails to fulfil its contractual obligations.

*Article 12*

The investment contract shall be entered in the register.
The register referred to in para 1, of this Article, shall be kept with the Federal Secretariat for the Economy.
The domestic organization of associated labour is obliged to file the application for entering the contract in the register within 30 days of the date of conclusion of the contract.
The contract concluded shall not be registered:
1. if the contract is inconsistent with the provisions of this Law or other regulations;
2. if the contract does not provide for business cooperation ensuring increase of production, productivity and exports, introduction and application of modern techniques, technology and organization of production and business operations in a domestic organization of associated labour, or if it does not contribute to advancement of scientific research work in a domestic organization of associated labour;
3. if the total resources provided by the contract to be invested by the parties to the joint venture are not sufficient for realization of the conditions set forth in item 2, of para 2, above;
4. if the conditions of business cooperation provided for by the contract do not correspond to the usual commercial conditions in which such cooperation is carried out in international economic relations;
5. if the contract concluded between the domestic organization of associated labour and the foreign party establishes business relations which essentially violate the equality of rights of the domestic organization of associated labour with those of the foreign party;
6. if the evaluation of the foreign party's non-financial participation (patent rights, licences, technology etc.) is unrealistic;

7. if the resources provided for by the contract to be invested by the foreign party are less than 1,500,000 dinars;
8. if the provisions of the contract are contrary to the interests of security and national defence.

The decision of the Federal Secretariat for the Economy on the application for registration of the investment contract shall be taken at the latest within two months from the date of application.
Prior to taking the decision, the Federal Secretariat for the Economy is obliged to obtain the opinion of the appropriate Federal Administrative body as to whether the provisions of the contract are contrary to the interests of security and national defence. The decision on the application for registration may not be taken contrary to this opinion. The decision on the rejection of the application for registration because the provisions of the contract are contrary to the interests of security and national defence is taken at the discretion of the administrative body and, in this respect, need not be substantiated.
An appeal against the decision of the Federal Secretariat for the Economy on the application for registration may be submitted to the Federal Executive Council within 15 days following the delivery of the decision.
The register is entered with the names and headquarters addresses of the firms which are parties to the contract, the total amount of resources invested in the joint venture and the contribution of each party, the date of conclusion of the contract and the application date for registration of the contract, the reference number and date of the decision on registration of the contract.
The parties concerned shall be informed by the Federal Secretariat for the Economy on the registration of the contract.
When registered, the contract becomes valid as from the date on which it was concluded.
The data contained in the contract, attached to the application for registration shall be kept in official confidence.
The register, in which the contract is entered, shall be available to the public.
The Federal Executive Council is authorized to issue, as required, further specific regulations for the application of the provisions of this Article.
The Federal Secretariat for the Economy, depending on the nature and the kind of business operations, shall prescribe, as required, in which cases the foreign party to the contract may invest total resources in a domestic organization of associated labour less than 1,500,000 dinars.

## *Article 13*

The domestic organization of associated labour in which resources are invested is liable to show separately in its accounts the net income earned by the joint venture, if the investment contract provides for participation by the foreign party in the income realized by the joint venture.
The foreign party is entitled to have access to the accounts showing the joint venture income.

## *Article 14*

If, on the basis of the investment contract, the foreign party's resources are invested

in a work organization, all basic organizations of associated labour, as units thereof, are jointly and severally responsible for the liabilities of the joint venture, unless otherwise provided for by the self-management agreement of association.
If, on the basis of the investment contract, the foreign party's resources are invested in a basic organization of associated labour, this basic organization is responsible for the liabilities of the joint venture up to the amount of all available assets (basic organization of associated labour with limited liability), unless the investment contract provides and the other basic organizations which form part of the same work organization approve that these basic organizations are also responsible to the extent exceeding the amount of the assets of the basic organization in which joint venture resources were invested.
The basic organization of associated labour in which the foreign party's resources are invested is not responsible for the liabilities of the work organization of which it is a part, i.e. the liabilities of the other basic organizations which form part thereof, or which are associated with another organization or with a union of organizations of associated labour, unless otherwise provided for by the investment contract with the approval of the other basic organizations.
The liabilities specified in para 1, and 2, of this Article, and the exclusion of liabilities specified in para 3, of this Article, are entered in the court register and these liabilities and/or exclusion of liabilities become effective as from the date of registration in the court register.

### *Article 15*

With the consent of the domestic organization of associated labour in which its joint venture resources are invested and of the parties to the contract, the foreign party may transfer its rights and obligations under the investment contract to another foreign individual or corporate body or another domestic organization of associated labour, unless otherwise provided for by the investment contract.

### *Article 16*

If the foreign party wishes to transfer its rights and obligations under the investment contract to another foreign individual or corporate body or another domestic organization of associated labour, it is first liable to offer the transfer of the rights and obligations, in a written form, to the domestic organization of associated labour in which its resources were invested.
The domestic organization of associated labour, unless otherwise provided for by the investment contract, is liable, within sixty days following the date of receipt of the offer, to deliver to the foreign party a declaration of acceptance or rejection of the offer.
If the foreign party, contrary to the provision of para 1, of this Article, transfers its rights and obligations under the investment contract without first offering these to the domestic organization of associated labour or if it transfers its rights and obligations under the investment contract under terms and conditions more favourable to the persons to whom the transfer is made than those offered to the domestic organization of associated labour, then the domestic organization in which the resources were invested may file a suit, with the appropriate economic court, that the transfer of the rights and obligations under the investment contract be annulled and the rights and

obligations under the investment contract be transferred to itself under the same terms and conditions.
The suit for violation of priority to the transfer of the rights and obligations under the investment contract may be submitted within thirty days from the date when the domestic organization of associated work became aware of the transfer and/or the more favourable transfer terms and conditions.
The transfer of the rights and obligations of the foreign party to another foreign party or domestic organization of associated labour is filed in the register specified in Article 12, of this Law. The application for the transfer of rights and obligations under the investment contract by the foreign party making the transfer shall be submitted within thirty days following the date when the transfer agreement was concluded.

*Article 17*

The foreign party shall pay the tax prescribed by a separate law on the earnings to which it is entitled, based upon its participation in the net income of the joint venture.

*Article 18*

The foreign party is entitled to transfer its earnings from the joint venture operation.
The transfer of earnings specified in para 1, of this Article, is effected according to the investment contract and in conformity with Government regulations on foreign exchange operations.
The foreign party may use the earnings acquired through the joint venture to increase its share of the resources of the joint venture or to conclude an investment contract with another organization of associated work and invest the earnings in joint venture operations, or to dispose of the earnings in Yugoslavia in some other way in accordance with the existing regulations.

*Article 19*

The foreign party is entitled to the transfer of resources, i.e. the residual resources invested in a joint venture if the investment contract is terminated through accomplishment of the business objectives, i.e. on expiry of the term of the contract, if the investment contract is annulled for the reasons provided for by this Law, or if the investment contract provides that the foreign party is entitled partially to withdraw the resources invested during the term of the investment contract.
The transfer of resources specified in para 1, of this Article, is effected in conformity with the existing regulations on foreign exchange operations.

*Article 20*

If the law is governing such investment changes after the investment contract has become legally effective then the relations set forth by the contract shall be governed by the provisions of the contract itself and the law in force at the time when the investment contract becomes effective, if such a solution is more favourable to the parties to the contract and unless certain questions are otherwise agreed upon between the parties in accordance with the amended law.

The provision of para 1, of this Article, does not refer to the obligatory payment to the social community.

### *Article 21*

Disputes arising in the performance of the investment contract between the domestic organization of associated labour and the foreign party shall be settled by the appropriate Yugoslav economic court, unless provided by the investment contract or by separate consent in a written form that these disputes shall be settled by a selected court (of arbitration) set up within the Chamber of Economy of Yugoslavia, by the Foreign Trade Arbitration Court of the Chamber of Economy of Yugoslavia, by a special court of arbitration appointed by the parties in accordance with the contract, or by a foreign court of arbitration.

### *Article 22*

A fine of 10,000 to 100,000 dinars shall be imposed on the domestic organization of associated labour for its failure, considered as a violation of business law, to file the application for registration of the concluded contract within thirty days following the date of conclusion of the contract (Article 12, para 3 above).
For the business violation specified in para 1, of this Article, the individual responsible in the domestic organization of associated labour shall also be fined and the fine shall range from 1,000 to 5,000 dinars.

### *Article 23*

A fine of 20,000 to 200,000 dinars shall be imposed on the foreign corporate body for its failure, considered as a violation of business law, to file the application for the transfer of rights and obligations under the investment contract within thirty days following the date of conclusion of the transfer agreement (Article 16, para 5 above).
For the business violation specified in para 1, of this Article, the individual responsible within the foreign corporate body shall also be fined and the fine shall range from 2,000 to 20,000 dinars.

### *Article 24*

A fine of 10,000 to 50,000 dinars shall be imposed on the foreign person for failure, considered as a violation, to file the application for the transfer of rights and obligations under the investment contract within thirty days following the date of conclusion of the transfer agreement (Article 16, para 5 above).

### *Article 25*

From the day on which it comes into force, this Law supersedes the provisions of Article 57, through Article 74, of the Law on the Resources of Work Organizations (*Official Gazette of SFRY*, No. 10/68, 24/68, 48/68, 42/69, 55/69, 28/70 and 34/71).

*Article 26*

This Law comes into force on the eighth day after its publication in the *Official Gazette of SFRY*.

# Bibliography

Adizes, I., 'Die Rolle des Managements in demokratischen (kommunalen) Organisationen; eine Untersuchung der jugoslawischen Selbstverwaltung, des israelischen Kibbuz und der peruanischen öffentlichen Betriebe', *Annalen der Gemeinwirtschaft*, No. 1, January/March 1972.

Adolfse, J.Th., *De Westeuropese Nationale Investeringsbanken voor buitenlandse ontwikkelingsfinanciering*, Stenfert Kroese, Leyden, 1970.

Ady, P.H. (ed.), *Private foreign investment and the developing world*, Praeger, London, 1971.

Aharoni, Y., *The foreign investment decision process*, Harvard Business School, Division of Research, Boston, 1966.

Balassa, B. and Bertrand, T.J., 'Growth performance of Eastern European economies and comparable Western European countries', *American Economic Review*, Papers and Proceedings, May 1970.

Baranson, J., *Industrial technologies for developing countries*, Frederick A. Praeger, New York and London, 1969.

Bergson, A., 'Market socialism revisited', *Journal of Political Economy*, Vol. 75, No. 5, October 1967.

Bhagwati, J.N., *Amount and sharing of aid*, Overseas Development Council, Monograph No. 2, Washington (D.C.), 1970.

Bicanic, R., *Economic policy in Socialist Yugoslavia*, Cambridge University Press, 1973.

Bilandzic, D., *Social self-government*, Medunarodna Politika Studies, No. 1, Belgrade, 1965.

Bivens, K.K. and Lovell, E.B., *Joint ventures with foreign partners. An international survey of business opinion and experience*, National Industrial Conference Board, New York, 1966.

Bogoev, K., 'The policy of more rapid development of the undeveloped Republics and Province', *Eastern European Economics*, Vol. x, No. 4, Summer 1972.

Bornstein, M. (ed.), *Plan and Market. Economic Reform in Eastern Europe*, Yale University Press, London and New Haven, 1973.

Broekmeyer, M.J., *De arbeidersraad in Zuidslavië 1950–1966; een hoofdstuk uit de bevrijding van de arbeid*, Boom, Meppel, 1968.

Broekmeyer, M.J. (ed.), *Yugoslav workers' self-management. Proceedings of a Symposium*, D. Reidel Publishing Co., Dordrecht, 1970.

Broekmeyer, M.J. and Cornelissen, I., *Arbeidersraad of ondernemersstaat; machten en machtsstrijd in Nederland en Joegoslavië*, Van Gennep, Amsterdam, 1969.

Bundesstelle für Aussenhandelsinformation, *Deutsch-jugoslawische Investitionsverträge*, Cologne, 1970.

Bundesstelle für Aussenhandelsinformation, *Die neuen jugoslawischen Gesetze über ausländische Investitionen*, Cologne, 1967.
Business International, *Ownership policies at work abroad*, New York, 1965.
Caves, R.E., 'International corporations: the industrial economics of foreign investment', *Economica*, No. 149, February 1971.
Chen-Young, P.L., *Report on private investment in the Caribbean*, Atlas Publishing Co., Kingston, 1973.
Clarke, W.M., *Private enterprise in developing countries*, Pergamon, Oxford, 1966.
Cobeljic, D., 'Le mécanisme de la coordination du plan national et des plans des entreprises en Yougoslavie', *Revue Economique*, May 1970.
Confederation of British Industry, *Yugoslavia Industrial Cooperation and Investment*, London, 1971.
Cviic, C., 'A survey of Yugoslavia: another way', suppl. *The Economist*, No. 6678, August 21, 1971.

Delfim Neto, A., 'Foreign capital, logic and development', *ADELA Monthly Bulletin*, October 1971.
Dimitrijevic, D., 'The financial structure in a changing economy: the case of Yugoslavia,' *Florida State University Slavic Papers*, Vol. 4, 1970.
Djilas, M., *The unperfect society: beyond the new class*, Harcourt, Brace and World, New York, 1969.
Domar, E.D., 'The Soviet collective farm as a producer cooperative', *American Economic Review*, Vol. LVI, No. 4, September 1966.
Dumas, A., 'La constitution d'un fonds d'accumulation dans un système socialiste d'autogestion: le cas de la Yougoslavie', *Tiers Monde*, No. 55, July/September 1973.
Dupont, C. and Keesing, F.A.G., 'The Yugoslav economic system and instruments of Yugoslav economic policy: a note', *IMF Staff Papers*, Vol. VIII, No. 1, November 1960.

Eremin, A., 'On the concept of "market socialism"', translated from Russian in *Problems of economics*, No. 4, August 1970.

Federal Chamber of Economy, *Jont investment and production – technical cooperation of Yugoslav economic organizations and foreign firms*, Belgrade, 1967.
Federal Planning Institute, *An outline of the concepts of the social plan of development of Yugoslavia from 1971 to 1975*, Belgrade, 1970.
Fellner, W., *Modern economic analysis*, McGraw-Hill/KogaKusha, Tokyo, 1960.
Franks, L.G., 'Do joint ventures still make sense in Europe?', *Worldwide Projects and Industry Planning*, Jan./Feb. 1972.
Friedmann, W.G., 'The contractual joint venture', *Columbia Journal of World Business*, Vol. VII, No. 1, Jan./Feb. 1972.
Friedmann, W.G. and Beguin, J.P., *Joint international business ventures in developing countries; case studies and analysis of recent trends*, Columbia University Press, New York and London, 1971.
Friedmann, W.G. and Kalmanoff, G., *Joint international business ventures*, Columbia University Press, New York and London, 1961.
Friedmann, W.G. and Mates, L., *Joint business ventures of Yugoslav enterprises and foreign firms; an international colloquium*, Institute of International Politics and Economy, Belgrade, 1968.
Furubotn, E.G. and Pejovich, S., 'Property rights and the behavior of the firm in a

socialist state: the example of Yugoslavia', *Zeitschrift für Nationalökonomie*, No. 3/4, 1970.

Furubotn, E.G. and Pejovich, S., 'Tax policy and investment decisions of the Yugoslav firm', *National Tax Journal*, Vol. XXIII, No. 3.

Gabriel, P.P., 'MNC's in the Third World: is conflict unavoidable?', *Harvard Business Review*, July/August 1972.

Gamarinikow, M., 'Industrial cooperation: East Europe looks West', *Problems of Communism*, No. 3, May/June 1971.

Gehrecke, S., 'Arbeiterselbstverwaltung und wirtschaftliche Effizienz (Jugoslawien)', *Osteuropa*, No. 9, September 1972.

Glickman, R.B., 'Yugoslav worker-management: speculations about change', *Florida State University Slavic Papers*, Vol. 4, 1970.

Glickman, R.B. and Sukijasovic, M., 'Yugoslav worker-management and its effect on foreign investment', *Harvard International Law Journal*, Vol. 12, No. 2, Spring 1971.

Glueck, W.F. and Kavran, D., 'Worker management in Yugoslavia', *Business Horizons*, No. 1, February 1972.

Goldman, M.I., *Soviet foreign aid*, Frederick A. Praeger, New York, 1967.

Gorupic, D., 'Trends in the development of workers' self-management – Yugoslavia', *Eastern European Economics*, Winter 1969/70.

Gorupic, D., 'The development of the self-managing organization of enterprises in Yugoslavia', *Yugoslav Survey*, Vol. XI, No. 3, August 1970.

Govedarica, S., 'Price system and policy', *Yugoslav Survey*, Vol. XIII, No. 3, August 1972.

Greener, M., *The Penguin Dictionary of Commerce*, Penguin Books, London, 1970.

Hauvonen, J.J., 'Postwar developments in money and banking in Yugoslavia', *IMF Staff Papers*, No. 3, November 1970.

Hauvonen, J.J., 'Money and banking in Yugoslavia since 1965', *Finance and Development*, No. 1, 1972.

Higgins, B., *Economic development, principles, problems and practices*, Constable and Co., London, 1959.

Hilten, H.W. van, *Joint ventures: enkele facetten van de joint business venture*, Kluwer, Deventer, 1968.

Hirschman, A.O., 'How to divest in Latin America and why', Princeton University, *Essays in International Finance*, No. 76, November 1969.

Hirschman, A.O. and Bird, R.M., 'Foreign aid – a critique and a proposal', Princeton University, *Essays in International Finance*, No. 69, 1968.

Holt, J.B., 'New roles for Western multinationals in Eastern Europe', *Columbia Journal of World Business*, Vol. VIII, No. 3, 1973.

Holt, S. and Stapleton, K., 'Yugoslavia and the European Community 1958–1970', *Journal of Common Market Studies*, No. 1, September 1971.

Hoorn, Th.P. van, and Koopman, C.A., 'De planning-procedure in een Joegoslavische onderneming met arbeiderszelfbestuur', *Economisch-Statistische Berichten*, No. 2821, October 27, 1971.

Horvat, B., *An essay on Yugoslav society*, International Arts and Sciences Press, White Plains (N.Y.), 1969.

Horvat, B., 'On the theory of the labour-managed firm', *Florida State University Slavic Papers*, Vol. 4, 1970.

Horvat, B., 'Business cycles in Yugoslavia', *Eastern European Economics*, No. 3/4, Spring/Summer 1971.

Horvat, B., 'Yugoslav economic policy in the post-war period: problems, ideas, institutional developments', *American Economic Review*, Vol. 61, No. 3, Part 2, Supplement, June 1971.
Horvat, B., 'An institutional model of a self-managed socialist economy', *Eastern European Economics*, No. 4, Summer 1972.
Horvat, B. and Raskovic, V., 'Workers' management in Yugoslavia: a comment', *Journal of Political Economy*, Vol. LXVIII, April 1959.
Hyson, C.D. and Weigel, D.R., 'Investment in the LDC's: the unresolved debate', *Columbia Journal of World Business*, January/February 1970.

Intitut za Spoljnu Trgovinu, *Model of a contract for joint foreign capital investment in Yugoslav companies*, Belgrade, 1970.
Institute of Comparative Law, *The legal system of foreign capital investment in Yugoslavia*, Belgrade, 1972.
International Bank for Reconstruction and Development, *Annual Report*, 1972.
International Bank for Reconstruction and Development, *World Bank Atlas*, 1972.
International Monetary Fund, *27th Annual Report on Exchange Restrictions*, Washington, 1973.

'Joegoslavië', *Wereldmarkt*, No. 36, Sept. 14, 1972.
Johnson, H.G., *Economic policies toward less developed countries*, Allen and Unwin, London, 1967.
Johnson, H.G., 'The multinational corporation as a development agent', *Columbia Journal of World Business*, May/June 1970.
'Joint ventures in Jugoslawien', *Nachrichten Aussenhandel*, No. 97, May 20, 1974.
Jovanovic, M., 'Changes in the Yugoslav banking system', *National Bank of Yugoslavia, Quarterly Bulletin*, No. 1, January 1973.
'Jugoslawische Selbstverwaltung und Auslandskapital', *Wissenschaftlicher Dienst Südosteuropa*, Nr. 5/6, May/June 1973.

Kastelein, T.J., 'Joegoslavië', *Intermediair*, No. 7, February 18, 1972.
Keller, E., 'Opportunities and problems of private investment in Latin America', *ADELA Monthly Bulletin*, April 1972.
Kennet, W., Whitty, L. and Holland, S., *Sovereignty and multinational companies*, Fabian Tract, No. 409, London, 1971.
Kim, S.H., *Foreign capital for economic development, a Korean case study*, Frederick A. Praeger, New York, 1970.
Kindleberger, Ch., *Economic development*, McGraw-Hill/KogaKusha, Tokyo, 1958.
Kindleberger, Ch.P., *American business abroad: six lectures on direct investment*, Yale University Press, New Haven and London, 1969.
Kommissie Internationale Samenwerking, *Verslag Joegoslavië-Hongarije reis*, Tilburg, 1973.
Koorenhof, A. Th. H., *Zuidslavië in de jaren 70*, Stichting Economische Publicaties, The Hague, 1971.
Korac, M., 'The socio-economic basis of the Yugoslav economic system: a theoretical analysis', *Ekonomist* (Zagreb), special issue in English, 1969.
Kraljic, I., 'Les règles de l'investissement étranger en Yougoslavie', *Moniteur du Commerce International*, December 11, 1972.
Kukoleca, S., 'Problems of business policy in a Yugoslav enterprise', *Florida State University Slavic Papers*, Vol. 2, 1968.

Lammers, C.J., 'Problemen en prestaties van het Joegoslavische zelfbestuur', *De Groene Amsterdammer*, January 24, 1973.
Lascelles, D., 'Constitutional amendments', *The Financial Times*, April 26, 1973.
Lefournier, Ph., 'Révolution culturelle chez Tito', *L'Expansion*, No. 63, May 1973.
Leman, G., *Stellung und Aufgaben der ökonomischen Einheiten in den jugoslawischen Unternehmungen*, Duncker und Humblot, Berlin, 1967.
Litvak, I.A. and Maule, Chr.J. (eds.), *Foreign investment and international business arrangements: the experience of host countries*, Frederick A. Praeger, New York, 1970.
Luben, D., 'La fonction de directeur dans l'entreprise autogérée yougoslave', *Economie et Humanisme*, No. 210, March/April 1973.
Lyall, K.C., 'Joint capitalist-socialist enterprise: a Yugoslav experiment', mimeo The Maxwell School, Syracuse University (N.Y.), December 1970.

Malmgren, H.B., *Trade for Development*, Overseas Development Council, Monograph No. 4, Washington (D.C.), 1971.
Markovic, M., 'De betekenis van het zelfbestuur voor het socialisme', *Oost-West*, Vol. 4, No. 7, July 1965.
Marsenic, D.V., 'The price system – development and problems', *Yugoslav Survey*, No. 3, August 1973.
Martin, E.M., *Development assistance, efforts and policies of the members of the DAC*, OECD, Paris, 1971.
Maurice, S.C. and Ferguson, C.E., 'Factor usage by a labour-managed firm in a socialist economy', *Economica*, February 1972.
Mazdar, L., 'Economic Development, 1947–1968', *Yugoslav Survey*, February 1970.
Meeker, G.B., 'Fade-out joint venture: can it work for Latin America?', *Inter-American Economic Affairs*, No. 4, Spring 1971.
Meister, A., 'Tendances de l'autogestion yougoslave', *Documentation sur l'Europe centrale*, Vol. x, No. 3, Louvain, 1972.
Meneghello-Dincic, K., 'L'autogestion yougoslave (1950–1972)', *La documentation française, Notes et Etudes Documentaires*, July 23, 1973.
Mensbrugghe, J. van der, 'Domestic savings in developing countries', *Finance and Development*, No. 1, 1972.
Mesa-Lago, C., 'Unemployment in a socialist economy: Yugoslavia', *Industrial Relations*, Vol. 10, No. 1, February 1971.
Milenkovitch, D.D., *Plan and market in Yugoslav economic thought*, Yale University Press, New Haven and London, 1971.
Miloskovic, S., 'Cooperation between the Yugoslav and foreign economies', *Yugoslav Survey*, May 1970.
Moore, R., *Self-management in Yugoslavia*, Fabian Research Series, No. 281, Fabian Society, London, 1970.
Mrkusic, Z., 'Organisation of foreign trade in Yugoslavia', *Florida State University Slavic Papers*, Vol. 3, 1969.

National Bank of Yugoslavia, *Annual Report*, 1971.
Neal, F.W. and Fisk, W.M., 'Yugoslavia: toward a market socialism', *Problems of Communism*, Vol. xv, No. 6, Nov./Dec. 1966.
Nedeljkovic, M., 'Neue Formen der wirtschaftlichen und finanziellen Zusammenarbeit mit ausländischen Unternehmen', in Bundesstelle für Aussenhandelsinformation, *Deutsch-jugoslawische Investitionsverträge*, Cologne, 1970, pp. 34–47.

'Neufassung der jugoslawischen Kooperationsverordnung', *Nachrichten für Aussenhandel*, No. 128, July 5, 1973.

Nikolic, M., 'Changes in the structure of industrial production, 1952–1972', *Yugoslav Survey*, May 1973.

Nurkse, R., *Problems of Capital Formation in Under-developed Countries*, Oxford University Press, New York, 1967.

Nykryn, J., 'A two-sided profile of multinational enterprises', *Soviet and Eastern European foreign trade*, Vol. 9, No. 1, Spring 1973.

OECD, *Investing in developing countries: facilities for the promotion of private investment in developing countries*, Paris, 1970.

OECD Committee on Invisible Transactions, *Foreign investment in Yugoslavia*, Paris, 1970 (second edition 1974).

OECD Development Centre, *Manual of industrial project analysis in developing countries*, Paris, 1968.

OECD Economic Surveys, *SFR Yugoslavia*, 1967–1972.

Ohlin, G., *Foreign aid policies reconsidered*, OECD Development Centre Studies, Paris, 1966.

Oppenheim, Sir Duncan, 'Official aid and private investment', *CBI Review*, September 1971.

Overlegorgaan Vakcentrales, 'Baas in eigen bedrijf', *Interlinks*, Vol. 2, No. 8, June 1970.

Paj, I., 'The development of the system of distribution of the social product and net income', *Yugoslav Survey*, Vol. XI, No. 3, August 1970.

Paj, I., 'The organisation of self-management in enterprises (managing bodies and their rights)', *Yugoslav Survey*, No. 1, February 1971.

Paj, I., 'The composition and some aspects of the activity of self-management bodies in enterprises', *Yugoslav Survey*, No. 4, November 1973.

Pavicevic, M., 'Transfer of foreign technology and the Yugoslav economy', *Yugoslav Survey*, No. 2, May 1973.

Pearson, L.B. et al., *Partners in development*, Frederick A. Praeger, New York, 1969.

Pejovich, S., 'The banking system and the investment behavior of the Yugoslav firm', in M. Bornstein (ed.): *Plan and market; economic reform in Eastern Europe*, Yale University Press, New Haven and London, 1973.

Pejovski, V., *Yugoslav investment policy*, Medunarodna Politika Studies, No. 3, Belgrade, 1965.

Pincus, J.A., 'How much aid for the have-not nations', *Columbia Journal of World Business*, September-October 1967.

Pincus, J.A., *Trade, aid and development*, McGraw-Hill, New York, 1967.

Planungsgruppe Ritter, *Transfer von Technologie in Entwicklungsländer. Empirische Untersuchung zur Kooperation deutscher Industrieunternehmen in Entwicklungsländern*, Forschungsauftrag des Bundesministeriums für wirtschaftliche Zusammenarbeit, Bonn, February 1972.

Plummer, J.L., 'Inter-firm production function analysis of Yugoslav industrial resource allocation', *Journal of Industrial Economics*, No. 1, November 1970.

Popov, S., 'Intersectoral relations of personal incomes', *Yugoslav Survey*, vol. XIII, No. 2, May 1972.

Popovic, S., 'The legal status of Yugoslav enterprises', *Florida State University Slavic Papers*, Vol. 4, 1970.

Radonovic, M., 'Joint investment by domestic enterprises, and business and financial cooperation between Yugoslav and foreign firms', *Yugoslav Survey*, No. 1, February 1968.
Rajkovic, V., 'An appraisal of the implementation of the economic reform and current problems', *Eastern European Economics*, No. 4, Summer 1970.
Ramaer, J.C., *International joint business ventures in developing countries*, International Chamber of Commerce, Paris, 1968.
Rankov, I.A., 'Economic problems of the foreign-exchange and customs systems', *Soviet and Eastern European Foreign Trade*, No. 2, Summer 1972.
Ratkovic, R.I., 'The evolution of the political system and the development of self-government in Yugoslavia', *Florida State University Slavic Papers*, Vol. 4, 1970.
Rokic, V., 'The Sisak Ironworks: novelties in management', *Yugoslav Life*, Vol. XVIII, No. 4, April 1973.
Rus, V., 'Influence structure in Yugoslav enterprises', *Industrial Relations*, Vol. 9, No. 2, February 1970.

Singleton, F., 'Three steps to self-management within an economic commonwealth', *The Times*, Special Supplement on Yugoslavia, February 2, 1972.
Stajner, R., 'The system of planning', *Yugoslav Survey*, Vol. XII, No. 1, February 1971.
Stambolic, P., 'A broader base for self-management', in special issue of *The Economic Reform in Yugoslavia*, Socialist Thought and Practice, Belgrade, 1965.
Stankovic, S., 'Ausländische Investitionen in Jugoslawien', *Osteuropäische Rundschau*, No. 11, November 1970.
'Statute of the SAVA factory for rubber, leather and chemical products', Kranj, 1970.
Stichting Maatschappij en Onderneming, *Arbeiderszelfbestuur in Joegoslavië; theorie en praktijk*, The Hague, 1972.
Stojkovic, K., *Foreign capital investment in Yugoslav enterprises*, published by the Yugoslav Export and Credit Bank, Belgrade, 1972 (2nd ed.).
Streeten, P., 'Obstacles to private foreign investment in the LDC's', *Columbia Journal of World Business*, May/June 1970.
Sukijasovic, M., 'Foreign investment in Yugoslavia', in Litvak, I. A. and Maule, Chr.J. (eds.), *Foreign investment and international business arrangements: the experience of host countries*, Frederick A. Praeger, New York, 1970.
Sukijasovic, M., *Yugoslav foreign investment legislation at work: experiences so far*, The Institute of International Politics and Economics, Belgrade, 1970 (2nd ed.).
Sukijasovic, M., 'Investment of foreign capital in the Yugoslav economy', *Yugoslav Survey*, Vol. XIV, No. 4, November 1973.
Sukijasovic, M. and Glickman, R.B., 'Yugoslav joint ventures: some legal problems', *Florida State University Slavic Papers*, Vol. 3, 1969.
Sutcliffe, R.B., *Industry and underdevelopment*, Addison-Wesley Publishing Co., London, 1971.

Theeuwes, J.A., 'Bedrijfseconomische aspecten van de medezeggenschap in Joegoslavië', *Economie*, No. 9, June 1968.
Thomas, H., 'Joegoslavië: een ontwikkelingsland', *Economisch-Statistische Berichten*, No. 2895, April 11, 1973.
Todoric, M., 'Current tasks in the development of the economic system and social-economic relations', in special issue of *The Economic Reform in Yugoslavia*, Socialist Thought and Practice, Belgrade, 1965.
Tomlinson, J.W.C., *The joint venture process in international business: India and Pakistan*, The MIT Press, Cambridge (Mass.) and London, 1970.

Tornquist, D., *Look East, look West: the socialist adventure in Yugoslavia*, Macmillan, New York, 1966.
Trajkovic, M., 'Yugoslav self-management and constitutional amendment xv', *Florida State University Slavic Papers*, Vol. 4, 1970.
Tugendhat, Chr., *The multinationals*, Eyre and Spottiswoode, London, 1971.

Union Européenne des Experts Comptables, Économiques et Financiers, *Les investissements étrangers dans les entreprises yougoslaves*, Belgrade, 1970.
UNCTAD, *Incentives for industrial exports*, New York, 1970.
UNIDO, *Domestic and external financing*, UNIDO Monograph on Industrial Development, No. 16, New York, 1969.
UNIDO, *Manual on the establishment of industrial joint venture agreements in developing countries*, New York, 1971.
UNIDO, *Politiques d'encouragement du développement industriel*, New York, 1971.
United Nations, *World economic survey – Part I: the financing of economic development*, New York, 1966.
United Nations, *Foreign investment in developing countries*, New York, 1968.
United Nations, *Panel on foreign investment in developing countries (Amsterdam, 1969)*, New York, 1969.
Uzair, M. and Syed, R.H., *International business cooperation: experience of Pakistan*, Karachi/Dacca, 1969.

Vanek, J., 'Decentralisation under workers' management: a theoretical appraisal', *American Economic Review*, Vol. LIX, No. 5, December 1969.
Vanek, J., *The general theory of labor-managed market economies*, Cornell University Press, Ithaca (N.Y.), 1970.
Vanek, J., *The participatory economy: an evolutionary hypothesis and a strategy for development*, Cornell University Press, Ithaca (N.Y.), 1971.
Vanek, J., 'The Yugoslav economy viewed through the theory of labor management', *World Development*, Vol. I, No. 9, September 1973.
Veljkovic, L., 'The meaning of the Economic Reform in Yugoslavia', in special issue of *The Economic Reform in Yugoslavia*, Socialist Thought and Practice, Belgrade, 1965.
Veljkovic, L. (ed.), *Economic development in Yugoslavia*, Medunarodna Politika Studies, No. 25, Belgrade, 1968.
Verburg, P., *Wie beslist er nu eigenlijk?*, Instituut voor bedrijfseconomie en accountancy, Universiteit van Amsterdam, 1972.
Vidakovic, Z., *Het tweede decennium van arbeiderszelfbestuur*, Van Gennep, Amsterdam, 1972.
'Von der Lizens zur Kapitaleinlage; neue Formen der jugoslawisch-westdeutschen wirtschaftlichen Zusammenarbeit', *Wissenschaftlicher Dienst Südosteuropa*, No. 1/2, January/February 1973.
Vratusa, A., 'Jugoslavia, 1971', *Foreign Affairs*, No. 1, October 1971.
Vucic, N., 'Finanzierungspolitik der Investitionen in Jugoslawien', *Oesterreichisches Bank-Archiv*, No. 2, February 1971.
Vucic, N., 'Aktuelle Fragen bezüglich fremden Kapitals in Jugoslawien', *Oesterreichisches Bank-Archiv*, No. 4, April 1971.
Vucic, N., 'Aenderungen im jugoslawischen Banksystem', *Oesterreichisches Bank-Archiv*, No. 8, August 1972.
Vucic, N., 'Probleme der jugoslawischen Finanzpolitik', *Osteuropa Wirtschaft*, No. 3, September 1972.

Wachtel, H. M., 'Wages in a labor-managed economy: the Yugoslav case', *Florida State University Slavic Papers*, Vol. 4, 1970.

Wachtel, H. M., 'Workers' management and interindustry wage differentials in Yugoslavia', *Journal of Political Economy*, No. 3, May/June 1972.

Ward, B., 'The firm in Illyria: market syndicalism', *American Economic Review*, No. 4, September 1958.

Ward, B., 'Marxism-Horvatism: a Yugoslav theory of socialism', *American Economic Review*, No. 3, June 1967.

Ward, B., 'Political power and economic change in Yugoslavia', *American Economic Review*, Papers and Proceedings, May 1968.

Wemelsfelder, J., 'Arbeiderszelfbestuur in de Joegoslavische industrie; afschrikwekkend of navolgenswaard voorbeeld', *Economisch-Statistische Berichten*, No. 2840, March 15, 1972.

Wemelsfelder, J., 'Kapitaalvoorzieningsproblemen in een op arbeiderszelfbestuur gebaseerde industrie. Het voorbeeld van Joegoslavië', *De Economist*, No. 2, 1973.

Wetsteijn, R., 'Arbeiderszelfbestuur als economisch experiment', *Economisch-Statistische Berichten*, No. 2733, February 11, 1970.

Willems, H., *Bedrijfseconomische aspecten van de internationale joint business venture in de ontwikkelingslanden*, Wolters, Groningen, 1963.

Wing, G. A., 'Impressions of a worker-managed economy', *Business Horizons*, No. 1, February 1971.

Winsemius, A. and Pincus, J. A., *Methods of industrial development*, OECD, Paris, 1962.

'Yougoslavie: assainir les entreprises', *Moniteur du Commerce International*, No. 11, December 11, 1972.

Yugoslav Bank for Foreign Trade, *Regulations on joint investments of domestic and foreign partners in Yugoslavia*, Belgrade, 1970 (2nd edition).

Yugoslav Chamber of Economy and Institute of Comparative Law, *The legal system of foreign capital investments in Yugoslav enterprises*, Belgrade, 1972.

Yugoslav Investment Bank, *Information on investments of foreign partners in Yugoslav enterprises*, Belgrade, 1970.

Zenoff, D., *Private enterprise in developing countries*, Prentice Hall, Englewood Cliffs (N.J.), 1969.

Zupanov, J., 'Yugoslavia: a socialist alternative', in Ch. De Hoghton (ed.), *The company, law, structure and reform in eleven countries*, Political and Economic Planning, London, 1970.

GPSR Compliance

*The European Union's (EU) General Product Safety Regulation (GPSR) is a set of rules that requires consumer products to be safe and our obligations to ensure this.*

*If you have any concerns about our products, you can contact us on ProductSafety@springernature.com*

In case Publisher is established outside the EU, the EU authorized representative is:

Springer Nature Customer Service Center GmbH
Europaplatz 3
69115 Heidelberg, Germany

**Batch number: 10830937**

Printed by Printforce, the Netherlands